Kyoto by Area

Essentials

Published by Time Out Guides Ltd
Universal House
251 Tottenham Court Road
London W1T 7AB
Tel: + 44 (0)20 7813 3000
Fax: + 44 (0)20 7813 6001
Email: guides@timeout.com
www.timeout.com

Managing Director Peter Fiennes
Editorial Director Ruth Jarvis
Business Manager Dan Allen
Editorial Manager Holly Pick
Assistant Management Accountant Ija Krasnikova

Time Out Guides is a wholly owned subsidiary of Time Out Group Ltd.

© Time Out Group Ltd
Chairman Tony Elliott
Chief Executive Officer David King
Group General Manager/Director Nichola Coulthard
Time Out Communications Ltd MD David Pepper
Time Out International Ltd MD Cathy Runciman
Time Out Magazine Ltd Publisher/Managing Director Mark Elliott
Production Director Mark Lamond
Group IT Director Simon Chappell
Marketing & Circulation Director Catherine Demajo

Time Out and the Time Out logo are trademarks of Time Out Group Ltd.

This edition first published in Great Britain in 2009 by Ebury Publishing
A Random House Group Company
Company information can be found on www.randomhouse.co.uk
Random House UK Limited Reg. No. 954009
10 9 8 7 6 5 4 3 2 1

Distributed in the US by Publishers Group West
Distributed in Canada by Publishers Group Canada

For further distribution details, see www.timeout.com

ISBN: 978-1-84670-129-0

A CIP catalogue record for this book is available from the British Library.

Printed and bound in Germany by Appl.

The Random House Group Limited supports The Forest Stewardship Council (FSC), the
leading international forest certification organisation. All our titles that are printed on
Greenpeace approved FSC certified paper carry the FSC logo. Our paper procurement
policy can be found at www.rbooks.co.uk/environment.

Time Out carbon-offsets all its flights with Trees for Cities (www.treesforcities.org).

Kyoto Shortlist

The **Time Out Kyoto Shortlist** is one of a series of guides that draws on Time Out's background as a magazine publisher to keep you current with what's going on in town. As well as Kyoto's key sights and the best of its eating, drinking and leisure options, the guide picks out the most exciting venues to have recently opened and gives a full calendar of annual events. It also includes features on the important news, trends and openings, all compiled by locally based editors and writers. Whether you're visiting for the first time, or you're a regular, you'll find the *Time Out Kyoto Shortlist* contains all you need to know, in a portable and easy-to-use format.

The guide divides central Kyoto into seven areas, each of which contains listings for Sights & Museums, Eating & Drinking, Shopping, Nightlife and Arts & Leisure, with maps pinpointing all their locations. At the front of the book are chapters rounding up these scenes city-wide, and giving a shortlist of our overall picks in a variety of categories. We include itineraries for days out, plus essentials such as transport information and hotels.

Our listings give phone numbers with the Kyoto area code (075). The international dialling code for Japan is 81. To call from outside Japan, follow this with the number given, dropping the initial '0'. Some listed numbers (beginning with 090) are mobiles.

We have noted price categories by using one to four yen signs (¥-¥¥¥¥),

representing budget, moderate, expensive and luxury. Major credit cards are accepted unless otherwise stated. We also indicated when a venue is NEW .

All our listings are double-checked, but places do sometimes close or change their hours or prices, so it's a good idea to call a venue before visiting. While every effort has been made to ensure accuracy, the publishers cannot accept responsibility for any errors that this guide may contain.

Venues are marked on the maps using symbols numbered according to their order within the chapter and colour-coded according to the type of venue they represent:

❶ Sights & Museums
❶ Eating & Drinking
❶ Shopping
❶ Nightlife
❶ Arts & Leisure

Map key	
Major sight or landmark	
Railway station	
Park	
College/hospital	
Neighbourhood	**GION**
Pedestrian street	
Main road	
Temple	卍
Airport	✈

Time Out **Kyoto** Shortlist

EDITORIAL
Editor Nicholas Coldicott
Deputy Editor Nicola Homer
Proofreaders Simon Coppock,
  Simon Cropper

DESIGN
Art Director Scott Moore
Art Editor Pinelope Kourmouzoglou
Senior Designer Henry Elphick
Graphic Designers Kei Ishimaru,
  Nicola Wilson
Advertising Designer Jodi Sher
Picture Editor Jael Marschner
Deputy Picture Editor Lynn Chambers
Picture Researcher Gemma Walters
Picture Desk Assistant Marzena Zoladz
Picture Librarian Christina Theisen

ADVERTISING
Commercial Director Mark Phillips
International Advertising Manager
  Kasimir Berger
International Sales Executive Charlie Sokol
Advertising Sales (Kyoto) Kitamura
  Susumu, Original Inc

MARKETING
Marketing Manager Yvonne Poon
**Sales & Marketing Director, North America
& Latin America** Lisa Levinson
Senior Publishing Brand Manager
  Luthfa Begum
Art Director Anthony Huggins

PRODUCTION
Production Manager Brendan McKeown
Production Controller Damian Bennett
Production Co-ordinator Kelly Fenlon

CONTRIBUTORS
This guide was researched and written by Michael Baxter, Dan Grunebaum, Madoka
Kagimoto, Greg Koch, Tomoko Kono, Michael Lambe and Chris Page. The editor would
like to thank Hiroaki Kakinuma, the JNTO, Yukiko Moriwaki, Ken Nishikawa, Campbell
Troy, Taeko Yamashita and Ken Yokoyama.

PHOTOGRAPHY
All photography by Chris McCooey, except page 93 Manabu Matsui/Disney.

Cover photograph: Toji Temple. Credit: © Jupiterimages.

MAPS
Maps by JS Graphics Ltd. (john@jsgraphics.co.uk). Maps are based on material supplied
by ITMB Publishing Ltd. Rail map by Mojoworks (www.mojoworks.jp).

About **Time Out**

Founded in 1968, Time Out has expanded from humble London beginnings into the
leading resource for those wanting to know what's happening in the world's greatest
cities. As well as our influential what's-on weeklies in London, New York and Chicago,
we publish nearly 30 other listings magazines in cities as varied as Beijing and
Mumbai. The magazines established Time Out's trademark style: sharp writing,
informed reviewing and bang up-to-date inside knowledge of every scene.

Time Out made the natural leap into travel guides in the 1980s with the City Guide
series, which now extends to over 50 destinations around the world. Written and
researched by expert local writers and generously illustrated with original photography,
the full-size guides cover a larger area than our Shortlist guides and include many
more venue reviews, along with additional background features and a full set of maps.

Throughout this rapid growth, the company has remained proudly independent,
still owned by Tony Elliott four decades after he started Time Out London as a single
fold-out sheet of A5 paper. This independence extends to the editorial content of all
our publications, this Shortlist included. No establishment has been featured because
it has advertised, and no payment has influenced any of our reviews. And, for our
critics, there's definitely no such thing as a free lunch: all restaurants and bars are
visited and reviewed anonymously, and Time Out always picks up the bill. For more
about the company, see www.timeout.com.

Don't Miss

Fushimi Inari Taisha p121

WHAT'S BEST
Sights & Museums

If you could measure a city by its monuments, Kyoto would be one of the world's greatest. Consider the numbers: 17 UNESCO World Heritage sites in Kyoto Prefecture, 14 within the city limits; around 1,600 temples, 400 shrines and more picture-postcard gardens than anyone can count. This city is home to just 1.2 per cent of Japan's population, but 20 per cent of its National Treasures.

The problem, of course, is deciding what to visit from this surfeit of attractions. It was in 1994 that UNESCO announced its 14 favourites, and you could do worse than follow its advice. The list flags most of the unmissable sights: Kiyomizu-dera (p84), Kinkaku-ji (p107), Ginkaku-ji (p97), Koke-dera (p121). However, sightseeing and heritage protection lists don't

always share the same criteria, and many visitors will find the lush gardens of Katsura Rikyu (p121), the 1,001 statues of Sanjusangen-do (p50) and the avenue of vermillion gates at Fushimi Inari Taisha (p121) more memorable sights than the UNESCO-backed Ujigami Jinja (p129) or Shimogamo Jinja (p72).

There are also temples that would be the highlight of most other cities, but barely make it on to the B-list here. Until the 15th century, Kennin-ji (p84) was among the most influential temples in the country. These days, even though it boasts a photogenic dry Zen garden, fabulous artworks and the grave of the monk who brought Zen to Japan, Kennin-ji is often overlooked in the scurry to reach the landmark temples at the foot of the nearby mountains. Shoren-in (p86) has

suffered from a similar fate, as a result of its far-too-famous neighbours, despite having once been a temporary Imperial Palace and possessing a garden that is associated with three of the biggest names of landscaping – Kobori Enshu, Soami and Jihei Ogawa. The garden, known for its great acoustics, hosts occasional *koto* and *shakuhachi* (bamboo flute) concerts (ask the tourist office for dates).

Be wary, though, of temple fatigue. The city may be awash with architectural masterpieces, but there comes a point when even the most dedicated temple-hopper wilts at the thought of seeing yet another ancient monument. Luckily, Kyoto is much more than an architectural time capsule, and exudes plenty of charm aside from the parts that were built centuries ago. You should not miss the modern art world in the Okazaki region, just south of Heian Jingu (p97). The Kyoto Art Map, available free at Gallery Haneusagi (p83) and Gallery Maronie (p53), will lead you to

www.treesforcities.org

Trees for Cities
Charity registration number 1032154

Travelling creates so many
lasting memories.

Make your trip mean something for
years to come - not just for you but
for the environment and for people
living in deprived urban areas.

Anyone can offset their flights,
but when you plant trees with
Trees for Cities, you'll help create
a green space for an urban
community that really needs it.

To find out more visit
www.treesforcities.org

Leave
Your
Mark

Create a green future for cities.

dozens of other independent galleries. Be sure also to visit the impressive National Museum of Modern Art, Kyoto (p101).

Fans of modern architecture can stroll Sanjo Dori to see the early 20th-century works of Kingo Tatsuno, Yasushi Kataoka and Shigenori Yoshii, or the designs of recent years, such as Kyoto Station (p48) and the Sfera Building (p82).

But the city's best new attraction is a forward-thinking museum devoted to an icon of modern Japanese culture: manga. The Kyoto International Manga Museum (see box p73) draws links from the comic books back through *kamishibai* story-card performances to *ukiyo-e* (pictures of the floating world) and even first millennium scrolls, but its eye is on the future. The museum holds symposiums pairing foreign graphic artists with local manga greats, invites DJs to perform inspired sets, and uses manga as a springboard for academic research.

The best way to treat Kyoto is not as a checklist of must-sees, but as a bubbling centre of culture, which happens to be furnished with more than its fair share of landmarks.

Gorgeous gardens

No other city in Japan comes close to Kyoto for exquisite gardens, many of which benefit from *shakkei* (borrowed scenery), whereby the city's scenic backdrop is incorporated into the fabricated landscape.

The history of the city can be traced in the gardens attached to its temples, shrines, palaces and villas. The peaceful Heian period (794-1185) saw imperial power flourish. With no great power struggles to contend with, nobles were free to spend time on aesthetic pursuits. Consequently, the gardens of Kyoto's early years were scenic and highly symbolic. Byodo-in (p128), in nearby Uji,

is the best example of the era's ambitious landscaping. Heian Jingu, though built in 1895, borrows consciously from the designs of the earlier era.

Zen arrived from China in the 12th century, coinciding with the rise of the samurai. The monks and warriors shared an austere aesthetic, reflected in the *karesansui* (dry Zen garden). Devised to aid the priests in their meditation, rather than for admiring, the dry gardens consist of a small area of raked gravel broken up by rockwork and dabs of greenery.

Few gardens in the world have undergone as much analysis as Ryoan-ji (p110), which is an irony, given that analysing is exactly what you aren't supposed to do. Ignore the speculation of academics over what the layout might mean, and simply enjoy it for what it is: a minimalist, elegant aid to contemplation that has captivated people for half a millennium.

A surprising number of gardens are attributed to Enshu Kobori (1579-1647). If all the claims are true, he must have been a busy man. The gardens of Nijo Castle (p70), Sento Gosho (p72) and Konchi-in (a sub-temple of Nanzen-ji, p100) are among those with convincing evidence of a Kobori connection.

In the 17th century, under the introverted regime of the shogun, the nobles were again free to bury themselves in artistic passions. The era brought three of the city's greatest gardens: Katsura Rikyu (p121), Shugaku-in Rikyu (p122) and Sento Gosho. All three are gardens of leisure, to be strolled in rather than studied.

When the shogun was deposed in 1868, Japan opened its ports to foreign trade and influence. Glimpses of these ideas showed up in the garden of Murin-an (p100), where Heian Jingu landscaper Jihei Ogawa

blended elements of English lawns with the Japanese stroll garden.

And finally, there's Kyouen (p88), a 21st-century take on those ancient Zen gardens. It may not last as long or inspire as much awe as its city siblings, but it's a garden and dining complex that only Kyoto could produce.

Planning ahead

A little preparation goes a long way in Kyoto. It's not just hotels and restaurants that require advance booking: some of the city's best palaces, gardens and temples demand that you apply for permission well in advance.

For some attractions, it's as painless as filling out an online form; for others the archaic application procedure demands that you write to the venue with your request and await their reply. To see the moss garden of Saiho-ji (p121), you'll need to send them a selection of preferred dates, with a stamped, self-addressed postcard. About two weeks later, you should receive a reply specifying a date and time for your visit. Write to

the following address: Saiho-ji, 56 Jingatani-cho, Matsuo, Nishikyo-ku, Kyoto, 615 8286.

The Imperial Household Agency asks for reservations to visit its properties (Kyoto Gosho, Sento Gosho, Katsura Rikyu, Shugaku-in Rikyu). The easiest way to apply is online. For more information, visit http://sankan.kunaicho.go.jp. But bear in mind that you'll need to have an address in Japan to receive the permission card. You can also visit the Household's office on the western side of Kyoto Gyoen to secure a pass in person. The office is open on week-days, 8.45am-noon, 1-4pm, but closed on national holidays and over the New Year (29 December-3 January).

In peak season, apply at least a week in advance; off-peak, two days' notice is usually enough. Bring your passport and they will reserve a place for you on their guided tours. Access to all the imperial properties is free, and the Kyoto Gosho tour is in English, although visitors must be aged 18 or over.

With so many trips that are easy to plan, it may be tempting to skip these sights, but all five are worth the effort of advance preparation.

Kiyomizu-dera p84

Kitcho p117

WHAT'S BEST
Eating & Drinking

The great news for gourmands is that Kyoto is obsessed with food. With good reason, too. This is a city of culinary perfectionists, some of whom are working to recipes that have been handed down through a dozen generations. After 300 years of practice, a dish ought to be delicious.

Now the bad news: for all the quality, there's not much variety. Local culinary pride is so strong that there seems little interest in what the rest of the world, or even the rest of Japan, has to offer. With a few notable exceptions, most of them listed here, if you want to eat well in Kyoto, eat Kyoto's food.

Many restaurants specialise in one type of cuisine. Tempura restaurants serve tempura and only tempura. Soba shops sell soba. Some places go further by offering just a single set meal. Dine at Daiichi (p110) and you won't need a menu – all it serves is turtle hotpot. Guests at Warajiya (p52) eat a similar meal, but with eel in place of turtle, Toriiwaro (p113) does likewise with chicken, and Seigen-in (p112) offers simmering bowls of tofu.

In the *kaiseki* restaurants that serve Japan's version of haute cuisine, you can sometimes choose the number of courses for your meal (pick the shortest – it will still be more than most people can manage), but there won't be a menu. At Nakahigashi (p104), your dinner is partly determined by what the chef foraged from the riverbanks that morning. Even in the humblest ramen shop or rice bowl joint, the kitchen is often staffed by artist-technicians.

Oku p89

Put yourself in their hands and reap the rewards of their obsession.

The flipside, of course, is that you might not share the palate or preferences of the chef. Taste buds groomed on greasy foods may miss the subtlety of a radish in broth as a full course, and anyone who finds raw fish adventurous will surely struggle with milt, a local delicacy. If you don't know what milt is, there's a clue in the Japanese name for this fishy product: *shirako* (literally 'white children').

This city guide was released shortly before Michelin's first look at Kyoto, and there ought to be plenty to please the inspectors. For locals, though, the culinary survey is likely to prove contentious. Debates have raged for decades, centuries even, over which is the best *kaiseki*, soba, tempura or tofu restaurant. In a city where only perfection is good enough, offering two stars would be an affront to many establishments. Locals who have long touted their favourite eaterie as the finest in the world, won't want to hear that it's not.

Whatever the ratings, and whether the restaurants embrace or reject their stars, there are more meals-of-a-lifetime in this small city than any place of similar size. Kyoto is the birthplace of *kaiseki*, perhaps the pinnacle of Japan's dining scene. Amazingly, these multi-course feasts of fine dining began as a warm-up to a bowl of green tea. The most formal tea ceremonies could be interminably long, and a few bites to eat helped ensure that participants weren't distracted by rumbling bellies.

Fast forward a few centuries. The meal still concludes with a bowl of tea and is often served in a private dining room styled on a tearoom, but the food is no longer the support act. Calling it 'seasonal' doesn't begin to describe the timeliness of *kaiseki*. Your maid's kimono, the room's flowers, the scroll on the wall and the food on your plate will all reflect the season, month or even the day of your meal. The small dishes arrive in succession until, or usually well after, you are sated. It's not a cheap experience. The most exclusive restaurants (Kitcho, p117; Douraku, p50) can charge more than ¥20,000 for lunch and up to ¥50,000 for

SHORTLIST

Best new
- Il Ghiottone Cucineria (p123)
- Iyemon Salon (p57)
- Oku (p89)

Meal of a lifetime
- Harise (p51)
- Kanga-an (p75)
- Kikunoi (p88)
- Nakahigashi (p104)

Cheap eats
- Issen Yoshoku (p88)
- Mikoan (p57)
- Yorozuya (p90)

Best café
- Café Bibliotic Hello (p72)
- Oku (p89)
- Sarasa Nishijin (p106)

East meets West
- Il Ghiottone (p86)
- Tamaki (p77)

For carnivores
- Hafuu (p74)
- Junidanya Honten (p88)

For herbivores
- Kanga-an (p75)
- Seigen-in (p112)

Summer balconies
- Misoguigawa (p66)
- Shougetsu-an (p66)

Top tempura
- Tenyu (p58)
- Yoshikawa Tempura (p58)

Night bites
- Honke Dai-ichi Asahi (p51)
- Uroco (p67)

Best sake
- Shuz (p66)
- Yoramu Sake Bar (p77)

dinner. But part of the price tag is for details that might not mean much to the average diner: calligraphy masterpieces on the wall, perhaps, or precious antique plates and bowls. There are cheaper options that involve no culinary compromise. Harise (p51), Nishiki (p117) and Kanga-an (p75), which serves a vegetarian version, are all good value – which is not to say cheap. Many *kaiseki* places also offer bento lunch boxes at a greatly reduced price. Expect to pay about ¥5,000 for a take-out meal from Doraku, Kanga-an or Kikunoi (p88).

If even a ¥5,000 lunch sounds ludicrous, you can still eat fabulously well without resorting to the budget chains. Ramen shops, with their clattering pans and air thick with grease, are about as far removed from *kaiseki* as it gets, but that's no bad thing – no one wants to see operas every night of the week. *Nishin soba* (smoked mackerel on buckwheat noodles) is a local favourite that developed in the days when the city, hemmed in by mountains, had little access to fresh fish. Kyoto is also famed for its high-quality tofu, and the streets

Get the local experience

Over 50 of the world's top destinations available.

around Nanzen-ji (p100) are known for their *yudofu* (tofu hotpot) restaurants. Junsei is the most celebrated. For good honest home-style cooking, look for *obanzai*. This Kyoto-only rustic grub is served as a tray of small portions – a kind of Japanese tapas. The restaurant named after the cuisine is a good place at which to try it (p75), as is Oku (p89), where the recipes are crafted by one of the area's star chefs.

Veggie Kyoto

Japan was once a vegetarian country, thanks to a decree issued by the nation's 40th emperor. How things change: *bonito* broth is the basis of much of Japan's modern cuisine, and meat is plentiful and popular. But Kyoto is blessed with a great variety of vegetables, and the city's long Buddhist heritage means that many chefs know how to cook a meatless meal. Zen temples Ryoan-ji (p110), Kanga-an (p75), Daitoku-ji (p120) and Tenryu-ji (p116) all have vegan restaurants in their grounds. Elsewhere, many chefs will tweak their menus to accommodate herbivores if asked in advance. Tamaki (p77), Misoguigawa (p66), Il Ghiottone (p86), Il Viale (p77) and Honke Owariya (p74) are all receptive to requests.

Night bites

Like everything else in Kyoto, the eateries close early. It's not unusual to call last orders at 9pm. *Kaiseki* and *shojin ryori* restaurants have their last sittings even earlier, often as early as 7pm, due to the length of the meal. If you're peckish late at night, your best best is to head to Kiyamachi in the Downtown district, where a handful of kitchens stay open until the small hours, and many bars offer cheap grub.

Eating alfresco

Each summer, restaurants along the Kamo river between Nijo and Gojo erect outdoor balconies, which are known locally as *yuka* or *kawadoko*. Eating alfresco, with a beautiful view of the lantern-lit river, is a tradition thought to date back to the 16th century. Not surprisingly, it's incredibly popular, and it's necessary to make reservations a long time in advance. The nearby districts of Takao and Kibune have similar riverside balconies each summer.

First time unlucky

There's one local custom that visitors won't find endearing. *Ichigen-san okotowari* means, roughly, 'no first-time visitors'. Sometimes, this rule is what it claims to be – guests must be introduced via a regular patron. At other times, it's an excuse to turn away anyone that might lack the appropriate decorum (read: youths and foreigners). Most geisha teahouses fall into the former category, while small cocktail bars often take the latter approach. Since such bars tend to be overpriced, think of the policy as a great way to avoid overrated establishments. All the bars reviewed in this book welcome first-timers.

Getting there

Finding modern restaurants is easy; most have websites and clear signage. Older establishments can be more problematic. Often, the only way to identify them is the Chinese character on a small sign or split curtain. Before heading to dine at a traditional restaurant, ask your hotel concierge or ryokan staff to write the name, or better still, find a photo of the façade online.

Ninenzaka p20

WHAT'S BEST
Shopping

The most striking thing about Kyoto's shopping streets is what's not there. International superbrands have homogenised most of the world's cities, but along the most commercial shopping drag in Kyoto, Shijo Dori, you'll find just a handful of famous names. The street's most eye-popping piece of modern architecture belongs not to Tiffany or Gucci, but to the venerable Fukujuen (p59), which has been a supplier of green tea since 1790.

Distinctive local stores continue to hold their own here. Although you could purchase brand-name trainers in the Puma store, you could equally walk a couple of blocks to Sou-Sou (p62) for a pair of split-toe athletic shoes – the result of a collaboration between a kimono designer and Le Coq Sportif.

Shops such as Oku, Sfera Archive and Kyoto Design House (p61) sell items that have been staples of Kyoto life for centuries, but bring them right up to date with the latest techniques and contemporary materials. Omo (p78) offers kimonos, perhaps teamed with a sash made from English upholstery. Once a traditional wallpaper manufacturer, Karacho (p61) applies its expertise in woodblock printing to decorating lampshades, greetings cards and business cards, among other products. If you didn't know that the bag-maker Ihee belonged to a 400-year-old cotton trader, you might assume this modest chain was one of the city's freshest faces. Kyoto doesn't cling to its heritage – it draws on its rich legacy to inspire new creations. The hottest

stores are the ones that blend the old and the new seamlessly.

That's not why the tourists come, though. The draw for most visitors is the *shinise* – family-run specialist shops with a century or more of history. As the imperial seat, Kyoto lured the nation's top craftsmen, some of whose stores have survived into the modern era. The romantic idea of a Kyoto shop has an elderly proprietress brushing a broom across the pavement in front. A split curtain separates the outside world from her tubs of miso or displays of ornaments. The store doesn't have a website, and never will. It has survived for a century on word of mouth and passing trade.

Such stores continue to trade all over the city, and the passage of time has whittled them down to the finest examples. Shinzaburo Hanpu (p92), Kashogama (p95) and Funahashiya (p59) don't all look like the classic *machiya shinise*, but they are examples of how techniques passed down through generations keep pace with modern tastes.

Where to shop

Traditionally, shopping in Kyoto was divided by blocks. The city planners borrowed the idea of a grid system from the Tang dynasty Chinese capital, and the old city centre, now known as the Downtown and Gosho districts, still has this layout. Traditionally, each block in the grid had its own industry. There was a block for comb-makers, a block for fan-makers and a block for tofu shops.

Today, it's still possible to glimpse the old set-up as you wander around central Kyoto, but streets have a more distinctive character than blocks these days. Shinmonzen Dori in Gion is lined with antique stores, Gokomachi is the street for fashion, Ninenzaka and Sannenzaka in Gion offer a picturesque jumble of ancient stores, teashops and souvenir hawkers, and Shijo Dori provides department stores and big-brand shopping, although it also boasts an array of smaller and more interesting stores.

Best of all, Nishiki-koji Dori is home to six blocks of the market nicknamed 'Kyoto's kitchen'. Nishiki-koji market (p62) is a sensory overload, a riot of colours, aromas and jostling shoppers. Back in the 16th century, fishmongers supplying the Imperial Palace discovered that Nishiki-koji Dori was the perfect place to make a pit-stop. It's en route to the palace, close to residential blocks for easy side-custom, and sits directly above a source of pure water (many restaurants on the street still have their own wells tapping directly into the water table). In 1770, the market expanded to accommodate vegetables, and these days it sells the gamut of Kyoto ingredients, from green tea to dried yuba (soy milk skin).

Flea markets

A major temple and shrine each host the two largest flea markets. The first market, called Kobo-san after Kobo Daishi, founder of the Shingon sect of Buddhism, is held at Toji (p122) on the 21st of each month. The second, Tenjin-san, is held four days later at Kitano Tenmangu shrine (p107). Both offer everything from snacks to kimono to bonsai trees, and draw sizeable crowds. A smaller, but no less charming flea market takes place on the 15th of each month at a small temple in Northern Higashiyama (Chion-ji, www.tedukuri-ichi.com). Tezukuri-ichi ('handmade fair') is for local artists and craftspeople to sell their creations.

Opening hours

Store opening hours vary greatly, but as a rule of thumb, the older the establishment, the earlier it is likely to close. Most stores open at 10am or

Hanjiro p60

11am, with traditional stores closing about 6pm, and more contemporary shops staying open until 8pm or later. Many shops open on Sundays and take a day off midweek.

Location hunting

Kyoto's address system is an oddity. The most technically accurate addresses use blocks, or 'cho', plus a number to locate the building in the block. The problem is that the blocks aren't clearly named, and most people can't locate anything beyond the block they live or work on. Ask someone for directions to Benzaiten-cho, and there is virtually no chance of them being able to help, even if you happen to be standing on Benzaiten-cho. The solution, at least for locations on the central grid, is to use addresses that sound like directions. The address for Horaido (p60) reads Teramachi, Shijo-agaru – which translates roughly as 'On Teramachi Dori, up a bit from Shijo Dori'.

The suffix -*agaru* means 'go up', -*sagaru* means 'go down', *Nishi-iru* is 'go west', and *Higashi-iru* means 'go east'. When a building is on the corner, the address just lists the two streets, so the address of Ichimanben (p61), 'Sanjo Yanaginobanba', means that it's on the corner of Sanjo Dori and Yanaginobanba Dori. The obvious problem is that 'up a bit' isn't precise enough to find a shop unless it has a clear sign. Still, when you're on the grid, or in most parts of Higashiyama, it shouldn't cause many problems. Further out, where most addresses revert to '-cho', it can be harder. Take a map.

Credit cards

Credit cards are a part of modern life in Kyoto. So, the contemporary shops will probably accept them, but traditional establishments may not. Look for signs on the window or by the till. You can withdraw money using credit cards at major banks, but rarely at cashpoints.

Metro p105

WHAT'S BEST
Nightlife

If New York is the city that never sleeps, Kyoto is the one that likes to retire at a sensible hour with a mug of cocoa and a book. There are nightclubs, but you can count the good ones on the fingers of one hand, and they don't all party until sunrise. Trends move at a glacial pace, and many of the liveliest bars close by midnight, even at weekends. If you like your cities to light up at night, pay a visit to Osaka – only a 29-minute train ride away.

Of course, intimacy has its advantages. Venue hopping is a breeze when most of the bars and clubs are packed into a few blocks. When major acts visit Kyoto, they play in venues a fraction of the size they might fill in Tokyo or other clubbing capitals. Jeff Mills, Richie Hawtin, François K and Masters at Work have all played here, to crowds of 300 rather than 3,000.

A two-decade veteran that shows no signs of wearing out its welcome is Metro (p105), surely the world's only nightclub inside a subway station. The club features international names and plays an eclectic schedule of house, jazz, hip hop, reggae, '80s cheese and drag-queen disco in a typical month.

For ten years, Metro ruled the club scene in Kyoto, but then came World (p68), a 700-capacity club that inherited stone arches from the previous tenant, an Italian restaurant. Some of Tokyo's biggest names regularly play here. Look out for Emma, Sugiurumun, Shinichi Ozawa or Towa Tei.

A few blocks north is Sam & Dave (p68), which charges different entrance fees for ladies and gents, throws toga parties and Jack Daniel's nights, stages flair bartending shows, serves alcopops and draws clubbers in their early twenties.

Rounding off the list of clubs worth a look are Lab Tribe (p79), a big, black box that only tends to work when heavyweight acts such as Layo & Bushwacka! or DJ Krush

perform; Rub a Dub (p68), a basement cubbyhole with DJs spinning good sets of Jamaican 45s; and Urban Guild (p68), the most avant-garde club in the city.

Record store-bar Japonica (p74) is a great place to find out about upcoming parties, as are local listings magazines *Kansai Scene* and *Kansai Time Out*.

Gay Kyoto

In Japan, homosexuality flies below the cultural radar. The best advice is to head for Osaka, specifically the Doyama district, with its bars, clubs, saunas and sex joints. If you do stay in Kyoto, head for Daria (p94), the most welcoming gay spot.

Kiyamachi and Pontocho

The streets of Kiyamachi and Pontocho sleep all day and perk up at night. Kiyamachi is youthful and rowdy, playing host to the clubs World, Sam & Dave, Urban Guild and Rub a Dub. Pontocho is the classy neighbour, with plenty of cocktail bars and fine restaurants (visit Misogigawa). Linking the two are a dozen alleys packed with lively bars that open late.

Live houses

The scene consists mainly of domestic acts in smaller venues known as 'live houses'. The most beloved and atmospheric places to catch a show are two former sake brewhouses: Taku Taku (p124) and Jittoku (p114). Taku Taku is the larger of the two, the most central (a block south of our Downtown map) and boasts impressive alumni, including Roy Ayers, John Lee Hooker and Screamin' Jay Hawkins. These days you're most likely to hear hotly tipped Japrockers. Jittoku is worth the effort it takes to find it.

Kongo Nohgakudo p79

WHAT'S BEST
Arts & Leisure

Let's get straight to the geisha, or *geiko* as they are known in Kyoto, and *maiko*, their more colourful apprentices. These enigmatic women are as high on most must-see lists as the temples, pagodas and shrines. Tourists linger on Hanamikoji Dori each evening in the hope of glimpsing one of the entertainers scuttling to an appointment. The cobbled streets of Gion are beautiful, but throw in a *maiko* and you've got Kyoto's top photo opportunity.

Not everyone is happy about that. *Maiko*-hunting has become such a popular pursuit in Kyoto that the local tourist bureau issued a plea in 2009 for visitors to respect the ladies' privacy. They are, after all, on their way to work, dressed in a uniform worth many millions of yen.

It can also be hard to distinguish the master performance artists from tourists: *maiko* makeovers are becoming so popular that the

kimono-clad lady with a snow-white face may well be a day tripper wearing fancy dress.

There are several ways to make sure that you're seeing the real deal. The traditional way is to visit an *ochaya*, a teahouse where the ladies sing, dance, play games and pour drinks. But, unless you are fabulously well connected, you can forget this option: it's invitation only and frighteningly expensive. However, you can hire a *maiko* as a dinner companion; most top restaurants have connections to the teahouses, and if you're staying at a high-end hotel or ryokan, your concierge will be able to organise this. Expect to pay around ¥40,000 to spend two hours with a *maiko*.

Since 2009, the Gion Hatanaka ryokan (p143) has been hosting a 'Kyoto cuisine and *maiko* evening'. A geisha and a pair of *maiko* treat up to 40 guests to a less intimate approximation of an *ochaya* evening,

beginning with traditional dances and culminating in geisha games (think parlour amusements along the lines of 'rock, paper, scissors').

For most, it's the dancing rather than games that will impress, and each of the five geisha troupes stages seasonal performances, open to all, at their *kaburenjo* (arts theatres), with the option of a tea ceremony beforehand (see Calendar p29). They take bookings directly, or you can turn up on the day for the cheapest seats at the Miyako Odori.

Propping up the table of *maiko* options is Gion Corner. Although aficionados consider this the equivalent of listening to jazz in Disneyland, it offers a reasonably authentic trot through seven of the city's great arts, including tea ceremony, *ikebana*, *kyogen* comic theatre and a performance by *maiko* from the adjacent *kaburenjo*.

Traditional theatre

The most prolific performance art in Kyoto is the least fathomable. Noh performances take place several times each week, mainly in the Kongo (p79) or Kanze (p115) theatres, and tickets are affordable and easy to procure. To say Noh moves slowly would be a vast understatement. You could fall asleep in the dramatic pauses. The performances are highly stylised, and according to Kongo School *soke* (head) Hisanori Kongo, few Japanese people really comprehend what's going on. But, he says, there are various forms of beauty on stage, and each viewer should focus on the aspects that interest them. You should 'feel' Noh rather than try to understand the genre, says Kongo.

Noh is Japan's oldest performance art, predating *kabuki* by centuries. Its roots lie in *sarugaku* (literally 'monkey music'), a more upbeat,

---

SHORTLIST

Biggest festivals
- Aoi (p31)
- Gion (p31)
- Jidai (p32)

Quirkiest festival
- Karasu Zumo (p32)

Best cinema
- Kyoto Cinema (p64)

Best traditional theatre
- Kanze Nohgakudo (p105)
- Kongo Nohgakudo (p79)
- Minamiza (p95)
- Ooe Nohgakudo (p79)

Best karaoke rooms
- Super Jankara premium rooms (p64)

Places to glimpse a geisha
- Hanamikoji Dori (p80)
- Pontocho (p64)
- Shinbashi Dori (p80)
- Yasaka Shrine (p86)

Best bathhouse
- Funaoka Onsen (p114)

Favourite flea markets
- Kobo at To-ji (p122)
- Tenjin at Kitano Tenmangu (p107)

Best for kids
- Kaleidoscope Museum (p53)
- Toei Uzumasa Eigamura (p124)

Zen experience
- Shunko-in (p110)
- Taizo-in (p110)

Condensed culture
- Gion Corner (p95)

now-defunct art form originating in nearby Nara. A 14th-century father and son team took the serious side of *sarugaku* and turned it into a high art. The light-hearted leftovers became *kyogen*, now performed as comic interludes at Noh shows.

With powerful supporters such as shogun Yoshimitsu Ashikaga and Japan's unifier Hideyoshi Toyotomi, Noh flourished until the end of the 16th century, and around 2,000 plays were written. It was then declared formally perfect, schools were forbidden to create new plays, a hereditary system of performers was instituted, and Noh became frozen in time. Even now, troupes perform from a repertoire of around 250 plays, written more than half a millennium ago. New plays appear once every several years, but they are usually based on one of the ancient stories.

Two of the five major Noh schools have theatres in Kyoto. The Kongo theatre is the newest, and the only one to offer English language pamphlets that explain the storylines. If you happen to be in the city on 1st or 2nd June, the venue at which to see an outdoor, torchlit Noh performance is Heian Jingu (tickets cost ¥3,000 at the gate, and ¥2,500 in advance from ticket offices, p97).

A less esoteric theatrical option is *kabuki*, with a narrative style and pace that will be more familiar to Western minds. The art form was born in Kyoto, with the earliest performances reportedly taking place on the banks of the Kamogawa river. Each December, Gion's Minamiza stages the country's pre-eminent *kabuki* event, the season-opening *kaomise* (literally 'face showing') run. The rest of the year, however, *kabuki* jostles for space on the bill with other, more modern, forms of theatre. Catch it if you can.

Karaoke crazy

When you need a break from the highbrow, there's karaoke. Hire a private room, pick a song and flex your vocal chords with only your friends to mock you. The place to head is Super Jankara (p64), which offers premium rooms with chandeliers, disco balls and better drinks. Telephones on the wall are for ordering drinks or food.

Sporting chances

Kyoto has yet to embrace the pleasures of modern ball games. The city has a football team, Kyoto Sanga FC, in the top-tier J-League, but visiting crowds often outnumber home fans at the Nishi-Kyogoku Stadium. There's more enthusiasm for baseball, and the Hanshin Tigers, in particular, even though Kyoto has to share the team with Osaka and Kobe. Their Hanshin Koshien Stadium is an hour away by train in Nishinomiya, situated between Osaka and Kobe.

Bathing and beauty

To enjoy an authentic hot spring, you will need to take a day trip to one of the nearby resorts. Ohara (p126), Kibune and Kurama all lie within easy reach of Kyoto and offer mineral-rich bathing in the photogenic countryside. In the city, there are several *sento* (bathhouses with artificially heated water), and Funaoka Onsen (p114) stands out as the best. Its rich mix of nostalgic architecture and a variety of baths has made it the city's most popular place to soak, as well as a genuine tourist attraction. If you make the trek to the countryside, you'll be rewarded with great scenic vistas. If you decide to visit Funaoka, you'll have to make do with views of ceramic tiles and body art.

Calendar

Autumn Leaves p32

Kyoto's 2,000 temples and shrines host several festivals throughout the year, so there's usually something going on somewhere, and it's likely to be colourful, upbeat and fun. You'll find participants in period costumes and onlookers in kimono or *yukata*, praying for good fortune and connecting with their forebears in all manner of captivating ways, from burning effigies to hurling soy beans.

Most festivals are free, but the geisha dances command advance booking and fees of around ¥5,000. As the *kaburenjo* (training centres) usually only open for one short period each year, when the tickets go on sale, they are hot commodities.

Perhaps because the city is so rich in religious festivals, it is conspicuously short on secular events such as art fairs, film or music festivals, although during warmer seasons you'll discover small, impromptu parties on the banks of the Kamogawa river, around Sanjo Bridge.

If you wish to avoid the crowds, stay away from the cherry blossom or autumn leaves seasons. Other major holidays include New Year (28 December to 4 January) and Golden Week (29 April to 5 May), when many stores and restaurants close, and accommodation prices rise.

For full listings of forthcoming festivals, and maps to their sites, visit the Tourist Information Centre on the ninth floor of Isetan in Kyoto Station (p52).

January

1-5 **Hatsumode**
Shinto shrines
The first shrine visit of the year, with Yasaka and Heian Jingu drawing the biggest crowds.

Toshiya

4 **Kemari Hajime**
Shimogamo Jinja
Men in Heian period costume play an ancient ball game.

2nd Mon **Seijin no Hi (Coming of Age Day)**
Yasaka Jinja and other locations
People turning 20 years old in this financial year head to shrines in their best kimonos and suits for blessings.

15 **Tezukuri-ichi Market**
Chion-ji
A market of handmade arts and crafts held in the grounds of a temple near Kyoto University. The market takes place on the 15th of every month.

Sun nearest 15 Jan **Toshiya**
Sanjusangen-do
Around two thousand young men and women in kimonos re-enact an ancient archery contest.

21 **Kobo-san Flea Market**
To-ji
The first flea market of the year takes place at Toji. There are antiques, food and vintage kimonos on sale. The market takes place on the 21st of every month.

25 **Tenjin-san Flea Market**
Kitano Tenmangu
A flea market to mark the death of Michizane Sugawara, for whom the shrine was built. The market takes place on the 25th of each month.

February

2-3 **Mibu Kyogen**
Mibu-dera
Staging of Mibu Kyogen, a performing art that is designated an Important Cultural Property.

3 **Setsubun**
Yoshida Jinja, Heian Jingu, Yasaka Jinja and elsewhere
Last day of lunar winter marked by hurling soy beans to exorcise demons.

14 **Valentine's Day**
Women give chocolate to men in the local take on the romantic festival.

Mid Feb-mid March
Plum Blossom Viewing
Kitano Tenmangu, Nijo Castle and elsewhere
The flowering of plum trees is greeted with more restraint than the approaching cherry blossom.

23 Godairikison Nin'no-e
Daigo-ji, Fushimi
Competitors test their strength by lifting oversized rice cakes.

25 Baikasai
Kitano Tenmangu
An outdoor tea ceremony performed by *geiko* and *maiko* under lovely plum blossom.

March

Mid March Kyoto Hanatoro
Streets and major temples in Higashiyama are lit by lanterns.
www.hanatouro.jp/e/index.html

Mid March Start of the Football Season
www.j-league.or.jp/eng

Mid March Kyoto City Half Marathon
Heian Jingu
This annual half marathon draws 8,000 runners.

Mid-late March Osaka Grand Sumo Tournament
Osaka Prefectural Gymnasium
The spring grand sumo tournament takes place a short ride from Kyoto.

14 White Day
A follow-up event to Valentine's Day, in which guys give chocolate to girls.

15 Saga Nenbutsu Kyogen, Taimatsu Shiki
Seiryo-ji
A kyogen play takes place in the afternoon and *otaimatsu* (giant torches) are burned in the evening to commemorate the Shaka Buddha.

15-17 Kiyomizu-dera Seiryu-e
Kiyomizu-dera
An effigy of the guardian dragon Seiryu is paraded around the temple.

Late March-early April Hanami (Cherry Blossom Viewing)
Maruyama Park and elsewhere
See box p30.

April

First weekend Kamogawa Sakura Festival
Kamogawa riverside, between Shijo and Sanjo food stalls
Spotlight cherry blossom and performance art along the Kamo riverbank.
www.sakura-matsuri.com

First weekend Kyoto Yosakoi
Kyoto Ward Office square, Shinpukan, Karasuma Dori and elsewhere
More than 70 amateur dance troupes perform around the city.
www.sakuyosa.com

Early April Start of the Baseball Season

1-30 Miyako Odori
Gion Kobu Kaburenjo, Gion
Cherry blossom-themed dances are performed by Gion's *geiko* and *maiko*.
www.miyako-odori.jp

3 Kiyomizu Seiryu-e
Kiyomizu-dera
An effigy of the guardian dragon Seiryu is paraded around the temple.

2nd Sun Yasurai Festival
Imamiya Jinja
Men dressed up as demons parade through the streets to appease disease-spreading birds.

Mid April Benishidare
Heian Jingu
Classical music concert amid spot-lit cherry trees.

Mid-late April Kitano Odori
Kamishichiken Kaburenjo
The *geiko* and *maiko* of the Kamishichiken troupe perform plays and dances.
www.maiko3.com/event/kitano.html

21-29 Mibu Kyogen
Mibu-dera
A performance of Mibu Kyogen (mimed Buddhist morality plays) in Mibu-dera temple.

Temples of bloom

Cherry blossom

Tourists flock to Kyoto at New Year and for each of the three major festivals (**Aoi** p31, **Jidai** p32 and **Gion** p31), but the city is never so packed as in April when the cherry trees bloom, or November when the maple and gingko trees turn crimson and gold. The Zen-inspired Japanese concept of beauty embraces transience and imperfection, which makes the fleeting spectacles of *sakura* (cherry blossom) and *koyo* (autumn colours) popular subject matter for poets, photographers and painters. Nature's annual spectacles are so important in Japan that the TV news bulletins track the blossom and foliage fronts.

Heian Jingu, Tenryu-ji and Chion-in all look their finest in *sakura* season, but for gourmet revelry, head to **Maruyama Park** (p85). Combining four of Japan's key passions – alcohol, food, photography and seasonal beauty – the day-long celebrations centre on the giant *shidarezakura*

(weeping cherry tree), which reaches its dramatic height when illuminated each evening.

The **Philosopher's Path** (p102) is the most famous and revered cherry blossom stroll. Kyoto doesn't get more congested than this path in peak season, but it doesn't get much more enchanting either.

You can also take in the scenery from wooden boats that travel part of the Biwa-ko canal each April and early May (¥1,000). The three-kilometre ride from nearby **Nanzen-ji** (p100) to the Ebisugawa Dam takes 25 minutes, although you can expect to wait up to four hours to board. A better idea, perhaps, is to make a reservation (well in advance) at **Nishiki** (p117), where a cherry tree branch will likely brush the window of your private dining room.

In autumn, it's hard to find a temple that doesn't dazzle with seasonal colours, but **Tofuku-ji** (p122), in southern Kyoto, should be top of your must-visit list. The vast Zen complex dates back to 1236 and boasts dry Zen gardens, landscape gardens and several historic structures, but it all takes second billing in November when tourists cram on to the wooden Tsuten Bridge to view the sea of red, gold and green leaves below.

After jostling with the hordes on the bridge, walk through the complex and turn right out of the Muharamon exit. Take the first right, and immediately to your left you'll see Toko-ji, a tiny temple that opens only in November. Here, you can enjoy a far more Zen experience, sipping green tea and admiring the garden with no hint of the commotion going on just a few hundred metres away.

29 April-5 May **Golden Week**
A string of national holidays, which together form one of Japan's most popular holiday periods.

May

Ongoing Golden Week (see April)

1-24 May **Kamogawa Odori**
Pontocho Kaburen-jo
Geiko and *maiko* perform traditional dances in an event dating back to 1872.

1 May-20 Sept **Kawadoko Noryo**
Al fresco food and drink along the Kamo and Kibune rivers.

3 **Yabusame Shinji**
Shimogamo Jinja
Archery in Heian-period dress.
www.shimogamo-jinja.or.jp

5 **Kurabeuma-e Jinji**
Kamigamo Jinja
Horse race with jockeys in traditional costumes, staged here since 1093.
www.kamigamojinja.jp

15 **Aoi Festival**
Kyoto Gosho to Shimogamo Jinja, Kamigamo Jinja

One of Kyoto's big three festivals. Costumed participants retrace the imperial procession.

3rd Sun **Mifune Festival**
Kurumazaki Jinja
Boats carry imperial-costumed participants up the Oji river in Arashiyama.

June

Ongoing Kawadoko Noryo (see May)

10 **Tuesai Festival**
Fushimi Inari Taisha
Girls in Heian period costumes perform otomai dance to pray for a good harvest.

30 **Nagoshi no Harai**
Kitano Tenmangu
Sinners step through a five-metre wreath to atone for the sins of the first six months of the year.

July

Ongoing Kawadoko Noryo (see May)

1-31 **Gion Festival**
The biggest and best festival with geisha, floats and portable shrines parading along Shijo Dori.

Kemari Hajime p28

August

16 **Daimonji Gozan Fire Festival**
The Chinese characters carved into Kyoto's mountains are set alight.

16 **Toro Nagashi**
Hirosawa-no-ike and Miyazu Bay
Multi-coloured lanterns are floated on rivers and bays throughout Japan.

September

1st Sun **Hassakusai**
Matsuo Taisha
Sumo wrestling and traditional dramas to pray for peace and good harvest.

9 **Karasu Zumo (Crow Sumo)**
Kamigamo Jinja
Officials leap from foot to foot while cawing like crows, followed by amateur sumo by youngsters.
www.kamigamojinja.jp

15-17 **Kiyomizu-dera Seiryu-e**
Kiyomizu-dera
Effigy of the guardian dragon Seiryu is paraded around the temple.
3rd Mon **Respect for the Aged Day**
Public holiday honouring the elderly.

October

2nd Mon **Sports Day**
Public holiday commemorating the 1964 Olympics.

Weekend of 2nd Mon **Mibu Kyogen**
Mibu-dera
Recital of Mibu Kyogen, a comedic performance art designated as an Important Cultural Property.
www.kyoto.zaq.ne.jp/mibu

22 **Jidai Festival**
Kyoto Gosho to Heian Jingu
To celebrate the founding of Kyoto, 2,000 people in traditional costumes parade from Gosho to Heian Jingu.

November

3 **Culture Day**
The former Meiji Emperor's birthday is now a public holiday dedicated to culture and the arts.

8 **Hitaki Festival**
Fushimi Inari Taisha
A bonfire of more than 200,000 prayer sticks to pray for good harvest.

15 **Shichi Go San (Seven Five Three Festival)**
Heian Jingu, Yasaka-jinja and other shrines
In this traditional rite of passage, five-year-old boys, and three- and seven-year old girls dress up in their finest costumes and head for the shrine.

Mid-late Nov **Koyo (Autumn Leaves)**
Tofuku-ji, Arashiyama and elsewhere
See box p30.

Second Sun **Arashiyama Maple Leaf Festival**
Togetsu-kyo Bridge area
Costumes, music, dancing and maple-leaf scenery.

30 Nov-26 Dec **Kichirei Kaomise Kogyo**
Minamiza
The highlight of the kabuki calendar marks the start of a new theatrical year.
www.shochiku.co.jp/play/minamiza/index.html

December

Ongoing Kichirei Kaomise Kogyo
(see Nov)

Mid Dec **Arashiyama Hanatoro**
Lanterns illuminate the bamboo forest and other areas of Arashiyama.
www.hanatouro.jp/e/index.html

23 **Emperor's Birthday**
A public holiday to mark the birth of the current Emperor.

31 **Okera Mairi**
Yasaka Jinja
Prayers for health and happiness in the coming year.

Itineraries

Kyoto Revamped

With geisha still clip-clopping down cobbled streets, artists hand-painting kimonos and chefs sticking with centuries-old recipes, it's clear that Kyoto isn't a city of gratuitous change. Locals grumble about the development of their city, but most visitors will be struck by how well the place has kept its looks. Even in the urban heart of Kyoto, classic townhouses, storehouses and bathhouses resist the wrecking ball. Although most have outlived their intended use, these buildings are being renovated and repurposed, usually with plenty of their original features preserved. This tour covers some of the best revamps.

Begin by checking into a *machiya*. The traditional wood and clay townhouse was the combined residence and workplace for merchants and craftsmen. Such vernacular buildings exist elsewhere in Japan, but the Kyoto version, known as *Kyo-machiya*, is considered to be the archetype, and is as integral to the city's visage as its temples, shrines and painted ladies.

Although it may look attractive, the fragile residence of clay and wood doesn't measure up to modern fire or earthquake regulations, and is ill equipped to cope with Kyoto's cold winters or humid summers. So the unsentimental post-war years saw a construction boom replace many with more practical structures.

Luckily, the 21st century has been kinder to the *machiya*. To preserve the old face of Kyoto – and cash in on people's affection for the city – businesses are snapping up classic townhouses and transforming them into cafés, bars, beauty salons, boutiques, restaurants and even a golf driving range.

Iori, a company fronted by author Alex Kerr, is leading the way in converting historic *machiya* into guesthouses. The company currently runs nine houses around the city,

Sarasa Nishijin p37

craftsmanship and fuses it with modern technology to create dishwasher-proof designs with a modern aesthetic. Rather than relying on traditional retail displays, Oku lets you eat and drink from its dishes, with a menu of gourmet treats that includes a gorgeous slow-steamed custard pudding with anise and vanilla.

For dinner, head into town to the ramen shop **Gogyo** (p54) on Yanaginobanba Dori. This building was once the home of Oyuki, a geisha who caused a sensation when, in 1904, she quit her profession and married the wealthy George Morgan, nephew of JP. After George's death, Oyuki spent a couple of decades on the Riviera before living out her retirement in this sizeable townhouse.

Oyuki died in 1963, and these days her front room is a rowdy open kitchen with pans clattering and flames roaring each time a customer orders the 'burned ramen' of noodles and pork in a rich, black flambéed soup. Your doctor would probably not recommend it, but ramen fans do.

After dinner, ask the staff to lead you to the bar. A backdoor opens onto the tiniest of gardens, with a path of stepping stones leading to Oyuki's old storehouse. Inside, you'll find one of Kyoto's best-hidden bars. Look for the ostentatious vault – proof that the previous owner wasn't short of a yen or two. The menu includes a range of original shochu-based cocktails. After drinks, head home to the *machiya*, roll out your futon and get a good night's sleep.

Around 10am the next morning, ride the Karasuma or Tozai subway line to Karasuma Oike Station. Take Exit 2 and look for the large orange building on Karasuma Dori. This is the former Tatsuike Primary School and current **Kyoto International Manga Museum** (see box p73).

each offering the kind of luxury that you might expect of a high-end hotel or ryokan (with prices to match); **Iori Sanbo Nishinotoin-cho** (p139) is one of the latest additions. For a more moderate *machiya* experience, visit **Suisen-Kyo Shirakawa** (p143). If you can live without a concierge and buffet breakfast, staying in a *machiya* is a fun way in which to connect with Old Kyoto.

After dropping off your luggage, head to Gion, a time warp of teahouses and stone streets. On a narrow street just south of Shijo Dori, you'll find **Oku** (p89), a café that typifies Kyoto's gift for modernising without homogenising. In a pristine *machiya* with a tiny Japanese rock garden, staff serve exquisite local food on fine lacquerware and ceramics. So far, so Kyoto. But the brilliant white interior with purple fabric seating, the oh-so-beautiful staff and the speakers playing mellow electronica make it clear that this is no preservation project. The café is a showcase for a new local brand of tableware that takes traditional

Iori Sanbo NIshinotoin-cho p35

On clement weekends, you'll spot legions of costumed manga fans in what used to be the playground. Inside, kids lay around on stairwells reading manga, just as they do in schools across Japan, but without the threat of reprimand. The curators have made a determined effort to keep the primary school feel, even pumping out the school song from speakers into one classroom-turned-exhibition space.

From here, walk north to Nijo Dori and turn right. A few blocks along, you'll spot a *machiya* hiding behind a banana tree. **Café Bibliotic Hello!** (p72) is a kimono store turned café and one of the city's best-loved conversions. Current owner Mitsunari Koyama stripped most of the ceiling away to give the place a bright, airy interior. He furnished it with a medley of modern tables, chairs and sofas, as well as the two-storey bookshelves that account for part of the peculiar name. Koyama says the 'Hello!' was inspired by a popular proverb, 'ichigo ichie',

which means, roughly: 'Every encounter is but once in a lifetime.' In this case, it tells you to expect warm service with your pasta or sandwich.

When you leave the café, turn right, and then left at the first corner. Walk south to Sanjo Dori, and stop at the stone building on the corner. These days it's home to **Ichimanben** (p61), a great place at which to pick up an affordable kimono, but it was built to house a branch of an insurance company and reinforced with steel as an early effort at earthquake-proofing. Architects Kingo Tatsuno and Yasushi Kataoka collaborated on this 1914 building at a time when Western ideas flowed into Japan. Tatsuno, the son of a samurai, had studied at the Royal Academy of Arts in London and returned to Japan with a taste for stately stone and brick architecture.

In the old days, Sanjo Dori was an economic hub and the city's main thoroughfare, so when Japan began to embrace Western

influences, Sanjo was first in line for trophy architecture, much of which survives today.

A few blocks west of Ichimanben stands another Tatsuno building, this one constructed for the Bank of Japan, but now home to the **Museum of Kyoto** (p54). The red brick with stripes of granite and turreted green roofing will be familiar to anyone who has seen his most famous creation, Tokyo Station, or Nakagyo Post Office, just a few yards away on Sanjo Dori.

The museum is not a world-class attraction, but will hold the attention of anyone wishing to see how this city has developed during the last 1,200 years.

After you've visited the museum, jump in a taxi and ask for **Funaoka Onsen** (p114), which lies in the Nishijin textile area. Until as recently as the 1960s, public bathing was commonplace in Japan, with private bathrooms never a feature of traditional machiya design. Although the bathhouse business has slumped as modern home plumbing has taken over, Funaoka remains a popular Kyoto institution.

Gents should enter via the blue curtain, ladies by the red, then undress and place clothes in a basket. Proceed to the showers and scrub yourself thoroughly before entering the tubs. Men will often find themselves sharing baths with yakuza gang members, but although they can be louder than other bathers, they won't bother you.

There's nothing remotely revamped about Funaoka Onsen – it's pure nostalgia, right down to the wood-relief panels depicting scenes of Japanese troops invading Manchuria. The reason it's on this itinerary, other than being a key Kyoto experience, is to set the scene for your next stop – the café **Sarasa Nishijin** (p112).

Museum of Kyoto

Turn right out of Funaoka and walk three blocks east. The most time-worn building on the block, with an arched doorway resembling Funaoka's entrance, was also once a public bathhouse. The floor plan, wooden beams and bright green tiles are remnants of its first life, but Sarasa is now a fun café, with wood floors, leather sofas and handmade furniture. Grab coffee and some cake and – pardon the pun – soak up the atmosphere.

From here, it's a short cab ride to **Jittoku** (p114), where you'll wrap up your day listening to some live music. Aim to arrive shortly after 7pm to grab the best seats. This former sake brewery underwent the slightest of renovations to become an atmospheric live venue. Although the brewing ceased in the early 1970s, booze still flows through the place as a vibrant crowd sits on old sake barrels, eating, drinking and listening to live music. Jittoku is open to all kinds of music, but there's a good chance you'll be listening to blues, rock, folk or pop.

Taizo-in

The New Philosopher's Path

Kyoto has one itinerary that has become a massive tourist attraction: the Philosopher's Path. The route was reportedly taken each day by Kitaro Nishida, founder of the Kyoto School of Philosophy and perhaps Japan's greatest modern thinker. Nishida was known for fusing Eastern and Western ideas to create theories of self-awareness and absolute nothingness, which no amount of scenic strolling will help you to comprehend. Nor are you likely to develop any profound concepts of your own. It is, after all, just a pretty walk.

So here is an alternative path for philosophers to ponder some of the city's biggest ideas. The route takes a little preparation, which can all be done online in English. First, book a 'Living in Zen' class via the website of **Taizo-in** (p110),

then email **Shunko-in** (p110) to reserve a room for the same night.

The session at Zen temple **Taizo-in** begins at 9am with some meditation. English-speaking priest Daiko Matsuyama explains the posture and purpose of meditating, and allows his guests to decide whether they wish to be 'encouraged by the stick of compassion' (clouted with a wooden bat). The course proceeds with a calligraphy workshop, a stroll through the temple's renowned garden, then a casual tea ceremony, before ending with a beautiful *shojin ryori* lunch of seasonal vegetarian dishes. The articulate, engaging priest also introduces the temple's greatest treasure – a 700-year-old painting that explains much about both Taizo-in and Zen. In the 15th century, shogun Ashikaga Yoshimochi ordered 31 Zen priests to answer

the seemingly impossible question, 'How do you catch a catfish with a gourd?' The priests wrote their solutions above an ink-and-wash painting of a fisherman drawing near a catfish, the last remaining masterpiece of Josetsu, father of the Sumi-e style. Answers ranged from 'Wax the gourd' to 'It's no use thinking about this, let's cook rice and drink catfish soup instead.' The difference between the laity who refuse to ponder the impossible, and the Zen monks who routinely do, according to Matsuyama, is the difference between a man who stares at a pointing finger, and one who follows the finger's direction.

When the session ends at 1pm, walk north – enlightened or baffled – until you reach the **Shunko-in** sub-temple, where you'll be spending the night. After checking in, head straight back out and exit the temple complex **Myoshin-ji** (p107) via the north gate. From here it's only a ten-minute walk to **Ryoan-ji** (p110), home to one of the most polarising attractions in the city. For some, the *karensansui* (dry mountain water) garden is a masterpiece, for others

it's just a bunch of stones. Some say the garden is a mirror to your soul, with positive people seeing beauty, and discontented ones finding nothing of value. The garden has 15 rocks encircled by moss and raked white gravel. To convey the Zen idea that only the enlightened can see the truth, the rocks are arranged to prevent you from viewing all 15 at once, no matter where you stand. Visitors who stand over six feet tall should thus be delighted to find that they can see it all at once, enjoying the view of the enlightened.

For philosophers, the garden offers a chance to ponder the meaning of the layout. Although the designer's intention is unknown, a multitude of theories have been proposed, with the most recent coming from a team of Kyoto University researchers. They discovered that, when viewed from one angle, the stones resembled the branches of a tree.

From Ryoan-ji, it only takes five minutes by bus or 20 minutes on foot to reach **Kinkaku-ji** (p107), another Zen temple, at which you

can ponder how a religious school with tenets of simplicity and austerity came to be home to a pagoda of brilliant gold (blame the shogun who built the structure).

Now it's time to head downtown (via bus 12 or 59) for a coffee at **Salon de thé François** (p86). Named after the French painter Jean-François Millet, the café was set up in 1934 as a hub of progressive politics and philosophical debate. In 1936, as fascism rose in prominence on domestic and international fronts, the salon's owner helped establish an underground anti-fascist newspaper. The owner and the interior designer of the Salon de thé François were imprisoned for their beliefs, but their café continued to thrive and is now a Registered Tangible Cultural Property.

After your coffee, it's time to have dinner at an establishment with a more contemporary agenda. **Mikoan** (p57) is run by a nun from **Higashi Hongan-ji** (p46), and as you will soon notice from the decor, she is passionate about pacifism. There are posters campaigning for freedom in Burma, flyers for pacifist movies, a flag bearing the text of the war-renouncing Article 9 of Japan's Constitution, and perhaps

Mikoan

incongruously, an image of Che Guevara. For every Burmese Milk Tea sold, the owners donate money to that country's democracy campaign. Naturally, the food is also pacifist, with a vegetarian menu of Japanese home cooking. If carnivores are struggling with the idea of two meatless meals in one day, try the mock *kara-age* for a decent approximation of chicken (and consider that meat was once prohibited on religious grounds).

After dinner, head back to **Shunko-in**. Walking through the hushed enclave to reach your room is an experience you won't soon forget. The next morning, join the meditation session with vice-abbot Takafumi Kawakami, then follow his tour of a temple that has plenty to teach the world about religious tolerance. In 1587, Japan's shogun banned Christianity, forcing devout followers to worship in secret. One such 'hidden Christian' married the grandson of Shunko-in's founder, and the temple gave refuge to persecuted believers. If you look closely, you can still find Christian imagery at the temple, including painted screen doors that hide symbols of the Holy Trinity, the Virgin Mary and the resurrection, and a Jesuit bell from Kyoto's first Christian church. Add to this a framed verse from Mohammad, written by a visiting Iraqi artist, and you have the city's most diverse place of worship. Appropriately, vice-abbot Kawakami graduated in religious studies, specialising in conflict management.

Shunko-in was also the site of philosophical discussions on the future of Buddhism between DT Suzuki, chief exporter of Zen to the West, and Shinichi Hisamatsu, a philosopher, Zen scholar and student of Kitaro Nishida, the man whose daily walk has become such a tourist attraction.

Gion Hatanaka p44

Do Kyoto in a Day

It's one of the world's most beautiful cities, with more temples and treasures than anyone could hope to see in a lifetime. So why on earth would you schedule just one day in Kyoto? But for those who pop in on a whirlwind tour of Japan, here's how to get a measure of the city in less than 24 hours.

Start early. If you're coming from Tokyo, the first bullet train reaches Kyoto a few minutes past 8am. Take the central exit from the station, look straight ahead and you should spot the eaves of the nearest temple, **Higashi Hongan-ji** (p46) – your first stop, and a great place in which to reflect on the extraordinary power that Buddhism once enjoyed in Japan.

The temple belongs to a subsect of Jodo Shinshu, a branch of Buddhism once seen as a threat to Japan's rulers. The 16th-century warrior Oda Nobunaga so feared the sect's swelling ranks of monks and peasants that he decided to torch their temples and massacre the members. In the early 17th century, Shogun Ieyasu Tokugawa took a more tactical approach, offering land for a breakaway faction to build a new temple. And so was born Higashi Hongan-ji.

As you marvel at the main hall, which claims to be the largest wooden structure in the world (a claim that is also made by Nara's **Todai-ji**, p125), remember that this is the fifth incarnation. Whenever fire has razed the temple, followers have funded a swift reconstruction. It's not just cash that they have donated. In the corridor between the Founder's Hall and the Amida Hall, you'll find a rope woven from locks of female followers. In 1895, when the buildings were constructed, the employees of the temple wove the tresses into heavy-duty ropes to haul the wooden beams into place.

Around 9am, walk a block south to **Kyoto Tower** (p48). This gaudy piece of 1960s kitsch would blend

Gion

in better in Blackpool or Niagara
Falls, but its panoramic observation
deck is the best place from which to
size up the city. The free telescopes
allow you to zoom in on distant
temples (and remind you to keep
your curtains drawn should you
ever stay within peeping distance
of Kyoto Tower).

Then it's time for breakfast. Kyoto
is renowned for its immaculate
restaurants and exquisite cuisine,
but the **Dai-ichi Asahi** (p51)
ramen shop is nothing like that. It's
cramped, noisy and thick with the
aroma of its signature soy ramen.
There are scores of more stylish
noodle joints in town, but luckily
for Dai-ichi Asahi, it's broth rather
than decor that makes or breaks a
ramen shop. Customers have been
crowding into this place for more
than six decades. There are two
noodle shops on the street – step
into the one with the yellow awning.
At this time of day you should find
vacant seats, but if there's a queue
outside, it will move fast. Once in,

park yourself on one of the tiny red
chairs and simply ask the staff for
'ramen'. It's no delicate way to start
the day, but it's tasty, filling and
makes a contrast to the fancy food
that you'll be eating later on.

Next, head back to the station,
find bus stop D2 and take a 100,
206 or 208 bus to **Sanjusangen-do**
(p50). If the thought of riding on a
bus worries you, grab a cab instead
– it should cost less than ¥800.

So many of Kyoto's temples do
their dazzling on the outside, but
Sanjusangen-do ('The Hall of
Thirty-three Bays'), has a relatively
plain façade, concealing a splendid
interior. The 750-year-old main hall
is home to a three-metre, gold-plated
statue of Kannon, goddess of mercy,
flanked by a further 1,000 Kannons,
each standing 1.7 metres tall and
staring serenely at her visitors.

Across the street from
Sanjusangen-do stands the
National Museum (p48), a
grand piece of Western-influenced
architecture on the grounds of a

former imperial estate. Although the permanent collection is closed to the public until 2013, the special shows, usually of works loaned by temples or the Imperial Household, are always worth a visit.

Now, head for the centre of the city. This time, we advise you to take a taxi – look for cabs with a heart on the roof for the cheapest rates. Ask for the street junction of Shijo-Shinkyogoku, then walk a block north to the start of Kyoto's main food market **Nishiki-koji market** (p62). As you may need to refuel by now, munch your way along this 400-metre stretch, collecting a multi-course feast as you go. Start with some rice crackers from Terakoya Hompo, followed by tuna sashimi-on-a-stick from Kimura, then *nerimono* (steamed dumplings of minced fish) from Hokyuan, and a salad of sweet potato and black beans from Inoue. Take a seat at Daiyasu for a grilled oyster, then join the queue opposite to pick up soy milk doughnuts at Konnyamonja for dessert. Finish up with a brew at Kaneta Coffee, or a green tea from Tsuruya Kakujuan.

When you've finished eating, head south a block and turn left on to Shijo Dori. This is the main shopping thoroughfare, and the only part of the city to have succumbed to homogenising megabrands. But it's not without its charms – the **Fukujuen store** (p59) has a basement in which you can sample various kinds of green tea from one of Japan's top suppliers, and **Karan Koron** (p61) sells elegant Japanese knick-knacks, which make great souvenirs.

After crossing over the river, turn left towards Kawabata Dori and take the fourth right on to Shinmonzen Dori (look for the red street umbrellas). If you're looking for some quality mementos, this street of antique stores has

everything that you could wish for. Try **Art Yoshikiri** (p91) for woodblock prints, or **Yume Koubou** (p94) for antiques. These stores are mini-museums with owners won't mind you browsing.

When you approach the end of Shinmonzen Dori, look to your right. On the opposite side of the street, you'll see a stone pillar with Chinese character carvings. This marks the entrance to **Chion-In** (p82), whose 24-metre-high wooden gate posed as the entrance to Edo Castle in *The Last Samurai*.

Chion-In is the seat of Jodo sect Buddhism, whose philosophy is, roughly: don't try to be clever, just chant. This relatively effortless path to enlightenment proved popular with peasants and nobles alike, and the temple counted among its patrons the Tokugawa shogunate – it funded several grand buildings and you can spot the family's hollyhock crest on the beams).

ITINERARIES

Chion-In

Chion-In is also known for its seven wonders, although only three of them are on show to the public, and 'wonder' might be a touch hyperbolic for a collection that includes a big wooden spoon, an umbrella lodged in the rafters and a pair of plain wooden coffins. The most interesting, although least mysterious, are the 'nightingale' floorboards of the cloisters, designed to sing (read: creak) with every footstep to help protect the Tokugawas and other visiting dignitaries from surprise attacks. While you're here, make sure that you visit the stroll gardens.

Leave Chion-In by the same grand gate, and turn left. A few yards south is the bright orange entrance of **Yasaka Jinja** (p86), a seventh-century Shinto shrine. The grounds are open around the clock, and at their most beautiful when the lanterns are lit every evening. There's a good chance of seeing the painted white face and colourful kimono of a *maiko* around here, but

Kyoto Tower p41

KYOTO TOWER HOTEL

the challenge is to distinguish bona fide entertainers from the tourists who pay for maiko makeovers when they come to town. If the girls look a little wobbly on their wooden shoes, or are photographing each other with their mobile phones, they're probably pretenders.

However, you won't need to gaze at the girls in the street, because you'll have booked a table at **Gion Hatanaka** (p87, reserve online in English, a few days ahead), where genuine *geiko* and *maiko* entertain visitors. In 2009, this ryokan began hosting events that allow visitors to glimpse the otherwise insular world of the geisha. The fun kicks off at 6pm with a dance performance by a pair of apprentices, accompanied by a *geiko* on *samisen*. The waiting staff then bring a lacquer box of seasonal delicacies, while the girls pour drinks and chat to guests. The *maiko* are about 17 years old and have absorbed themselves in studying traditional dance, dress and etiquette rather than watching Hollywood movies, so English conversation is rudimentary.

The evening wraps up with drinking games and photo opportunities, before visitors are turfed out at 8pm, which is your cue to climb into a cab and ask for Rokkaku Gokomachi. Just west of that crossing is the lantern-lined entrance of **K'Ya** (p57), one of the city's best bars, and a great place for a nightcap. This converted townhouse stocks several hundred scotches, and creates original cocktails, including a Laphroaig-flavoured flaming espresso, paired with homemade scented chocolates.

If you're heading to Tokyo next, grab a cab to **Kyoto Station** (p48) about 9pm. Those heading south can spend another hour, while anyone heading to Osaka can stay here until 11pm.

Kyoto by Area

Kyoto Station p48

Kyoto Station Area

Kyoto doesn't make a great first impression. Whether you love or loathe the 15-storey cubism of Kyoto Station, as soon as you step outside, you'll find the area short of photogenic gifts. Shabby concrete buildings and a gaudy orange-and-white tower greet you. There's no nightlife, few shops and little in the way of popular leisure facilities.

So it says much about Kyoto that even here you'll discover a historic garden, a UNESCO World Heritage Site and one of the city's oldest temples. It has some gourmet treats too: the area lies between the site of the ancient entrance to the city and the grand Kiyomizu Temple, and some of the old tea houses that served pilgrims are still open for business, although they dish up grander meals today. It's not an area you'll fall in love with, but it has its moments.

Sights & museums

Costume Museum

5F Izutsu Building, Shinhanaya-cho Dori, Horikawa Higashi-iru, Shimogyo-ku (075 342 5345/www.iz2.or.jp/english). Kyoto Station (JR, Karasuma, Kintetsu lines). **Open** 9am-5pm Mon-Sat. **Admission** ¥400. **Map** p47 A1 ❶

This museum is like a vast doll's house, built with a staggering eye for detail. Palm-sized dolls dressed in period costume recreate scenes from Japanese history, often with reference to *The Tale of Genji*, the thousand-year-old story of imperial courtships. The displays are created by tailors to Kyoto's monks, priests and nuns. Every six months, they unveil a new scene, scrupulously crafted with details of the era. Visitors can don costumes and pose for pictures.

Higashi Hongan-ji

Karasuma Dori, Shichijo-agaru, Shimogyo-ku (075 371 9210/www.higashihonganji.jp).

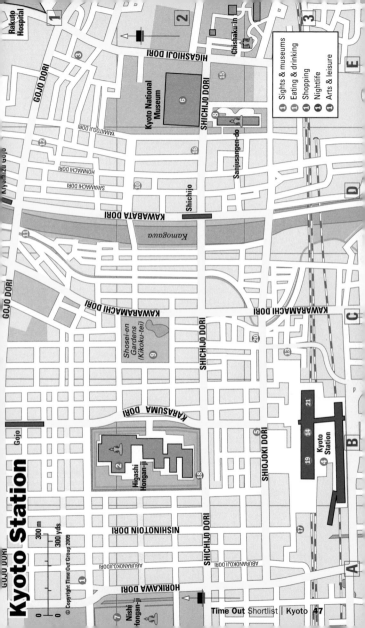

Kyoto Station

Rakuto Hospital

GOJO DORI

Chishaku-in

HIGASHIOJI DORI

Kyoto National Museum

SHICHIJO DORI

Sanjusangen-do

YAMATOOJI DORI

Kawazu-gojo

HONMACHI DORI

SAYAMACHI DORI

Shichijo

KAWABATA DORI

Kamogawa

GOJO DORI

KAWARAMACHI DORI

Shosei-en Gardens (Kikoku-tei)

SHICHIJO DORI

KAWARAMACHI DORI

KARASUMA DORI

Higashi Hongan-ji

SHIOJOKI DORI

Kyoto Station

GOJO DORI

NISHINOTOIN DORI

SHICHIJO DORI

ABURANOKOJIDORI

HORIKAWA DORI

ABURANOKOJI DORI

Nishi Hongan-ji

0   300 m
0   300 yds

© Copyright Time Out Group 2009

Gojo

Sights & museums
Eating & drinking
Shopping
Nightlife
Arts & leisure

Time Out Shortlist | Kyoto **47**

Kyoto Station (JR, Karasuma, Kintetsu lines). **Open** *Mar-Oct* 5.30am-5.30pm daily. *Nov-Feb* 6.20am-4.30pm daily. **Admission** free. **Map** p47 B2 ❷

The temple closest to Kyoto Station exists thanks to a shogun's paranoia. By the 17th century, the Jodo Shinshu sect of Buddhism had grown powerful enough to worry Shogun Ieyasu Tokugawa. When it became embroiled in a succession dispute, he drove the wedge in by offering land for a breakaway faction to build a temple on. Higashi Hongan-ji opened in 1602, a few hundred metres away from rival Nishi Hongan-ji (p50), and the sect has been divided ever since. Fire razed the newer Hongan-ji four times, the current structures date from only 1895. Among the temple's exhibits are tools used in the most recent reconstruction, including a wooden sledge for transporting timber and a 375kg rope made from the hair of temple followers – regular ropes of the era were too weak to hoist such heavy timber. After a major renovation, the Main Hall is set to reopen in October 2009.

Kanjiro Kawai Memorial House

569 Kanei-cho, Gojo-zaka, Higashiyama-ku (075 561 3585). Gojo Station (Keihan line). Bus 206. **Open** 10am-5pm Tue-Sun. **Admission** ¥900. **Map** p47 E1 ❸

The former home and atelier of master potter and sculptor Kanjiro Kawai is a museum of his artworks and an immaculate townhouse that shows how a wealthy artist lived during the early 20th century. Kawai was one of the leaders of the Japanese folk craft movement, and his home has been preserved remarkably well, with many examples of his work and a multi-level kiln in the backyard.

Kyoto National Museum

527 Chayamachi, Higashiyama-ku (075 541 1151/www.kyohaku.go.jp). Shichijo Station (Keihan line). **Open** 9.30am-5pm Tue-Sun. **Admission** ¥500. **Map** p47 E2 ❻

The National Museum is worth a visit just to see the building. Constructed in the 1890s, this neo-classical gem by Tokuma Katayama has been designated an Important Cultural Property. It now functions as the special exhibition hall, which stages regular, fascinating shows of Chinese and Japanese art and artefacts. The museum's permanent collection, which is housed in a newer and less photogenic Collection Hall, is closed until 2013 as the wing undergoes renovations.

Kyoto Station

Karasuma Dori, Shiokoji-sagaru, Shimogyo-ku (075 352 5441/ www.kyoto-station-building.co.jp). Kyoto Station (JR, Karasuma, Kintetsu lines). **Map** p47 B3 ❹

In 1997, a little over 1,200 years after the city was founded, Kyoto got a grand new station, just a few blocks away from the site of Rashomon, the original entrance gate to the city. Architect Hiroshi Hara's creation is futuristic and rugged; in other words, the antithesis of Kyoto. The protests have subsided as Kyoto-ites have learned to live with, or love, this steel-and-glass giant, with a theatre, hotel and department store.

Kyoto Tower

Karasuma Dori, Shichijo-sagaru, Shimogyo-ku (075 361 3215/ www.kyoto-tower.co.jp). Kyoto Station (JR, Karasuma, Kintetsu lines). **Open** 9am-9pm (last entry 8.40pm) daily. **Admission** ¥770. **Map** p47 B3 ❺

From the outside it's an eyesore, and inside it's even worse, but the Kyoto Tower, opposite Kyoto Station, is a great place at which to get your bearings. The 100m-high panoramic observation deck has free telescopes offering close-ups of all kinds of city details, from the carved roof tiles of nearby Higashi Hongan-ji (p46) to the crowds along the balcony of the distant Kiyomizu-dera (p84).

Fabric of life

Kimono-clad Kyoto.

Costume Museum p46

The kimono is elegant, graceful and feminine. It's also bulky, restrictive and difficult to tie. So it's not without reason that the once everyday attire is now reserved for special occasions in most of Japan.

In Kyoto, however, the kimono is still a popular garment. It's the uniform of the geisha, of course, but also of shop and ryokan staff; it's everyday wear for the city's more traditional residents, and a popular outfit with out-of-towners visiting their cultural heartland.

The tourists like to dress in elaborate, formal designs, but locals who don daily kimonos are likely to choose a subtler and more modern-looking garment. 'Traditional styles are very formal, but for daily wear, colourful pop designs are more comfortable,' says a spokesperson for **Sou Sou** (p62), a local brand from Katsuji Wakisaka. Current Sou Sou designs include black fabric scattered with Japanese script and red cloth decorated with numerals.

At **OMO** (p78), kimono stylist Motoko Morita offers tailor-made or prêt-à-porter designs. Her fabrics suit contemporary tastes, and can be paired with vivid *obi* (kimono belts), made from the upholstery of French sofas.

But Kyoto is never a city to abandon its culture, and the traditional kimono patterns are popping up in unorthodox places. French restaurant, **Tamaki** (p77), employs kimono shawls as tablecloths, and Zen temple **Kanga-an** combines kimono cloth with tatami mats for its flooring.

Local brand Mizra decorates its jeans with kimono fabric, and last year, Toyoaki Kuwayama, the scion of a kimono-making family, launched **Kyoto Denim** (p52), a line of jeans with traditional kimono designs on the pockets and waistbands. He uses a laborious dyeing process known as *kyo-yuzen,* which has been handed down through generations of his family and is traditionally reserved for high-end kimonos.

Nishi Hongan-ji

*Horikawa Dori, Hanayacho-sagaru,
Shimogyo-ku (075 371 5181/www.
hongwanji.or.jp). Kyoto Station
(JR, Karasuma, Kintetsu lines).*
Open *Jan, Feb* 6am-5pm daily. *Mar,
Apr* 5.30am-5.30pm daily. *May-Aug*
5.30am-6pm daily. *Sept, Oct* 5.30am-
5.30pm daily. *Nov, Dec* 6am-5pm daily.
Admission free. **Map** p47 A2 **7**

The head temple of Jodo Shinshu
Buddhists is the closest World Heritage
landmark to Kyoto Station. The original
temple was built in the Higashiyama
district during the 13th century, but
wars and politics forced it to relocate
several times before Hideyoshi
Toyotomi granted the sect the land for
its current site in 1591. There are now
more than 10,000 sub-temples of Nishi
Hongan-ji scattered throughout Japan.
The precinct has impressive examples
of decorative architecture from the
Momoyama period (1573-1615) and a
beautiful garden, although only part of
the complex is open to the public.

Sanjusangen-do

*657 Sanjusangen-do, Mawari-cho,
Higashiyama-ku. Shichijo Station
(Keihan line).* **Open** *1 April-15 Nov*
8am-5pm daily. *16 Nov-31 Mar*
9am-4pm daily. **Admission** ¥600.
Map p47 E2 **8**

Built during the 12th century for
emperor-turned-monk Go-Shirakawa,
Sanjusangen-do has several claims to
fame. The 120m-long main hall is the
longest wooden building in Japan;
it was the site of one of the most famous
duels of Musashi Miyamoto, the legendary Japanese swordsman; and each
January it plays host to an archery contest. But when you step inside that long
hall, you'll see why this is such a popular temple. A breathtaking 1,000 golden
statues of the Bodhisattva Kannon stand
in orderly rows, facing their visitors to
offer them protection. In the centre sits
a 3m-tall Kannon, the work of an 82-
year-old master sculptor, Tankei, back in
1254. Photography is prohibited.

Shosei-en Gardens

*Kamijuzuya-cho, Karasuma Dori,
Shimogyo-ku (075 371 9210/www.
higashihonganji.jp). Kyoto Station
(JR, Karasuma, Kintetsu lines).*
Open 9am-4pm daily. **Admission**
¥500. **Map** p47 C2 **9**

The creators of this sizeable garden
couldn't have imagined that future
generations would see fit to build budget hotels and a gaudy tower on
its perimeter. This National Historic
Site, belonging to Higashi Hongan-ji,
was created in the 17th century to
resemble the Shiogama coastline of
northern Japan, and although the
grounds haven't been nearly as well
maintained as many gardens in the
city, it's still a charming place to visit
when you're near the station.

Eating & drinking

Douraku

*304 Shomen-cho, Honmachi Dori,
Higashiyama-ku (075 561 0478/
www.dourakurou.jp). Shichijo Station
(Keihan line).* **Open** noon-2pm,
5-8pm Tue-Sun. **¥¥¥¥**. **Kaiseki**.
Map p47 D2 **10**

Douraku was established almost
400 years ago as a teahouse for nobles.
The fifth-generation owner transformed
it into a restaurant, and by the Meiji era
it had become an official supplier to the
household of the imperial family. The
current (tenth-generation) chef serves
the most formal multi-course cuisine in
vast, hushed private rooms. It's richer
than some *kaiseki*, and with over a dozen
dishes, you can expect to leave stuffed
and up to ¥50,000 poorer. For a taste of
Douraku without breaking the bank,
order a lunchtime bento box (¥5,500).

Efish

*798-1 Nishi Hashizume-cho, Kiyamachi
Dori, Gojo-sagaru, Shimogyo-ku (075
361 3069/www.shinproducts.com).
Gojo Station (Keihan line).* **Open**
11am-10pm daily. **Café/bar**.
Map p47 D1 **11**

This cosy riverside café was once the home of local designer Shin Nishibori, whose creations continue to furnish the place. In the daytime, it dishes up great sandwiches and coffee; by night it operates as a chic bar, drawing in the local design crowd.

Harise

294 Fukuro-cho, Daikoku-machi, Gojo-sagaru, Higashiyama-ku (075 561 5021/www.harise.com). Gojo Station (Keihan line). **Open** 11.30am-2pm, 5-9pm Mon, Wed-Sun. **¥¥¥¥. Kaiseki. Map** p47 D1 ⑫

This unforgettable restaurant began life in 1656 as a humble teahouse for pilgrims en route to Kiyomizu-dera (p84), but these days it serves something far grander. The maid will usher you into a private room, furnished with a sumptuous array of cushion seats. Twelfth-generation masterchef Tomoyuki Morimoto then serves a multi-course feast of Kyoto cuisine that perfectly balances colours, textures and tastes. *Kaiseki* can sometimes be a stiflingly formal affair, but Morimoto's culinary creations are playful enough to make the fine dining fun.

Honke Dai-ichi Asahi

845 Mukaihata-cho, Higashi Shiokoji-cho, Shimogyo-ku (075 351 6321/www. honke-daiichiasahi.com). Kyoto Station (JR, Karasuma, Kintetsu lines). **Open** 5.30am-2am daily. **¥. No credit cards. Ramen. Map** p47 C3 ⑬

It's not much to look at, but this bustling 29-seater ramen shop is perennially popular, with lines of people waiting to get in most lunchtimes. There's only one kind of ramen on offer: a rich, soy-flavoured soup with pork and noodles, made to a recipe that hasn't changed since the store opened more than 60 years ago. It closes for just three and a half hours each day.

Kyodofu Fujino

11th floor, Isetan, Kyoto Station, Karasuma Dori, Shiokoji-sagaru,

Efish

Shimogyo-ku (075 352 5401/www. shop/fujino_kyoto/index.html). Kyoto Station (JR, Karasuma, Kintetsu lines). **Open** 11am-10pm daily. **¥¥. Tofu. Map** p47 B3 ⑭

Kyoto Station contains a warren of restaurants; some are great, but most are not. The pick of the bunch is this tofu specialist, which serves an extra silky local version known as *kyodofu*. In winter, try the *yudofu*, a broth of tofu and local vegetables; in summer, the speciality is *hiya yakko* (chilled tofu with soy sauce, chopped leek and spices). Although the interior may be forgettable, the 11th-floor view of the Higashiyama mountains will linger in your memory for some time.

Touzan Bar

Hyatt Regency Kyoto, 644-2 Sanjusangen-do, Mawari-cho, Higashiyama-ku (075 541 3201/ www.kyoto.regency.hyatt.jp). Shichijo Station (Keihan line). **Open** 5pm-midnight daily. **Bar. Map** p47 E2 ⑮

As you would expect to find in a luxury hotel, the Hyatt Regency's bar is

an upmarket place serving superlative drinks. Less predictable is the decor, with scrap ironware, antique locks, confectionery moulds, kimono fabric and a mosaic of vintage books, spines to the wall, inexplicably combining to create an alluring and stylish interior. Leading designer Takashi Sugimoto has also overseen the soundtrack of funk and jazz classics.

Warajiya
Shichijo Dori, Honmachi Higashi-iru, Higashiyama-ku (075 561 1290). Shichijo Station (Keihan line). **Open** 11.30am-2.30pm, 4-7pm Mon-Fri; 11.30am-7pm Sat, Sun. **¥¥¥**. **Eel**. **Map** p47 D2 ⑯

Eel porridge may sound like a cockney breakfast, but it's actually the gourmet speciality at this historic address. Every guest receives the same five-course meal, including the porridge and a sliced-eel soup at Warajiya. The 400-year-old restaurant lists legendary warlord Hideyoshi Toyotomi as a former guest, although he is likely to have enjoyed a cup of tea rather than the fishy feast served these days.

Shopping

Bic Camera
927 Higashi Shiokoji-cho, Shimogyo-ku (075 353 1111). Kyoto Station (JR, Karasuma, Kintetsu lines). **Open** 10am-9pm daily. **Map** p47 A3 ⑰

This seven-floor superstore is the biggest electronics outlet in town. One of those floors is devoted to toy-dispensing gumball machines.

Chouya
161 Nishi Sakai-cho, Shichijo Dori, Shinmachi Higashi-iru, Shimogyo-ku (075 205 2117). Kyoto Station (JR, Karasuma, Kintetsu lines). **Open** 1-8pm daily. **Map** p47 B2 ⑱

Vintage kimono and *haori* (kimono jackets) at cheap prices make this tiny boutique a great place in which to pick up a souvenir. Prices start at just ¥1,000.

Isetan
Kyoto Station, Karasuma Dori, Shiokoji-sagaru, Shimogyo-ku (075 352 1111). Kyoto Station (JR, Karasuma, Kintetsu lines). **Open** 10am-8pm daily. **Map** p47 B3 ⑲

This branch of a Tokyo-based department store is operated by the local train company and lies within Kyoto Station. Despite its rather soulless design, the 11 floors of fashion, food, interior goods, dozens of restaurants and, on the ninth floor, huge tourist information centre with internet access make it worth a look.

Kyoto Denim
79-3-104 Koinari-cho, Shimogyo-ku (075 352 1053/www.homay.jp). Kyoto Station (JR, Karasuma, Kintetsu lines). **Open** 10am-8pm daily. **Map** p47 C3 ⑳

Toyoaki Kuwayama, the son of a kimono-maker, launched the Kyoto Denim brand in 2008, and opened this dedicated store the same year. He uses *kyo-yuzen*, a painstaking kimono dyeing technique, to add elegant and traditional motifs to the waistbands and pockets of women's jeans. The process of hand-drawing and dyeing each pair takes a full week, and prices reflect this. Sadly, cuts are made with the Japanese physique in mind, so no-one with a waist measuring above 76cm need pay the shop a visit. (See box p49).

Arts & leisure

Kyoto Gekijo
Kyoto Station, Karasuma Dori, Shiokoji-sagaru, Shimogyo-ku (075 341 2360/www.kyoto-gekijo.com). Kyoto Station (JR, Karasuma, Kintetsu lines). **Map** p47 B3 ㉑

Modern dramas and musicals are the staples of this pristine 875-seat theatre inside Kyoto Station. You'll need to speak Japanese to follow most of the shows. The lobby has a branch of Ticket Pia, Japan's leading ticket agency, where you can pick up tickets for concerts, sports events and plays.

Nishiki-koji market p62

Downtown

Central Kyoto

The commercial heart may be light on sights, but it's loaded with everything else you could ask of a city. You can shop till you drop, eat till you pop, sip world-class cocktails, catch a show or take in art. This is the best place to see Old Kyoto battle New Kyoto, with tea bowls and baseball caps for sale on the same block, nouvelle cuisine served in classic townhouses and temples tucked quietly between coffee shops.

Shijo is the main shopping drag, though perhaps the least interesting. Foodies should head straight for Nishiki-koji, whereas fashionistas should visit Gokomachi or Sanjo. Small, centuries-old temples coexist with an eclectic range of shops and cafés along the pedestrian arcades of Teramachi and Shinkyogoku. Street signs are few and scattered, but the area is laid out on a grid, making navigation a breeze.

Sights & museums

Gallery Maronie

Kawaramachi Dori, Shijo-agaru, Nakagyo-ku (075 221 0117). Kawaramachi station (Hankyu line). **Open** noon-8pm Tue-Sat; noon-6pm Sun. **Admission** free. **Map** p55 D2 ❶
Three galleries and a select store make up this Tadao Ando-esque concrete complex. Each gallery hosts a unique show, with displays spanning a wide spectrum of arts and crafts, ranging from portraits to fashion, glassware and abstract installation art. The second-floor store sells work by exhibitors past and present, most of them local.

Kaleidoscope Museum of Kyoto

706-3 Dongeinmae-cho, Aneyakoji Dori, Takakura Nishi-iru, Nakagyo-ku (075 254 7902/www.k-kaleido.org). Karasuma Oike station (Karasuma, Tozai lines). **Open** 10am-6pm Tue-Sun. **Admission** ¥300. **Map** p55 B1/C1 ❷

The city's most hands-on museum is one of its most charming. The friendly staff encourage you to get touchy-feely with exhibits such as kaleidoscopes made from dustbins, mobile phones and violins. If you're suitably inspired, you can join a workshop in the café to make your own polychrome toy.

Museum of Kyoto

Takakura Dori, Sanjo-agaru, Nakagyo-ku (075 222 0888/www.bunpaku.or.jp). Karasuma Oike station (Karasuma, Tozai lines). **Open** 10am-7pm Tue-Sun. **Admission** ¥500. **Map** p55 C1 ❸

A former branch of the Bank of Japan, the building is arguably more impressive than its exhibits and has limited English signage. But the museum is worth a look for its models and audiovisual guides to the city's 1,200-year history. It also screens classic Japanese movies on a daily basis.

Rokkakudo

Rokkaku Dori, Higashinotoin Nishi-iru, Nakagyo-ku (075 221 2686/www.ikenobo.jp/rokkakudo). Karasuma Oike station (Karasuma, Tozai lines). **Open** 6am-5pm daily. **Admission** free. **Map** p55 B2 ❹

Poor little Rokkakudo doesn't get much attention in a city packed with far grander temples, but it's central and historic enough to warrant a quick look. It was built in 587, predating the city, well before Buddhists were rich enough to jazz up their temples with opulent art. This tiny, hexagonal temple claims to be the birthplace of ikebana, as well as the site of a vision that led Buddhist monk Shinran to found the Jodo Shinshu sect

Eating & drinking

Café Independants

B1 1928 Building, Sanjo Gokomachi, Nakagyo-ku (075 255 4312/www.cafe-independants.com). Sanjo station (Keihan line). **Open** 11.30am-midnight daily. ¥. **Café**. **Map** p55 D1 ❺

Neither the food nor drink is memorable here, but the setting certainly is. The building was created in 1928 as an office for the Mainichi newspaper company. When the journalists moved out, cafés and galleries moved in, the best of which lie in the basement. With crumbling brick walls, flaking paint and rusty artwork as decor, Independants provides a counterpoint to the elegant city. Live bands and DJs often perform in the evenings, with genres ranging from acoustic folk to thumping techno.

Gogyo

452 Jumonji-cho, Yanaginobaba Dori, Takoyakushi-sagaru, Nakagyo-ku (075 254 5567/www.ramendining-gogyo.com/shop_kyoto/index.html). Kawaramachi station (Hankyu line). **Open** 11.30am-3.30pm, 5pm-midnight daily. ¥. **Ramen**. **Map** p55 C2 ❻

One of the city's ramen landmarks is housed in a gorgeous *machiya* that couldn't be further removed from the brash interiors of many ramen joints. The signature *kogashi* (burned) ramen is a hearty, full-bodied dish with a soy- or miso-based soup that has been flambéed in 300°C lard. Other menu items reflect the store's roots in the southern island of Kyushu, which is renowned for its raw horse meat.

Hale

198-1 Higashi Uoyacho, Nishiki-koji, Fuyacho Nishi-iru, Nakagyo-ku (075 231 2516). Karasuma station (Hankyu line), Shijo station (Karasuma line). **Open** 11.30am-2.30pm Tue, Wed; 11.30am-2.30pm, 6-9pm Thur-Sun. No credit cards. ¥. **Vegetarian**. **Map** p55 C2 ❼

With only three tables and a prime location on Nishiki-koji market, this vegetarian restaurant fills up fast for lunch. There's more chance of a seat, and more choice of food, when it opens for dinner after the market has gone silent. The food is home-cooked Japanese veggie fare, such as deep fried tofu, steamed Kyoto vegetables and brown rice stir-fry.

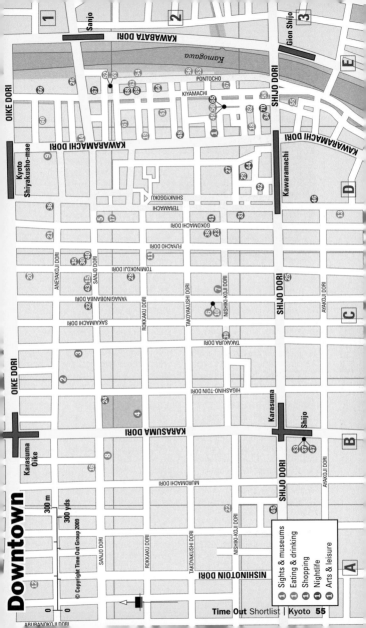

Downtown

Karasuma Oike

Karasuma Shijo

OIKE DORI

KAWABATA DORI

KAWARAMACHI DORI

SHIJO DORI

SHIJO DORI

KARASUMA DORI

NISHIKI-KOJI DORI

Kamogawa

Sanjo

Gion Shijo

Kyoto Shiyakusho-mae

PONTOCHO

KIYAMACHI

Kawaramachi

SHINKYOGOKU

TERAMACHI

GOKOMACHI DORI

FUYACHO DORI

TOMINOKOJI DORI

ANEYAKOJI DORI

SANJO DORI

YANAGINOBANBA DORI

SAKAIMACHI DORI

ROKKAKU DORI

TAKAKURA DORI

HIGASHINO-TOIN DORI

TAKOYAKUSHI DORI

AYAKOJI DORI

MUROMACHI DORI

ROKKAKU DORI

TAKOYAKUSHI DORI

NISHIKI-KOJI DORI

SANJO DORI

NISHIINOTONSHIN DORI

ABURANOKOJI DORI

300 m

300 yds

© Copyright Time Out Group 2009

● Sights & museums
● Eating & drinking
● Shopping
● Nightlife
● Arts & leisure

Drink your greens

Top-grade tea without the ceremony.

Iyemon

'A lot of people are intimidated by tea because it's a high-society art,' says Soei, perhaps Kyoto's best-known tea master. 'Many of them don't know what to do.'

It's hardly surprising. The art of tea incorporates a slew of rules on topics including how to open a door, how to walk, when to bow, what to say, where to look, how to sit, how to sip and the appropriate contents of one's heart.

Soei has been studying tea since 1985 and teaching for more than a decade, but he still winces at the term 'tea master', saying that the pursuit takes a lifetime and 40 minutes to master.

It's enough to put anyone off drinking the stuff. Fortunately 2008 brought along several new establishments that give the drink a contemporary, accessible twist. **Marukyu Koyamaen** (p57), one of the oldest and biggest names in Japanese tea, has opened the first Kyoto salon in its 300-year history. In a simple, modern

interior, the tea titan offers classic brews alongside matcha-flavoured cakes and ice-cream.

Meanwhile, drinks giant Suntory teamed up with a local café operator to open **Iyemon Salon** (p57), a green-tea lounge for the Starbucks set. While teahouses are traditionally tiny and austere, the Iyemon is spacious, lavishly appointed and draws the attention of hip young locals with its range of teas and tea-flavoured café grub. The only orthodoxy is the choice of tea supplier – the 200-year-old **Fukujuen** (p59).

Fukujuen made a splash of its own at the end of 2008 with a dazzling flagship store that combines traditional clay, granite and latticework with aluminium, LEDs and steel. In the basement you can try 25 styles of tea or mix a bespoke blend to suit your palate; a third-floor French restaurant serves dishes such as roast lamb with pan-fried tea; whereas up on the fourth floor, you can borrow a traditional tea room and enjoy a bowl of matcha without anyone to notice when you flout the rules.

Rounding out the notable new venues is **Ranhotei** (p123), a café opened by Soei. Born in Canada as Randall Channell, the tea master has become a local celebrity, in part as a cross-cultural curiosity, but also for his ability to elucidate tea culture in English or Japanese. Guests at Ranhotei can book Channell for an hour-long tea primer – your best chance to figure out how a cup of tea became Japan's most hallowed drink.

Iyemon Salon

Sanjo Dori, Karasuma Nishi-iru,
Nakagyo-ku (075 222 1500/www.
iyemonsalon.jp). Karasuma Oike
station (Karasuma, Tozai lines).
Open 8am-11.30pm daily. **¥**. **Café**.
Map p55 B1 ❽
The hallowed green tea meets modern
café culture. See box p56.

Kerala

2F KUS Building, Kawaramachi, Sanjo-
agaru, Nakagyo-ku (075 251 0141).
Kyoto Shiyakusho-mae station (Tozai
line). **Open** 11.30am-2pm; 5-9pm daily.
¥¥. **Indian**. **Map** p55 D1 ❾
If only they had put as much effort into
the decor as the food: it's an Indian
restaurant-by-numbers interior, but
Kerala serves the best curries in town.
The menu is enormous and makes a
few nods to the local cuisine in dishes
such as tofu curry.

Kura

452 Jumonji-cho, Yanaginobanba
Dori, Takoyakushi-sagaru, Nakagyo-ku
(075 212 8701). Kawaramachi station
(Hankyu line). **Open** 7pm-3am daily.
Bar. **Map** p55 C2 ❿
Enter the Gogyo ramen shop (p54) and
ask for the bar. If there's space, the staff
will lead you to their backyard and
what used to be a storehouse. Inside,
you'll find a stylish cocktail bar, with
a counter on the first floor and a small
lounge upstairs.

K'Ya

105 Yaoya-cho (075 241 0489).
Open 6pm-3am, Mon, Wed-Sun.
Bar. **Map** p55 C2 ⓫
Kyoto's best bar? K'Ya is certainly a
strong contender. The *machiya* setting
is sublime, as are the drinks. The bartender honed his skills in Tokyo's
Ginza district – home to the world's
most meticulous cocktail craftsmen –
before returning to dazzle Kyoto. Try
his Gaelic espresso, a coffee- flavoured
with flaming Laphroaig and paired with
Laphroaig-scented fresh chocolates.

Marukyu Koyamaen

Nishinotoin Dori, Oike-sagaru (075
223 0909). Karasuma Oike station
(Karasuma, Tozai lines). **Open**
9.30am-6pm Mon,Tue, Thur-Sun.
¥. **Café**. **Map** p55 A1 ⓬
Esteemed Uji-based tea supplier
Koyamaen has been cultivating fine
tea since the 17th century, but it took
until 2008 to establish a store in Kyoto.
The backstreet location enhances the
mellow atmosphere, as customers sip
freshly milled *matcha* in a smart, modern salon or traditional tearoom.

Mikoan

Teramachi Dori, Shijo-sagaru,
Shimogyo-ku (075 361 2200/
www.mikoan.com). Karasuma
station (Hankyu line), Shijo station
(Karasuma line). **Open** 5-11pm
Mon-Fri; noon-11pm Sat; noon-8pm
Sun. No credit cards. **¥**. **Shojin ryori**.
Map p55 D3 ⓭
Temples come in all shapes and sizes,
but they don't usually look like this: a
city-centre house with a cluttered
restaurant counter running through
what was once the living room. You
probably won't believe it's a place of
worship, until you see the Buddha on
the kitchen shelf between the Bailey's
and the cassis liqueur. Mikoan is run
by a nun and her mum, both of whom
are passionate peace activists. They
serve vegetarian Japanese fare, and the
dinner set (four dishes plus soup and
rice for ¥1,000) is probably the best
value meal in the city.

Ogawa Coffee

96 Nakajima-cho, Sanjo, Kawaramachi
Higashi-iru, Nakagyo-ku (075 251 7700/
www.oc-ogawa.co.jp/shop/kyoto_sanjo)
Sanjo station (Keihan line). **Open**
9am-9pm Mon-Thur, Sun; 9am-10pm
Fri, Sat. **¥**. **Café**. **Map** p55 D1 ⓮
Ogawa is one of Japan's classic coffee
shops, predating Seattle's mega chain
by 19 years. In the last decade it has been
upstaged by the foreigners, but it still
makes better coffee, as shown by Akihiro

Okada of this Sanjo branch, who won the Japan Barista Championship in 2008. Since his triumph, Okada has been touting his talent on nationwide tours, but still brews here each Friday.

Setsu Gekka

Sacra Building, Sanjo Dori, Tominokoji Nishi-iru, Nakagyo-ku (075 231 0070/ www.kyoto-setsugekka.com). Karasuma Oike station (Karasuma, Tozai lines). **Open** 7pm-4am Tue-Sat; 7pm-1am Sun. **Bar**. Map p55 C1 ⑮

Almost two decades ago, this former bank was renovated into a two-storey cocktail complex with a quartet of bars. The best seats are in the entrance-level Salon, with a high ceiling and the furnishings of an aristocrat's reading room, and the lower-level Ka bar, dressed in brilliant gold *washi* by paper artist Eriko Horiki. The speciality is a green tea and chestnut cocktail called Soueki.

Somushi

Karasuma Dori, Sanjo Nishi-iru, Nakagyo-ku (075 253 1456/www. somushi.com). Karasuma Oike station (Karasuma, Tozai lines). **Open** 11am-9pm Mon,Tue, Thur-Sun. ¥¥. **Korean**. Map p55 B1 ⑯

Somushi serves healthy Korean fare. Forget about mountains of meat and *kimchi*: the brief food menu here includes Somushi gozen, a nine-dish version of Korean court cuisine, and *shojin bibimbap*, a meat-free dish of rice and veg. The longer drink list is just as nutritious, with mugwort shakes, ginseng-flavoured juices and a dozen herbal teas. Best of all, it's set against a fantasy of clay walls and dark beams, which could have been designed for a film set.

Tenyu

Gokomachi Dori, Sanjo-sagaru, Nakagyo-ku (075 212 7778). Kyoto Shiyakusho-mae station (Tozai line), Sanjo station (Keihan line). **Open** 11.30am-1.30pm Mon, 5-9.30pm Mon, Wed-Sun. ¥¥¥¥. No credit cards. **Tempura**. Map p55 D1/D2 ⑰

This cosy tempura restaurant comes from the people behind the Tawaraya ryokan. Guests of the inn can take dinner here as part of their room fee, but the rest of us have to fork out at least ¥8,000 for *kaiseki*-style tempura of shrimp, fish and local vegetables.

Tsukiji

Hitosujime Higashi-iru, Kawaramachi, Shijo-agaru, Nakagyo-ku (075 221 1053). Kawaramachi station (Hankyu line). **Open** 11am-11pm daily. ¥¥. **Café**. Map p55 D3/E3 ⑱

Velour seats, smoke-stained plaster walls and classical music set the old-time tone of this two-storey tea salon. Crammed with antiques, it opened in 1934 and has barely changed since. Don't expect frappucinos, or even cappuccinos: the small menu of teas, coffees and cocktails is just as retro as the setting.

Uoshin

Ajibiru, 238 Yamazaki-cho, Kawaramachi Dori, Sanjo-sagaru, Nakagyo-ku (075 223 1431). Sanjo station (Keihan line). **Open** 11.30am-11pm daily. ¥¥. **Sushi**. Map p55 D2 ⑲

To use its full name, Ganso Bucchigiri Sushi Uoshin serves sushi, but not the wafers of fish you might imagine. Here, they claim to slice the fish three times thicker than usual. The 'spilling over' *ikura* lives up to the promise of its name and is served on a spoon to catch the tumbling salmon roe. The atmosphere is casual and lively, the prices are reasonable and the fish is superb.

Yoshikawa Tempura

Tominokoji, Oike-sagaru, Nakagyo-ku (075 221 5544/www.kyoto-yoshikawa. co.jp). Kyoto Shiyakusho-mae station (Tozai line). **Open Counter** 11am-2pm, 5-8.30pm Mon-Sat. **Tatami room** 11am-2pm, 5-8.30pm daily. ¥¥¥. **Tempura**. Map p55 C1 ⑳

This small room was originally the tearoom of the adjoining Yoshikawa ryokan (p141), but became a tempura

Fukujuen p59

It was a merchant's house during the early 20th century, but now Zezekan Pocchiri is one of Kyoto's best-looking Chinese restaurants. Shark's fin features prominently on the menu, including in a 'beautiful person' course menu, which is designed to give your looks a boost with the collagen-rich ingredients. After dinner, head to the garden where a former storehouse is now home to a great bar serving seasonal fresh fruit cocktails.

Shopping

Aritsugu

Nishiki-koji Dori, Gokomachi Nishi-iru, Nakagyo-ku (075 221 1091). **Open** 9am-5.30pm daily. **Map** p55 D2 ㉓
If you're looking for kitchenware, this is the place to go to. Aritsugu has been supplying the city's top chefs with pots, pans, peelers and handmade knives since the 16th century, and is famous nationwide. You'll find it at the eastern end of Nishiki-koji market.

shop in the 1950s. Customers sit round a counter while chef Satoru Okita holds court, frying outstanding seafood and vegetables. There are various sets, but you'd need to have a hearty appetite not to be sated by the smallest (¥6,000).

Yukei Salon de Thé

Anekoji, Fuyacho Higashi-iru, Nakagyo-ku (075 212 8883). Kyoto Shiyakusho-mae station (Tozai line). ¥. **Café**. **Open** 11am-7pm Mon, Wed-Sun. **Map** p55 D1 ㉑
In 2007, the owner of the top-end Tawaraya inn (p55) designed this tea salon. It's a serene spot, with classical music and a moss garden. It's more modern than you might expect from the historic inn. Walls are art-gallery white, the furniture is Danish and the shelves hold art tomes on subjects like Eames furniture and graffiti. The drinks (green tea, earl grey, coffee) are first class.

Zezekan Pocchiri

Nishiki-koji Dori, Muromachi, Nishi-iru, Nakagyo-ku (075 257 5766). Karasuma station (Hankyu line), Shijo station (Karasuma line). **Open** 11am-2pm, 5-10pm daily. ¥¥¥. **Chinese**. **Map** p55 A2 ㉒

Bape

B1F Horie Building, Sanjo Dori, Karasuma Higashi-iru, Nakagyo-ku (075 255 5855/ www.bape.com). Karasuma Oike station (Karasuma, Tozai lines). **Open** 11am-7pm daily. **Map** p55 B1 ㉔
Hoodies, hats, trainers and toilet paper with the ape logo from Nigo's urban casual superbrand.

Fukujuen

Shijo Tominokoji, Shimogyo-ku (075 221 2920/www.fukujuen-kyotohonten. com). Karasuma station (Hankyu line), Shijo station (Karasuma line). **Open** 10am-7pm daily. **Map** p55 C3 ㉕
One of the big names in Japanese tea. See box p56.

Funahashiya

Sanjo Ohashi, Nishi-zume, Nakagyo-ku (075 221 2673). Sanjo station (Keihan line). **Open** 10am-8pm daily. **Map** p55 E1 ㉖

KYOTO BY AREA

This neighbourhood has changed dramatically during the century since Funahashiya opened, with a pizzeria, supermarket and a Starbucks growing up. This handsome wooden store has outlasted its original peers by offering a range of locally baked rice crackers. The most popular flavours include *sansho* (Szechuan pepper) and *shichimi*, a Japanese blend of chilli and spices.

Gallery by Spinns

2F, 538-1 Nakano-cho, Shimogyoku Dori, Shijo-agaru, Nakagyo-ku (075 212 7511/www.galleriebyspinns.com). Kawaramachi station (Hankyu line). **Open** 11am-8pm daily. **Map** p55 D2 ㉗
Filling in gaping holes on the fashion scene in Kyoto, this vast concrete store opened in late 2008 with new and used threads from mainly imported brands, including designer names like Marc Jacobs, Raf Simons and Neil Barrett.

Hakuchikudo

Fuyacho, Rokkaku-agaru, Nakagyo-ku (075 221 1341/www.hakuchikudo.co.jp). Kyoto Shiyakusho-mae station (Tozai line). **Open** 10am-6pm Mon, Tue, Thur-Sun. **Map** p55 C2 ㉘
Approaching its 300th anniversary, this paper fan specialist stocks around

Lisn p61

100 designs, ranging from classic motifs to modern manga images. These days they also sell online, but that's no reason to miss this beautiful store. Expect to pay ¥5-¥12,000.

Hanjiro

Mimatsu Kaikan, Nakano-cho, Shinkyogoku Dori, Shijo-agaru, Nakagyo-ku (075 257 5871/www.hanjiro.co.jp/shop/shop-kyo.htm). Kawaramachi station (Hankyu line). **Open** 11am-8pm daily.
Map p55 D3 ㉙
The decor is so dazzling that it's hard to focus on the clothes at this gargantuan boutique. Design elements include about 60 chandeliers suspended from a 9m-high ceiling, gilt-framed mirrors galore, live chipmunks, old bathtubs, Elvis-bust fountains and vintage ravioli cans. Somewhere in the middle of it all is a wide range of new and used clothing that is popular with Kyoto's hip twentysomethings. Across the street, a branch of the Wego chain offers similar clothing in the shell of an old cinema.

Height

Tominokoji Dori, Sanjo-agaru, Nakagyo-ku (075 212 8827/www.height.jp). Sanjo station (Keihan line). **Open** noon-8pm daily. **Map** p55 C1 ㉚
This select shop for B-boys likes its clothing bold, colourful and plastered with slogans. It stocks a mix of domestic and international brands that can make Stussy and Bape look conservative.

Horaido

Teramachi, Shijo-agaru, Nakagyo-ku (075 221 1215/www.kyoto-teramachi.or.jp/horaido). Kawaramachi station (Hankyu line). **Open** 10am-8.50pm daily. Closed every 2, 12, 22 of mth.
Map p55 D3 ㉛
Tea bowls priced from ¥2,000 to ¥50,000 (try to spot the difference), colourful tea caddies and a wide range of teas have kept this Teramachi store

in business since 1803. The store has English-language printed explanations of the various teas, as well as a genial, English-speaking boss to answer any questions. Even though Teramachi now has hip-hop clothing stores and chain restaurants, Horaido remains resolutely old-fashioned, with a time-worn interior and traditional opening hours (the owner says that closing on certain days of the week, rather than the month, is a new-fangled idea that he has yet to adopt).

Ichimanben

Sanjo Yanaginobanba, Nakagyo-ku (075 256 8282/www.ichimanben.com). Karasuma Oike station (Karasuma, Tozai lines). **Open** 11am-8pm daily. **Map** p55 C1 ㉜
In the remnants of a building by Tatsuno Kingo, the architect of Tokyo Station and the Bank of Japan, this kimono store offers all-in-one 'debut' sets for ¥18,900, or vintage kimono from as little as ¥5,000.

Karacho

Cocon Building, Karasuma Dori, Shijo-sagaru, Shimogyo-ku (075 353 5885/ www.karacho.co.jp). Karasuma station (Hankyu line), Shijo station (Karasuma line). **Open** 11am-7pm Mon, Wed-Sun. **Map** p55 B3 ㉝
Karakami is the traditional wood-block-printed *washi* paper that adorns some of Japan's poshest walls and sliding doors. Kyoto's Karacho, established in 1624, is the only atelier still creating *karakami* in the authentic way, handpressing centuries-old woodblocks – although these days they apply their designs to business cards, envelopes and lampshades.

Karan Koron

Shijo Dori, Kobashi Nishi-iru, Shimogyo-ku (075 253 5535/ www.karancolon.jp). Gion Shijo station (Keihan line), Kawaramachi station (Hankyu line). **Open** 10.30am-8pm daily **Map** p55 E3 ㉞

Named for the onomatopoeia of a geisha's shoes clip-clopping on cobble-stones, Karan Koron is a chain of cute stores that sells delightful Japanese textiles and knick-knacks.

Kyoto Design House

Niwaka Bldg., Tominokoji Dori, Sanjo-agaru, Nakagyo-ku (075 221 0200/ www.kyoto-dh.com). Kyoto Shiyakusho-mae station (Tozai line). **Open** 11am-8pm daily. **Map** p55 C1 ㉟
If your friends back home won't put up with receiving tourist tat as souvenirs, this is the place to pick up the hottest contemporary Japanese design goodies. A trio of local design luminaries select the merchandise, usually featuring sophisticated twists on classic Kyoto lifestyle items. In April 2009, the store moved from its bland former home to the gleaming Niwaka Building, which was designed by Japanese star-chitect Tadao Ando.

Kyukyo-do

Teramachi Aneyakoji, Nakagyo-ku (075 231 0510/www.kyukyodo.co.jp). Kyoto Shiyakusho-mae station (Tozai line). **Open** 10am-6pm Mon-Sat. **Map** p55 D1 ㊳
One of Teramachi's oldest tenants, this store first opened for business in 1663. It stocks a range of Japanese goods, from incense to calligraphy tools. But it's best known for making top quality *washi* and other paper products.

Lisn

Cocon Building, Karasuma Dori, Shijo-sagaru, Shimogyo-ku (075 353 6466/www.lisn.co.jp). Karasuma station (Hankyu line), Shijo station (Karasuma line). **Open** 11am-8pm daily. **Map** p55 B3 ㊲
Shoyeido is a 300-year-old incense giant that creates the traditional aromas you'll smell in temples and ryokan across the city. Lisn is their sexy new sub-brand of sticks and cones with contemporary fragrances, such as 'Gorgeous' and 'True Happiness'.

Mindtrive

371 Funaya-cho, Gokomachi, Takoyakushi-sagaru, Nakagyo-ku (075 211 4361/www.mindtrive.com). Kawaramachi station (Hankyu line). **Open** noon-8pm daily. **Map** p55 D2 ❸❽

This select gents' fashion store stocks some of the hottest domestic brands, including the sleek monochromatic designs of Kazuyuki Kumagai's Attachment label and the eccentric, avant-garde Julius line.

Nishiki-koji Market

Nishiki-koji, Nakagyo-ku (www.kyoto-nishiki.or.jp). Karasuma station (Hankyu line), Shijo station (Karasuma line). **Open** 9am-6pm daily. **Map** p55 C2 ❸❾

Kyoto's premier food market is always bustling, partly because it's so narrow, but also because it offers such an extraordinary array of gourmet treats. Most of the 130 shops lining this covered arcade are devoted to eating and drinking, and as you make your way along the 400m stretch, the aromas of fish, green tea, chestnuts, doughnuts and much more will jostle for your attention. Opening times vary, but they are usually 9am-6pm.

Sanjo by Pagong

32 Nakano-cho, Sanjo Dori, Tominokoji Higashi-iru, Nakagyo-ku (075 257 3723/www.pagong.jp). Kyoto Shiyakusho-mae station (Tozai line). **Open** 11.30am-8pm, Mon, Tue, Thur-Sun. **Map** p55 C1 ❹❶

A textile-dyeing company with a history stretching back to 1919 runs the Pagong brand, best known for its aloha shirts with kimono patterns. The label also applies its bold designs to shirts, skirts, dresses and boxer shorts.

Sistere

2F, 381-1 Funayacho, Gokomachi Dori, Takoyakushi-sagaru, Nakagyo-ku (075 241 0693/www.sistere.jp). Kawaramachi station (Hankyu line). **Open** noon-8pm, Mon, Tue, Thur-Sun. **Map** p55 D2 ❹❶

The city's hippest boutique occupies the second floor of a Tadao Ando building, selling designs by Kyoto's Yutaka Kojima. See box p63.

Sou-Sou

Futasujime Higashi-iru 2-kenme, Shinkyogoku Dori, Shijo-agaru, Nakagyo-ku (075 212 8005/www.sousou.jp). Kawaramachi station (Hankyu line). **Open** 11am-8pm daily. **Map** p55 D3 ❹❷

The Kyoto brand Sou-Sou produces hip reinventions of Japanese workwear. The ground floor offers split-toe trainers based on *tabi* footwear. In the basement, you'll find the menswear and on the top floor, you can see the results of a collaboration with Le Coq Sportif: sports bags, jackets and shoes emblazoned with classic prints. The store opposite sells ladieswear, including made-to-order kimonos.

Stavecation

2F Arimoto Building, 6 Nakanomachi, Sanjo Dori, Yanaginobanba Higashi-iru, Nakagyo-ku (075 213 4506/www.stavecation.com). Karasuma Oike station (Karasuma, Tozai lines). **Open** 1-9pm Mon-Fri; noon-8pm Sat, Sun. **Map** p55 C1 ❹❸

It began life as a skater-influenced streetwear boutique, but this store has soared upmarket over the last decade. It now stocks monochromatic menswear such as the military-tinged Siva label. It's not easy to find, but look for a kimono store called Wafufu, then head upstairs.

Nightlife

Greenwich House

577-5 Nakano-cho, Shinkyogoku Dori, Shijo-agaru, Nakagyo-ku (075 212 5041/ www.greenwich-house.com). Kawaramachi station (Hankyu line). **Open** 1-5pm, 6pm-midnight. Mon, Tue, Thur-Sun. **Map** p55 D3 ❹❹

Jazz joints are intimate in Kyoto, but there's nowhere quite like this skinny bar. At a push, it can hold 15 people, but the manager still books quartets to perform, so you might find yourself

Sistere act

Kyoto's reputation for craftsmanship and refined taste hasn't helped it to grow much of a fashion scene. You'll find a few respectable boutiques and local outposts of Tokyo labels, but little homegrown high fashion. One conspicuous exception is **Sistere** (p62) a boutique from self-taught Kyoto-ite Yutaka Kojima. The label works with traditional artisans to realise Kojima's concepts of asymmetrical 'ugly beauty' in palettes of smoke and black.

Time Out (TO): How did you start as a designer?

Yutaka Kojima (YK): Like a flash.

Time Out (TO): Tokyo is a major fashion hub with media attention and hungry buyers. Kyoto isn't. Why do you base yourself in the Old Capital?

Yutaka Kojima (YK): I grew up in Kyoto. I hate the fact that fashion in Tokyo has become so political. You have to see so many people, and someone is always pushing. It's easier to create something in Kyoto. There's freedom here.

TO: How does being in Kyoto affect your design?

YK: Well, many craftsmen work in Kansai (Western Japan), so there's more opportunity to meet and work together. Kyoto is a place of silk production and high-quality dyeing, thanks to its kimono-making history. My designs are often inspired by the craftsmen's techniques. I just transform what they do into real clothes.

TO: Many modern Kyoto brands adopt kimono patterns or cuts, playing on the romance that people associate with the city's heritage. You don't seem tempted to take that route.

YK: I grew up in Western-style outfits, so the kimono is not a realistic reference for me. But the spirit of the old craftsmen can be transferred from kimono to Western clothing. As you can see on the street, not many people wear kimonos, so craftsmen have to change direction or lose custom. Those who shift to new genres can stay in business and supply people like Comme des Garçons or Yohji Yamamoto.

TO: How do you collaborate with people whose experience is in traditional garments?

YK: After selecting the threads, I take my idea to a craftsman. Sometimes they tell me that my idea won't work, but they find it interesting to try. From their trials, new ideas emerge.

TO: You held your first exhibition in Tokyo, and recently opened a branch there in 2009.

YK: Right. At the end of the day, it's the centre of everything.

TO: Last question: Tokyo or Kyoto?

YK: Kyoto.

KYOTO BY AREA

sharing elbow space with the trumpeter. Greenwich House is a fun and friendly place, which mostly hosts vocal jazz. Entrance is free and drinks are cheap. The building houses a school for students of the koto, a traditional Japanese string instrument, and from 3pm each Saturday and Sunday they play in the bar.

Mojo

39-1 Tsukibokocho, Shijo Dori, Shinmachi Higashi-iru, Shimogyo-ku (075 254 7707/www.kyoto-mojo.com). Karasuma station (Hankyu line), Shijo station (Karasuma line). **Open** varies. **Map** p55 A3 **45**

There's an unusual entrance policy at this black basement box: foreigners get in free so long as they promise to talk about the show on their return home. Expect to see unsigned local punks and rockers tearing up the small stage (the crash barrier in front is evidence of how rowdy things can get). The venue handpicks most of the acts, which keeps the quality high. The free-entry offer applies only to events organised by Mojo, but that means most of them.

Toga Toga

B1F, Camera no Naniwa, Termachi Dori, Shijo-sagaru, Shimogyo-ku (075 361 6900/http://park20.wakwak. com/~togatoga). Kawaramachi station (Hankyu line). **Open** varies. **Map** p55 D3 **46**

Acoustic, folk and pop shows dominate the schedule at this light, airy live venue that could do with a better bar.

Arts & leisure

Kyoto Cinema

3F, Cocon Karasuma, Karasuma Dori, Shijo-sagaru, Shimogyo-ku (075 353 4723/www.kyotocinema.jp). Karasuma station (Hankyu line), Shijo station (Karasuma line). **Open** varies. **Map** p55 B3 **47**

Built by starchitect Kengo Kuma, Cocon Karasuma is filled with design-related concept stores (including Karacho and Lisn, p61). It's home to this art-house cinema, which plays impressive Euro and Japanese indie flicks.

Super Jankara

296 Naraya-cho, Kawaramachi, Takoyakushi-agaru, Nakagyo-ku (075 212 5858/www.jankara.ne.jp/super). Kawaramachi station (Hankyu line). **Open** 11am-6am daily. **Map** p55 D2 **48**

If you're going to make a mockery of your favourite song, why not do so with smoke machines, glitter balls and disco lights at Super Jankara (super jumbo karaoke), Kyoto's seven-storey, 81-room karaoke behemoth? The fancy gimmicks and gadgets are only available in the 'premium' rooms, but they cost as little as 40 yen extra per person per hour. As with most karaoke in Japan, rooms are hired by groups for private ignominy.

Kiyamachi/Pontocho

You'll notice from the listings that there's little to do here but eat, drink or dance. For centuries, these two streets have formed one of the city's great nightlife hubs, silent by day and bustling by night.

The half-kilometre Pontocho is narrow, dark and enigmatic – exactly the kind of street you'd steer well clear of in most cities. Luckily, street crime is unheard of here, so you're as safe walking down this shadowy stretch as you are in any other street in Kyoto. A geisha theatre graces the northern end of Pontocho, and decades ago this was an alley of exclusive establishments for well-to-do geisha patrons. These days it is more accessible, but no less atmospheric.

Kiyamachi is equally steeped in history. Ryoma Sakamoto, a key figure in the overthrow of the shogunate, was killed here. It was also a major trade route, thanks to the Takase canal that runs down

the middle. Unlike Pontocho, Kiyamachi has been transformed architecturally, and is now lined with concrete buildings full of bars, clubs and cheap restaurants that attract young crowds.

Eating & drinking

A Bar

2F, Reiho Kaikan, 336 Kamiya-cho, Nishi-kiyamachi Dori, Shijo-agaru, Nakagyo-ku (075 213 2129). Kawaramachi station (Hankyu line), Gion Shijo station (Keihan line). **Open** 5pm-midnight daily. **¥**. **Izakaya**. Map p55 E2 ④⑨

The proprietor also owns part of a mountain, and has used the timber he has sourced there to turn a city-centre bar into a mock log cabin. Over the years, the customers have given it an urban makeover with graffiti, stickers, flyers and business cards covering the walls. It's not as boorish as it sounds, and if you're seated at the long centre table, you'll soon be engaged by friendly fellow punters. There's an impressive 70-item menu of cheap and cheerful *izakaya* grub.

Café La Siesta

336 Kamiya-cho, Nishi-kiyamachi Dori, Shijo-agaru, Nakagyo-ku (075 634 5570/http://shop.cafelasiesta.com). Kawaramachi station (Hankyu line), Gion Shijo station (Keihan line). **Open** 5pm-2am; Mon, Wed-Sun. **Bar**. Map p55 E2 ⑤⓪

A year after it opened, Café La Siesta hosted a performance by a musician who used vintage computer games as part of his act. The games proved so popular that retro gaming became the new attraction. You can now sip a Bonus Stage or One-up cocktail as you battle eight-bit enemies on the vintage Nintendo or try to recall some death moves at the full-size Streetfighter machine. The food is surprisingly good, and there are plenty of vegetarian options on the menu.

Pontocho

Ing

2F Royal Building, Nishi-kiyamachi, Takyakushi (075 255 5087). Sanjo station (Keihan line). **Open** 6pm-late Mon-Thur; 6pm-5am Fri, Sat. **Bar**. Map p55 E1 ⑤①

This sepia-lit dive is a vaguely Rolling Stones-themed bar (hence, apparently, the name – which is the middle syllable of the band's name). But the reason behind the joint's enduring popularity among expats is the unpretentious vibe, oddball owner Hako and the likelihood of the atmosphere being boisterous long into the small hours of the morning.

Kuro

Pontocho, Kaburenjomae, Nakagyo-ku (075 211 4796/www.temas.jp). Sanjo station (Keihan line). **Open** 6pm-1am daily. **Bar**. Map p55 E2 ⑤②

One of Pontocho's newest faces, Kuro opened in summer 2008 and hit all the right notes from the start. Good drinks at great prices, a stylish all-black interior ('kuro' means black) and bubbly, fun staff see the bar busy on most nights. If you visit this bar, you'll find that the Asahi Jukusen is a cut above the usual draft beers.

Mimasuya

157 Matsumoto-cho, Pontocho, Sanjo-sagaru 4-chome, Nakagyo-ku (075 213 4445/www.the-la-mart.com). Sanjo station (Keihan line). **Open** Mon-Fri 5pm-midnight; Sat, Sun noon-2am. **¥¥.**
Modern Japanese. Map 55 E2 ㊳
A romantic Pontocho address plus Kyoto cuisine with a river view usually adds up to a steep bill, but Mimasuya is refreshingly casual and affordable. The young staff serve high-quality local cuisine, including plenty of tofu and seafood. It's the kind of unfussy fare that you'll find in fancier places at twice the price. There are private rooms, but try to snap up a window seat with a view of the Kamo river.

Misoguigawa

Pontocho Higashigawa, Sanjo-sagaru, Nakagyo-ku (075 221 2270/www.misogui.jp). Sanjo station (Keihan line). **Open** 11.30am-1.30pm, 5.30-8.30pm Tue-Sun. **¥¥¥. French.**
Map p55 E2 ㊴
They call it 'French *kaiseki*', but the cuisine here is classic French – it's the presentation that's *kaiseki*. In a finely preserved former teahouse, chef Teruo Inoue dispatches his creations in small portions on Japanese ceramics, and diners eat with chopsticks. The other major departure from French orthodoxy is the attitude of the chef: when you arrive, you'll be asked about food preferences, allergies and diets, and Inoue will create a meal accordingly.

Salon de thé François

Nishi-kiyamachi Dori, Shijo-sagaru, Shimogyo-ku (075 351 4042). Gion Shijo station (Keihan line), Kawaramachi station (Hankyu line). **Open** 10am-11pm daily. **¥. Café.**
Map p55 E3 ㊵
This tea salon dates from 1934, back when Kyoto was a centre of left-wing, anti-war politics. It was a gathering place for leading literati and philosophers, including author Osamu Dazai, and funnelled money to the then-banned

Japan Communist Party. These days it has a nostalgic appeal, with an interior last revamped in 1941.

Shougetsu-an

Jidou Koen Minamigawa, Pontocho, Shijo-aguru, Nakagyo-ku (075 223 1401). Kawaramachi station (Hankyu line), Gion Shijo station (Keihan line). **Open** noon-2pm (reservations only), 5-11pm daily. **¥¥. Modern Japanese.**
Map p55 E2 ㊶
This friendly restaurant on Pontocho provides glorious views of the Kamo river and serves authentic Japanese home-style *obanzai* cooking. Although their speciality is seafood, make sure that you try the *yuba* (soy milk skin), served sashimi-style in a sweet sauce or a creamy gratin. From May until the end of September, a *yuka* balcony over the river makes this an even more delightful place to dine at.

Shuz

212 Nabeya-cho, Higashi Kiyamachi Dori, Shijo-aguru, Nakagyo-ku (075 212 1104). Kawaramachi station (Hankyu line), Gion Shijo station (Keihan line). **Open** 7pm-late daily.
Bar. Map p55 E2 ㊷
Sake has fallen out of favour with Japan's youth in recent years, but the young people running this new bar still love the stuff, stocking a great selection of rice brews. They also have a decent menu of local dishes. Walk north on Kiyamachi from Shijo and turn right at the big red lantern.

Soirée

95 Shin-cho, Nishi-kiyamachi Dori, Shijo-aguru, Shimogyo-ku (075 221 0351). Gion Shijo station (Keihan line), Kawaramachi station (Hankyu line). **Open** noon-10.30pm, Tue-Sun. **¥.**
Café. Map p55 E3 ㊸
This time warp's eerie blue lighting may not be to everyone's taste, though it was installed on the advice of an expert, who claimed that women would look their best under such illumination.

Art lovers should check out the wonderful decor, which includes three original works by celebrated 20th-century artist Seiji Togo, who was a former regular here. Even though the pieces are each worth about ¥1 million, the owner won't part with them. The retro menu offers teas, coffees and a range of lurid jelly desserts.

Takaraya Ramen

122-5 Ishiya-cho, Pontocho, Nakagyo-ku (075 222 2778/www.takaraya.info). Sanjo station (Keihan line). **Open** 11.30am-3pm, 5.30pm-midnight Mon, Tue, Thur-Sun. No credit cards. **¥**. **Ramen**. Map p55 E1 ⑤⑨
The speciality here is *sumashi*, a one-of-a-kind nouveau ramen garnished with quirky ingredients such as mozzarella cheese, deep-fried burdock and thick chunks of smoky bacon. However, it's the soup that's the speciality here: 15 chefs spent 45 days developing the recipe, which is laboriously built à la *consommé*. There are six additional branches of Takaraya in the area, but only this one serves the *sumashi*. Hungry diners can order a side dish of rice, complete with raw egg, cucumber and kelp.

Trattoria da Nino

Futasujime, Aneyakoji Higashi-iru, Kawaramachi, Sanjo-agaru, Nakagyo-ku (075 211 3373/www.danino.jp). Kyoto Shiyakusho-mae station (Tozai line). **Open** 11.30am-2.30pm, 6-10.30pm Mon, Tue, Thur-Sun. **¥¥¥**. **Italian**. Map p55 E1 ⑥⓪
Chef Yukio Kato studied in Italy and returned with a culinary repertoire of top-end Tuscan dishes, including a signature homemade *picci pasta* with *boscaiola* sauce. Although the restaurant could be improved if there were a couple more waiting staff, the high quality of the food, combined with a well-chosen wine list and a rustic early-20th century townhouse setting make Trattoria da Nino a charming place in which to dine.

Up's Club

4F Kawaramachi Rokkaku Building, Rokkaku Dori, Kawaramachi Higashi-iru, Nakagyo-ku (075 255 0706). Sanjo station (Keihan line). **Open** 7.30pm-5am daily. **Bar**. Map p55 E2 ⑥①
One of the city's top funk DJs works this little black and red bar, serving cheap drinks to a soundtrack of syncopated beats from the '60s to the present day.

Uroco

Hitosujime-agaru Nishi-gawa, Nishi-kiyamachi Dori, Shijo-agaru, Nakagyo-ku (075 231 2772). Kawaramachi station (Hankyu line), Gion Shijo station (Keihan line). **Open** 6pm-3am daily. **¥¥**. **Izakaya**. Map p55 E3 ⑥②
Izakayas are traditionally rowdy, low-brow joints with a fondness for fried food. Uroco is one of a wave of upmarket versions with a modern Japanese interior and tasty, healthy dishes such as salmon, cream cheese and *yuba* roll, oven-roasted chicken and sashimi that melts in your mouth. With last orders at 2am, it's ideal for a late-night bite to eat.

Wabiya Korekido

Kaburenjo-seinan, Pontocho, Sanjo-sagaru, Nakagyo-ku (075 254 5656). Sanjo station (Keihan line). **Open** 5pm-2am Tue-Sun. **¥¥**. **Yakitori**. Map p55 E2 ⑥③
Grilled chicken liver is the most popular dish here, but most other bits of the bird are also on the menu. This gourmet restaurant changes its range of salts each day, and has a stunning, 100-strong collection of shochu.

Shopping

Evisu The Kyoto

190 Zaimoku-cho, Kawaramachi Dori, Shijo-agaru, Nakagyo-ku (075 213 1992/www.evisu.jp). Kawaramachi station (Hankyu line), Gion Shijo station (Keihan line). **Open** noon-8pm daily. Map p55 E2 ⑥④
The main branch of Osaka's brash denim brand fits right into rowdy Kiyamachi.

The two-tier store, with a stag's head and a life-size Superman dummy for decor, sells a miscellany of branded goods, from jeans and jackets to golf bags and fishing tackle. The store will custom-paint your products with their logo or Kiki character, a hybrid of Mickey Mouse and Hello Kitty.

Nightlife

Collage

3F, Reiho Kaikan, 336 Kamiya-cho, Nishi-kiyamachi Dori, Shijo-agaru, Nakagyo-ku (075 256 6700/www12. ocn.ne.jp/~collage/index2.html). Kawaramachi station (Hankyu line), Gion Shijo station (Keihan line). **Open** varies. **Map** p55 E2 ⑥⑤

This long black room began life as a members-only club and home of DJ legends Kyoto Jazz Massive. These days it's open to all, and specialises in soul, funk and jazz. Though it can be quiet on weekdays, it comes alive when Jazz Massive members take to the turntables on the second Saturday of each month.

Rag

5F Kyoto Empire Building, Kiyamachi, Sanjo-agaru, Nakagyo-ku (075 241 0446/www.ragnet.co.jp). Sanjo station (Keihan line), Kyoto Shiyakushomae station. **Open** varies **Map** p55 E1 ⑥⑥

Kyoto's biggest jazz club is a spartan black room with a schedule that veers from local student bands to legends such as Sadao Watanabe and Hiromasa Hino, so admission prices vary wildly. It's a cosy, upbeat and unpretentious place.

Rub-a-Dub

B1F Tsujita Bldg, 115 Ishiya-cho, Kiyamachi Dori, Sanjo-sagaru, Nakagyo-ku (075 256 3122). Sanjo station (Keihan line). **Open** 7pm-2am Mon-Thur, Sun; 7pm-4am Fri, Sat. **Map** p55 E1 ⑥⑦

Tatsufumi 'Nick' Yamamoto was a nuclear power plant worker who quit his job when he found himself dreaming about safety levels. After a spell in Jamaica, he returned to Kyoto and opened Rub-a-Dub, a basement club that, but for the Japanese faces, could have been lifted straight from Kingston. The steel bar serves Red Stripe, jerk chicken and rums, while DJs play reggae and dancehall 45s. The punters are young, lively and seem not to mind being pressed against each other.

Sam & Dave

3F FS-Kiyamachi Building, Zaimoku-cho, Kiyamachi, Sanjo-sagaru, Nakagyo-ku (075 211 8998/www.samanddave.jp). Sanjo station (Keihan line). **Open** 8pm-5am Wed-Sat; 10pm-5am Sun. **Map** p55 E2 ⑥⑧

Ignoring the Stax connotation, this vast club blasts contemporary R&B, hip hop and techno for a just-old-enough-to-drink crowd. Although it originated in lively Osaka, Sam & Dave has proved a hit in this most traditional of cities. Saturday night parties draw up to 800 young locals.

Urban Guild

3F Le New Kyoto Building, Kiyamachi, Sanjo-sagaru, Nakagyo-ku (075 212 1125/www.urbanguild.net). Sanjo station (Keihan line). **Open** varies. **Map** p55 E2 ⑥⑨

This avant-garde venue puts on entertainment ranging from local noise bands to an abstract mime artists. The audience sits at long wooden tables, tucking into Japanese-style pub grub. Bring an empty belly and open mind.

World

97 Shinmachi, Nishi-kiyamachi, Shijo-agaru, Shimogyo-ku (075 213 4119/ www.world-kyoto.com). Kawaramachi station (Hankyu line), Gion Shijo station (Keihan line). **Open** varies **Map** p55 E3 ⑦⓪

Subterranean stone arches, rattling bass and high-octane lights are hardly an original formula for clubbing, but it works here, drawing young fans to hear electronica and house from top-tier acts such as Mondo Grosso, Towa Tei and Fantastic Plastic Machine.

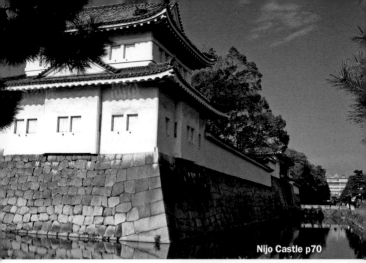

Nijo Castle p70

Gosho District

As you'll notice on the map, this area is dominated by 90 hectares of imperial palaces and gardens. For more than 500 years, this was the heart of court activity, with emperors and other blue bloods pursuing cultural refinement.

The area developed to serve its most eminent resident, with the neighbouring streets home to suppliers of imperial food, clothing, art and crafts. Although the emperor moved to Tokyo almost a century and a half ago, many of his old purveyors are still around, such as the Ippodo tea shop and the Owariya soba restaurant.

It was probably no accident that the first Tokugawa shogun built his Kyoto stronghold, Nijo Castle, just a few blocks away from the nobles. Even though it was never used as a primary residence, the castle was close enough to the court to remind its residents where the true power lay.

As bullet marks on some of the palace gates attest, the rivalry ended in conflict, with imperial troops returning power to the throne, along with ownership of Nijo Castle, in 1869.

These days, the district is a laid-back locale, with hushed backstreets hiding some impressive artisan shops and restaurants.

Sights & museums

Confectionery museum

Karasuma Dori, Kamidashiuri-agaru, Kamigyo-ku (075 432 3101).
Imadegawa station (Karasuma line).
Open 10am-5pm Mon,Tue, Thur-Sun.
Admission free. **Map** p71 B2 ❶
Although this single-room museum contains just a handful of exhibits, it's a free and fun diversion if you're in the area. Sporadic English texts trace Japan's confectionery culture from its eighth-century origins, describing the role of sweets in Christian missionary

work and the Zen origin of sweet buns, among other tales of historic trivia. The museum is attached to a store run by the venerable confectioners Tawaraya Yoshitomi.

Kyoto Gosho

Kyotogyoennai, Kamigyo-ku (075 211 1215/http://sankan.kunaicho.go.jp). Imadegawa station (Karasuma line). **Tours** 10am, 2pm Mon-Fri. **Admission** free. **Map** p71 B3 ❷

Although Kyoto held the imperial seat for more than a millennium, the 'Old Imperial Palace' that stands today served as an emperor's residence for just 14 years (1855-69). Previous incarnations succumbed to fire, natural and intentional, but were rebuilt each time with the same medley of architectural styles. The palace sits in an 11-hectare walled compound, which is open to the public from 23th to 29th April and 12th to 16th November. The rest of the year, visitors can apply online for one of the twice-daily, hour-long English-language tours. It's worth the effort: the gardens are magnificent, as is the Shishinden building, in which two of the last three emperors were enthroned.

Kyoto International Manga Museum

Karasuma Oike, Nakagyo-ku (075 254 7414/www.kyotomm.jp). Karasuma Oike station (Karasuma, Tozai lines). **Open** 10am-5.30pm Mon, Tue, Thur-Sun. **Admission** ¥500. **Map** p71 B5 ❸

You don't need to be a manga fan to be charmed by this vast but endearing museum, with a collection spanning three centuries and four continents. Comprehensive English signage narrates the history of the comic genre, and regular workshops, seminars and performances keep the place buzzing. See box p73.

Nijo Castle

541 Nijojo-cho, Nijo Dori, Horikawa Nishi-iru, Nakagyo-ku (075 841 0096/ www.city.kyoto.jp/bunshi/nijojo). Nijojo-mae station (Tozai line). **Open** 8.45am-4pm daily. Closed Tue in Dec, Jan, July and Aug. **Admission** ¥600. **Map** p71 A5 ❹

Built in 1603 as the Kyoto stronghold of shogun Ieyasu Tokugawa, Nijo Castle occupies vast grounds, including a garden and pond by master landscape designer Kobori Enshu. The buildings are bolder and golder than most of Kyoto's landmarks, with ostentatious carvings, dramatic murals and gold leaf galore, signifying the fine tastes of a warrior. Although it boasts squeaking 'nightingale' corridors and samurai guard quarters, the castle is unfortified, designed to flaunt more than to protect. When the shogunate fell in 1869, the fortress passed into imperial hands and became known as Nijo Rikyu (Nijo Imperial Villa). If you look closely, you can spot the hollyhock crest of the Tokugawas and the chrysanthemum mark of the emperor. An English-language audio guide is available for ¥500.

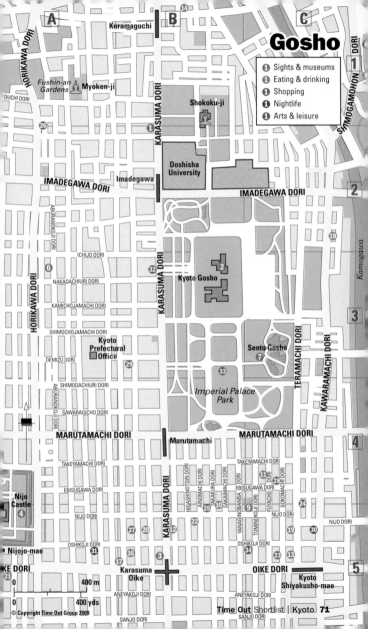

Nijo Jinya

137 Samboomiya-cho, Omiya Dori, Oike-sagaru, Nakagyo-ku (075 841 0972/www.nijyojinya.net). Nijojo-mae station (Tozai line). **Tours** 10am, 11am, 2pm, 3pm Mon-Tue. Thur-Sun. **Admission** ¥1,000. **Map** p71 A5 **5**

A treat for fans of ninja films, this former inn is packed with hidden passages, secret stairways and trapdoors. The 24-room residence used to host feudal lords on their visits to Kyoto, and the owner clearly took the safety of his guests seriously. The house was built in the late 17th century and was gradually modified with various security tricks and traps. Although the 50-minute tours take place in Japanese, an English pamphlet costs only ¥100 and volunteer interpreters are listed on the website. Reservations must be made in advance, by phone, in Japanese. Check the website for opening times.

Raku Museum

84 Aburahashizume-cho, Aburanokoji Dori, Nakadachiuri-agaru, Nakagyo-ku (075 414 0304/www.raku-yaki.or.jp). Buses 9, 12, 50 or Imadegawa station (Karasuma line). **Open** 10am-4pm Tue-Sun. **Admission** ¥700. **Map** p71 A3 **6**

Tea master Sen no Rikyu was one of the early admirers of *raku-yaki*, the ceramics of the Raku family. The clan is now in its 15th generation, with a reputation for producing the very finest tea bowls. This museum holds a collection of more than 1,000 examples of the family's work.

Sento Gosho

Kyotogyoennai, Kamigyo-ku (075 211 1215/http://sankan.kunaicho.go.jp). Imadegawa station (Karasuma line). **Tours** 10am, 2pm Mon-Fri. **Admission** free. **Map** p71 C3 **7**

When Emperor Go-Mizuno retired in the 17th century, a new palace was constructed for him in the imperial grounds. The building was razed in 1854, but his gardens remain, and are well worth a look. Designed by Kobori Enshu, the most acclaimed architect of his generation, the gardens are built around two large ponds. The pebbles on the beach were donated by a feudal lord from Odawara, 300 kilometres away, who had each stone selected for size and shape, then individually gift-wrapped in silk. The Imperial Household Agency conducts twice-daily, hour-long tours in English, but all visits must be approved in advance. It's essential to apply online.

Shimogamo Jinja

59 Izumikawa-cho, Shimogamo, Sakyo-ku (075 781 0010/ www.shimogamo-jinja.or.jp). Demachiyanagi station (Keihan line). **Open** 6.30am-5.30pm daily. **Admission** free. **Map** p71 C1 **8**

It's less mesmerising than most of its World Heritage peers, but this shrine is historic (thought to date from the sixth century) and hosts one of Kyoto's big three festivals (Aoi Festival, see p31). It's set in the Forest of Truth, a 12-hectare belt of untouched nature often used by film-makers to represent a primeval forest in period dramas. In the south-east corner of the grounds stands one of the 'Seven Wonders of Kyoto', a pair of evergreen trees growing inches apart. Although the trees have died three times, on each occasion a similar pair has grown in their place. They are now tied together with rope and considered auspicious for lovers.

Eating & drinking

Café Bibliotic Hello!

650 Seimei-cho, Nijo Dori, Yanaginobanba-higashi iru, Nakagyo-ku (075 231 8625/www.cafe-hello.jp). Kyoto Shiyakusho-mae Station (Tozai line). **Open** 11am-midnight daily. **¥**. No credit cards. **Café**. **Map** p71 C5 **9**

This century-old building began life as a kimono store, but the interior was revamped in 2002, transforming it into one of Kyoto's coolest cafés. Designer

Cartoon culture

When people talk of Kyoto as the cultural capital of Japan, they usually mean the cradle of kabuki, Noh, tea ceremony and *ikebana*. In other words: the classic stuff. For anything post-19th century, try Tokyo. That said, it was the former capital that created a world-class museum for one of Japan's most successful contemporary phenomena: manga.

The **Kyoto International Manga Museum** (p70) opened in 2006 as a collaboration between the city and Kyoto Seika University. It's part library (with 50,000 books for browsing, from a collection of more than 300,000), part museum (exhibits trace the history of manga and its place in global comic culture) part research facility (intellectual property management is a specialism of the four full-time researchers), part school (offering classes for aspiring artists), part convention centre (it hosted the International Manga Summit in 2008 and stages regular symposiums) and part social centre (the corridors and lawn are teeming with youths, often wearing manga-inspired costumes).

Comic books may seem an unusual topic for serious academic study. As museum director Shuzo Ueda puts it, 'manga isn't respected or important, it's just a part of life.' However, it's a ¥500 billion-per-year part of life, and Seika University recognises the cultural significance of a medium that has been documenting Japanese society for more than a century. Just as scrolls tell us how Japan lived during the Heian period (794-1192), so manga is an archive of more recent social history. You don't need to be fluent in Japanese to comprehend the 1940s cover depicting a hybrid of Dracula and Frankenstein's monster that has more than a passing resemblance to FDR.

The museum began life as a manga lab at the university. The academics wanted to expand the collection into a serious library, and began searching for a suitable space. Politics and prices ruled out Tokyo as a venue, but Kyoto had the perfect space: the former Tatsuike Primary School. Dwindling student numbers forced the school to close in 1995, but locals had helped fund its construction back in 1929, so still had a voice in the building's future. Plans to create a library and police station never found footing, but the manga museum won approval from the residents and city. The interior of the building still resembles the school, complete with teenagers lying around in corridors reading manga.

Café Bibliotic Hello! p72

Hafuu

*471-1 Sasaya-cho, Fuyacho Dori,
Ebisugawa-agaru, Nakagyo-ku (075
257 1581/www.hafuu.com). Kyoto
Shiyakusho-mae Station (Tozai line).*
Open 11.30am-1.30pm, 5.30-9.30pm
Mon, Tue, Thur-Sun. **¥¥¥**. **Beef**.
Map p71 C4 ⓫

Top-grade Japanese beef usually commands sky-high prices, but Hafuu is run by a veteran Kyoto butcher, so quality is high and prices (relatively) low. You could splurge on a seven-course set menu, but the most popular choice is the beef cutlet sandwich, available with regular beef (¥1,800) or premium wagyu (¥5,000).

Honke Owariya

*Kurumayacho Dori, Nijo-sagaru,
Nakagyo-ku (075 231 3446/www.
honke-owariya.co.jp). Karasuma Oike
station (Karasuma, Tozai lines).* **Open**
11am-7pm daily. **¥**. No credit cards.
Soba. Map p71 B5 ⓬

Kyoto's oldest soba restaurant began life in 1465 as a confectionery store. Gradually, its sideline in soba became more popular than the sweets, with a fanbase that included local temples and the imperial family. The secret, as always, is the soup – a rich, complex broth of Kyoto well water, three kinds of dried fish and top-grade Hokkaido kelp. The menu is unusually extensive, but the top picks here are the Hourai soba, with egg, mushrooms and shrimp, and the *rikyu-fu*, deep-fried, soy-flavoured wheat gluten. Thanks to its history of serving monks, Owariya also knows how to knock up a tasty vegetarian soba.

Japonica

*476 Kamihonnojimae-cho, Teramachi
Dori, Oike-agaru, Nakagyo-ku (075
211 8580/www.japonica-music.com).
Kyoto Shiyakusho-mae station (Tozai
line).* **Open** noon-10pm daily. **Bar**.
Map p71 C5 ⓭

A record store at the front, selling hiphop, house, soul and nu jazz on

furnishings, art books and modern café grub is hardly an original formula, but the blend of historic and contemporary detail has proved a big hit with young Kyoto-ites. The café added a bakery in 2008, which sells a small but tasty range of loaves and rolls until 11pm.

Chez Quasimodo

Takakura Dori, Nijo-agaru, Nakagyo-ku (075 231 2488). Karasuma Oike station (Karasuma, Tozai lines).
Open 6pm-midnight Mon-Sat.
Bar. Map p71 B5 ⓾

Sawaguchi was 55 years old when he wound down the family greengrocer business and converted his garage into a bar. If selling booze in your old garage sounds rough and ready, it couldn't be further from the truth. The bar is furnished with antiques, stocked with rare spirits and vermouths, and plays jazz from a Denon-Marantz-Tannoy set-up, which could power a small club. Throw in a wine collection, a log fire and a genial host and you've got a fantastic place to go to for an evening drink.

vinyl, draws DJs and other music lovers; the bar at the back keeps them here. The stripped-down space features enormous furniture and a pair of decks, as well as a bar with an impressive selection of domestic microbrews by the bottle.

Kanga-an
Kuramaguchi Dori, Karasuma Higashi-iru, Kita-ku (075 256 2480/www. kangaan.jp). Kuramaguchi station (Karasuma line). **Open** noon-9pm daily. ¥¥¥. **Vegetarian/Bar**. **Map** p71 B1 ⑭
A temple that no gastronome should miss (see box p76).

Kichisen
5 Morimoto-cho, Shimogamo, Sakyo-ku (075 711 6121/www.kichisen-kyoto.com). Demachiyanagi station (Keihan line). **Open** noon-1pm, 5.30-7pm daily. ¥¥¥¥. **Kaiseki**. **Map** p71 C1 ⑮
Chef Yoshimi Tanigawa made a national splash with a 2001 triumph on the *Iron Chef* TV show. His classic, unfussy version of Kyoto's ancient court cuisine is more orthodox than some *kaiseki* restaurants, but no less dazzling. Whether you notice or not, your food will be seasonal, right down to the tiniest detail, from ingredients to tableware to decor, the marks of a meticulous craftsman. The service by shaven-headed, kimono-clad male apprentice chefs is precise and courtly. Reservations essential.

Obanzai
199 Shimomyokakuji-cho, Koromodana Dori, Oike-garu, Nakagyo-ku (075 223 6623). *Karasuma Oike station (Karasuma, Tozai lines).* **Open** 11am-2pm, 5-9pm daily; closed Wed lunch. ¥. **Obanzai**. **Map** p71 B5 ⑯
Named after the local style of home cooking, Obanzai is almost a vegetarian restaurant (no meat, some fish stock) and offers a great value lunch buffet.

Tamaki p77

Le Petit Mec
186 Shimomyokakuji-cho, Koromodana Dori, Oike-agaru, Nakagyo-ku (075 212 7735). *Karasuma Oike station (Karasuma, Tozai lines).* **Open** 8am-8pm daily. ¥. **Bakery**. **Map** p71 B5 ⑰
Kyoto's fanciest bakery is a tiny, takeaway joint with an all-black interior and staff dressed in Comme des Garçons. It sells all the requisite baguettes, croissants and tartes as well as bite-size rolls with restaurant-grade French fillings, such as escargot and potato puree or roast pork with plums in red wine.

Risei
448-16 Kajii-cho, Kawaramachi Dori, Imadegawa-sagaru Futasujime, Kamigyo-ku (075 255 5652). *Demachiyanagi station (Keihan line).* **Open** 11am-6pm Wed-Sun. ¥. **Korean**. **Map** p71 C2 ⑱
Even Korean food is gently seasoned in Kyoto. Risei goes easy on spices and lets the beef and organic vegetables provide the flavours. The bibimbap and naengmyeon are as good as it gets in

A most intoxicating temple

Like most Zen temples, **Kanga-an** (p75) has an enchanting dry landscape garden with waves of raked stones. Unlike its peers, this house of worship allows you to view the garden from a fully licensed bar. Whereas other temples offer tea, Kanga-an serves whisky and shochu, draft Guinness, and glasses of Japan's tastiest big brewery beer, Kohaku Yebisu.

The elegant ten-seater counter bar was installed several years ago as a private retreat for the chief priestess and her friends. Since 2008, it has opened to the public, serving brews and spirits from 5pm to 1am daily.

It's not a bar that you are likely to stumble across. The temple is tucked away in a backstreet north of the old Imperial Palace, and the drinks are poured from behind an anonymous wooden door just left of the Main Hall. At night, with noone in sight and only a recording of bamboo flutes breaking the silence, it's hard to imagine that you're heading to a watering hole.

However, the bar is just a flourish in Kanga-an's culinary repertoire. The temple's speciality is *fucha ryori*, a vegetarian cuisine introduced to Japan in the 17th century by Chinese monk Ingen. Followers of Ingen's Obaku Zen are associated more with artistic prowess than asceticism, and Kanga-an's multi-course banquet measures up to this reputation.

Some dishes are as simple as a single broad bean or a square of tofu with a dab of wasabi. Others are more indulgent, such as orchid tempura or plums garnished with gold leaf. In line with *fucha ryori* tradition, all food is served on a communal platter – intended to make the meal chatty and informal. As you dine, you may notice chrysanthemum motifs dotted around – the sign of an imperial connection. Kanga-an was established in the 17th century on the orders of retired emperor Go-mizuno, who wanted a guardian temple to stop evil spirits reaching the Imperial Palace. The emperor became fond of kanga-an, and his calligraphy still furnishes one of the dining rooms.

This restaurant is fit for an emperor, and a meal here should be on every itinerary.

this price bracket. There's also a 12-strong menu of Korean teas in a homey spot furnished with Korean antiques.

Shinamo

454-3 Myomanjimae-cho, Teramachi Dori, Nijo-sagaru, Nakagyo-ku (075 223 3969/www.sinamo.com). Kyoto Shiyakusho-mae Station (Tozai line). **Open** 11.30am-11pm daily. **Wine bar**. Map p71 C5 ⑲

The extensive wine list runs from cheap plonk to vintage treats, all at incredibly affordable prices (glasses from ¥290), which is one reason this place is always full of couples on dates. The other reason is the interior, which employs mirrors and a wall of 90 table lamps to make this narrow strip of a room seem cosy and romantic. Decent Italian dishes dominate the food menu.

Tamaki

472-1 Kinbuki-cho, Ryogaemachi Dori, Nijo-sagaru, Nakagyo-ku (075 213 4177/www.tamaki-kyoto.com). Karasuma Oike station (Karasuma, Tozai lines). **Open** *Restaurant* 11.30am-2pm, 5-8pm Mon, Tue, Thur-Sun. **¥¥¥**. **French**. Map p71 B5 ⑳

The building is a 19th-century kimono merchant's house. The dining room looks onto a rock garden. The meal is a multi-plate parade, cooked from local ingredients. So far, so Kyoto. But chef Hiroyuki Aoike trained in classic French cuisine, and although your dinner might begin with fermented rice, the next course could be *potage de pois* or a gratin. Aoike's 'French *kaiseki*' is more delicate than orthodox French fare – and a lot more fun. A vegetarian set is available if booked in advance.

Il Viale

Horikawa Dori, Oike Nishi-iru, Nakagyo-ku (075 812 2366). Nijojo-mae station (Tozai line). **Open** noon-2pm, 6-9pm Tue-Sun. **¥¥¥**. **Italian**. Map p71 A5 ㉑

There's no à la carte menu here – you'll get what you're given, and like it. Take

a seat at the counter and watch unflappable chef Takemasa Watanabe create classic Italian dishes with home-made pasta, local veg and Italian hams. Watanabe is also a grappa fan, stocking more than 30 varieties.

Yoramu Sake Bar

Nijo Dori, Higashinotoin Higashi-iru, Nakagyo-ku (075 213 1512/www.sake bar-yoramu.com). Karasuma Oike station (Karasuma, Tozai lines). **Open** 6pm-midnight, Mon, Tue, Thur-Sun. Closed 1st Sun of mth. **Sake**. Map p71 B5 ㉒

If you want to explore sake but haven't a clue where to begin, this is your place. The Israeli owner has a professorial knowledge of the rice brew, and will recommend drinks to suit your tastebuds. He carries an impressive range of aged sakes and pairs them with an international menu of snacks, including falafel, fermented tofu and fried halloumi.

Shopping

Comme des Garçons

378 Kameyacho, Gokoumachi Dori, Oike-agaru, Nakagyo-ku (075 223 0370). Kyoto Shiyakusho-mae station (Tozai line). **Open** 11am-8pm daily. Map p71 C5 ㉓

Rei Kawakubo designed this store, along with the avant-garde fashion that fills it. A curving black entrance with a lacquer-like surface reveals a glimmering reflection of her creations. Inside, you'll find the surroundings as monochromatic as the fashion, with gorgeous staff to intimidate you.

Ippodo

Teramachi Nijo, Nakagyo-ku (075 211 3421/www.ippodo-tea.co.jp). Kyoto Shiyakusho-mae Station (Tozai line). **Open** *Store* 9am-7pm Mon-Sat; 9am-6pm Sun. *Café* 11am-5pm daily. Map p71 C4/C5 ㉔

Kyoto-ites will argue about the best green tea, but elsewhere in Japan one

brand reins supreme in the public mind: Ippodo. This former purveyor to the imperial family has been in business for three centuries, and based in this store since the 19th century. The store recently added a salon in which you can sample the teas before deciding which to buy.

Iremonya Design Labo

51 Matsuya-cho, Nijo Dori, Takakura Nishi-iru, Nakagyo-ku (075 256 5652/ www.iremonya.com). Karasuma Oike station (Karasuma, Tozai lines). **Open** 11am-7pm daily. **Map** p71 B5 ㉕
Kyoto designer Masaki Tokuda has a fascination with faces, adding smiles and sulks to furniture, stationery, socks and other goodies on sale in his two-tier store.

Kanoko

20 Horinoue-cho, Kamidachiuri Dori, Horikawa Higashi-iru, Kamigyo-ku (075 441 3114/www.kanoukou.com). Imadegawa station (Karasuma line). **Open** by appointment. **Map** p71 A1 ㉖
When Japan hosted the 2008 G8 Summit, the leaders' wives all received a Kanoko kimono sash. This family business has been supplying luxury sashes since 1889, and their beautiful creations have caught the attention of people in high places across the world, ranging from Japan's imperial family to French *Vogue* magazine and even the New York Metropolitan Museum of Art. If you would like to buy one, make an appointment and bring along plenty of money: kimono and sash sets start at around ¥400,000, and at the top end of the scale, belts alone can cost ¥2 million.

Omo

Muromachi Dori, Oshikoji-agaru, Nakagyo-ku (075 212 8676/www. moritamotoko.com/omo/omo/ index.html). Karasuma Oike station (Karasuma, Tozai lines). **Open** 11am-7pm Mon, Tue, Thur-Sun. **Map** p71 B5 ㉗

In a delightful store with a small garden, kimono stylist Motoko Morita will help you team a kimono with sash, bag and wooden *geta* shoes. The tailor-made kimonos are available in fun and informal designs, and vary in price from ¥30,000 to several hundred thousand yen, depending on your chosen material.

Wajigen Shizukuya

Ebisugawa-dori, Gokomachi Nishi-iru, Nakagyo-ku (075 211 0897/www. shizukuya.com). Kyoto Shiyakusho-mae station (Tozai line). **Open** 11am-7pm Sat, Sun; weekdays by appointment. **Map** p71 C4 ㉘
Women are spoiled for choice when buying kimono in Kyoto; men have to look a little harder. The best place to start from is the store of Tokyo-born tailor Soyu Hyogo. Other outlets produce men's kimonos for formal occasions, but Hyogo, who studied western and Japanese tailoring, designs his as everyday attire. You'll find classic gents' kimonos and jackets, as well as modern versions, complete with funky prints and even zips.

Yamada Matsu

Muromachi Dori, Shimodachiuri-agaru, Kamigyo-ku (075 441 1123/www. yamadamatsu.co.jp). Marutamachi station (Karasuma line). **Open** 10am-5.30pm daily. **Map** p71 B3 ㉙
It's not just green tea that gets the ceremonial treatment in Japan. The classical art of *kodo* involves burning wood chips for their aroma, and though it hasn't endured as well as other traditions, it still has a place in Kyoto's cultural scene. For two centuries, Yamada Matsu has been the leading wood chip supplier. It's not a pursuit to take up on a whim: hearths sell for around ¥60,000 and wood chips cost up to ¥30,000 per gram. The store offers one-off classes for anyone with a casual interest, and sells more affordable incense sticks, pouches and cones.

Nightlife

Lab Tribe
Kawaramachi Dori, Nijo-sagaru, Nakagyo-ku (075 254 1228/www. labtribe.net). Kyoto Shiyakusho-mae Station (Tozai line). **Open** times vary. Map p71 C5 ③⓪
For people who take their clubbing seriously, here's a big, black dancefloor with little to look at but the DJ. It doesn't always draw the big-hitting DJs, but a great sound system and an ebullient young crowd make Lab Tribe a good spot for fans of house or techno music.

Nano
632-3 Nijonishinotoin-cho, Oshikoji Dori, Nishonotoin Higashi-iru, Nakagyo-ku (075 254 1930). Karasuma Oike station (TK line); or Nijojo-mae station (Tozai line). **Open** varies. Map p71 A5 ③①
This 40-seater live music venue is incredibly intimate, if a bit sterile. It feels like the front room of someone's house. Events span the musical spectrum.

LabTribe

Arts & leisure

Kongo Nohgakudo
590 Totsumae-cho, Karasuma Dori, Ichijo-sagaru, Kamigyo-ku (075 441 7222/www.kongou-net.com). Imadegawa station (Karasuma line). **Open** varies. Map p71 B3 ③②
The Kongo Noh school, one of the nation's big five, has been performing for 26 generations. Their art form may draw only a fraction of the support it once enjoyed, but in 2003 the family opened this splendid 420-seat theatre in a purpose-built piece of modern architecture. Their 100-show-a-year schedule is prolific by Noh standards, and English-language plot summaries and even occasional simultaneous translations help make things more accessible. Still, given the notoriously glacial pace of performances, you'll be glad the seats are so comfy.

Kyoto Gyoen
Kamigyo-ku (075 211 6348). Imadegawa station (Karasuma line). **Open** 24 hours daily. Map p71 B3 ③③
Before the emperor moved to Tokyo, the palace grounds housed more than 200 estates for court nobles. Nowadays, most of the buildings have been razed and the grounds have been turned into a park, open to the public 24 hours a day. In terms of scenery, it can't begin to compete with the great gardens of Kyoto, but it's good for playing games.

Ooe Nohgakudo
Tachibana-cho, Oshikoji, Yanaginobanba, Nakagyo-ku (075 561 0622). Kyoto Shiyakusho-mae station (Tozai line). **Open** shows start at 1pm. Map p71 C5 ③④
Kyoto's oldest Noh theatre was built in 1908, and had its last major refurbishment nine years later. This 400-seat, two-storey wooden structure oozes atmosphere, but only stages four regular shows a year, in February, May, September and December. Call for this year's precise dates.

Hanamikoji

Southern Higashiyama

Get your cameras ready: this is Kyoto as you dreamed it would look. In Southern Higashiyama, you'll find cobbled streets and willow-lined canals, geishas tottering to wooden teahouses, and temples that give you goosebumps. The district developed to serve Yasaka Shrine pilgrims with refreshments, and its function remains largely the same, although there are many more temples and shrines to visit, and many more visitors, keeping prices high.

The historic pleasure quarters of Gion provide the entertainment, with once-in-a-lifetime restaurants, exclusive bars and *ochaya*, the teahouses in which geishas entertain. Although entering the teahouses is all but impossible for tourists, if you stroll along Shinbashi Dori in the evening, you can peek through the windows to see the painted entertainers at work. Hanamikoji, which bisects Gion vertically, is another popular geisha-spotting street, and leads you to the city's oldest Zen temple.

Souvenir hunters should head for Ninnenzaka and Sannenzaka, a pair of narrow streets leading to the area's most famous temple, Kiyomizu-dera. Locals may scoff, but these quaint lanes are lined with shops, some centuries-old, some modern and stocked with tourist bait. More serious, and affluent, shoppers might prefer Shinmonzen Dori, which is home to many of the city's best art and antique shops.

Southern Higashiyama

Kyoto Municipal Zoo

Sanjo

Higashiyama

Shoren-in

Chion-in

Maruyama Park

SHIJO DORI

Gion Shijo

GION

Kennin-ji

Kodai-ji

Kiyomizu-dera

YASAKA DORI

Rakuto Hospital

Kyoto National Museum

❶ Sights & museums
❶ Eating & drinking
❶ Shopping
❶ Nightlife
❶ Arts & leisure

0   300 m
0   300 yds
© Copyright Time Out Group 2009

33 takes a magical turn

The number 33 is sacred in Buddhism. The sutras tell of 33 deities guarding Shumisen, the celestial mountain at the centre of the universe. They describe how Kannon, bodhisattva of mercy, can take one of 33 forms when saving souls.

You'll find the number at most temples that worship Kannon. In Kyoto, **Sanjusangen-do** (Hall of 33 Bays, p50) has 33 alcoves built into its main hall and Southern Higashiyama's popular attraction, the **Kiyomizu-dera** (p84), honours Kannon by keeping its top treasures hidden for 33 years at a time.

The story of the treasures begins with a shogun named Sakanoue no Tamuramaro, who was walking on Mount Otowa and hunting deer to provide his pregnant wife with nourishing blood. He met a young priest who admonished the shogun for his murderous intentions. The priest convinced Sakanoue to rely on prayer rather than blood, and when mother and baby survived, the commander became a follower of Kannon. He funded Kiyomizu-dera's construction on the site of his encounter with the priest, and donated statues of three deities – Jizo, guardian of children, Bishamonten, god of war, and Kannon. Although the originals haven't survived, their replicas are enshrined in the inner sanctum of the main hall.

The threesome are making an appearance in 2009 to mark the 1,000th anniversary of the death of Emperor Kazan.

Sights & museums

Chion-in

400 Rinka-cho, Shinbashi Dori, Yamatoo-ji Higashi-iru, Higashiyama-ku (075 531 2111/www.chion-in.or.jp). Buses 12, 46, 201, 203, 206; or Higashiyama station (Tozai line). **Open** *9am-4pm daily.* **Admission** *Grounds free. Hojo Garden ¥400. Yuzen Garden ¥300. Both gardens ¥500.* **Map** p81 C2 ❶

The entrance to Chion-in, the head temple of Buddhism's Jodo sect, is as imposing as it is tragic. The world's largest and oldest wooden gate is 24m high, 50m wide and houses the coffins of the master builder and his wife, both of whom committed suicide after the grand creation went over budget. The original temple was built in 1234 on the site of sect founder Honen's death. Most of the current buildings date back to the mid 17th century, when the Tokugawa Shogunate funded a reconstruction. With such heavyweight backing, the architecture is imposing and includes a defensive 'nightingale corridor', with squeaky floorboards designed to sing like birds whenever anyone approached. The complex includes the 16th-century Hojo Garden, and the mid 20th-century Yuzen Garden, dedicated to the creator of *yuzen* dyeing.

Choraku-ji

626 Maruyama-cho, Higashiyama-ku (075 561 0589). Bus 206. **Open** *9am-5pm daily.* **Admission** *¥500.* **Map** p81 C3 ❷

Like a B-lister's house on the Hollywood Homes Tour, this temple struggles to impress amid such famous neighbours. It lacks the awesome dimensions of Higashiyama's most popular sights, and draws a tiny fraction of their crowds – which is precisely why you should visit. Climb the lantern-lined approach and head into the second building on your left. Order a bowl of green tea, sit on the edge of the garden

Kodai-ji p84

and enjoy the most peaceful place in the area. If you head further up, behind the main hall, you'll reach the graveyards and some great views of the city.

Ebisu Shrine
125 Komatsu-cho, Higashiyama-ku (075 525 0005/www.kyoto-ebisu.jp). Gion Shijo station (Keihan line). **Open** 24 hours daily. **Admission** free. **Map** p81 A3 ❸
Known locally as 'Ebessan', this shrine was established in 1202 as a guardian of Kennin-ji (p84). It sits in relative quiet for the majority of the year, but comes alive from the 8th to the 10th of January, when local business owners flock to honour Ebisu, the god of business, in the hope that they will have a prosperous and bountiful year.

Entoku-in
Shimokawaramachi 530, Kodaiji, Higashiyama-ku (075 535 0101/www. kodaiji.com/entoku-in). Buses 206, 207. **Open** 10am-4.30pm daily. **Admission** ¥500. **Map** p81 B3 ❹
After visiting Kodai-ji, step across the street to see Entoku-in, a sub-temple that for 19 years was the living quarters

of Nene, widow of warlord Hideyoshi Toyotomi. Enjoy the two gardens, including an impressive Momoyama-period creation, dating from the late 16th century.

Galerie 16
3F Togawa Building, 394 Sekisenin-cho, Sanjo Dori, Shirakawabashi-agaru, Higashiyama-ku (075 751 9238/ art16.net). Higashiyama station (Tozai line). **Open** noon-7pm Tue-Sun. **Admission** free. **Map** p81 B1 ❺
One of the city's best contemporary art spaces, Galerie 16 has been running since 1962. In 2007, it moved to new premises a few blocks south of the big Okazaki Park art museums. It's a small space with a big presence on the local art scene, and always worth a look.

Gallery Haneusagi
2F Hollyhock Building, Sanjo Dori, Jingumichi Higashi-iru, Higashiyama-ku (075 761 9606/www.haneusa.com). Higashiyama station (Tozai line). **Open** noon-7pm daily. **Admission** free. **Map** p81 C1 ❻
Textiles, video art, installations, sculpture and even paintings are shown at

KYOTO BY AREA

Maruyama Park

Japan loves to rank its attractions, and Kyoto's oldest Zen temple has been deemed the city's third greatest (Nanzen-ji, p100, enjoys the top spot). Among its highlights are a *karesansui* (dry Zen) garden, a 179sq m dragon ceiling and an art collection that features 60 screens by Kansetsu Hashimoto (p102). There's a kindergarten within shrieking distance of the Zen garden, so it's not always peaceful.

Kiyomizu-dera

1 Kiyomizu, Higashiyama-ku
(075 551 1234/www.kiyomizudera.or.jp).
Buses 100, 206, 207. **Open** 6am-6pm
daily. **Admission** ¥300; Tainai-meguri
¥100. **Map** p81 C4 ❾
If you only visit one temple in Kyoto, make it this World Heritage behemoth. From the balcony at the eastern edge of the complex, you can view an awesome sight: a massive hall and Noh stage supported by 139 wooden pillars. This architectural marvel was built in 1633 using not a single nail, but relying instead on wooden wedges.

The temple has a reputation for bestowing good fortune, with numerous ways to appeal to the gods. A natural spring has a sign that states confidently: 'You can make any wishes here and they will all come true'. In the north of the complex, young ladies close their eyes and try to walk between a pair of stones placed 18m apart. If they make it, legend says, they'll find true love. Just west of the Main Hall is the Tainai-meguri, a pitch-black tunnel that represents Buddha's intestine. Feel your way down the short, twisting path and you'll find a stone that can also grant wishes. Despite all this, some worshippers used to leap from the 13m-high stage, believing their prayers would be answered if they survived the drop.

this three-room modern art gallery. There's a new show each week, keeping things fresh and very varied.

Ii Museum

564 Komatsu-cho, Hanamiko-ji,
Shijo-sagaru 4-chome, Higashiyama-ku.
(075 525 3921/www.ii-museum.jp).
Buses 6, 207. **Admission** ¥1,500. **Map** p81 A3 ❼
Samurai helmets, swords and body armour are crammed into a huge townhouse in backstreet Gion. Early attempts at curation have been overwhelmed as the rooms overflow with donations of historical treasures. Among the more unusual exhibits is a handwritten report by a samurai, telling his master of his successful mission.

Kennin-ji

Komatsu-cho, Yamatoo-ji, Shijo-
sagaru, Higashiyama-ku (075 561
6363/www.kenninji.jp). Bus 206;
or Gion Shijo station (Keihan line).
Open 10am-4pm daily. **Admission**
¥500. **Map** p81 A3 ❽

Kodai-ji

526 Shimogawara-cho, Higashiyama-ku
(075 591 9966/www.kodaiji.com).
Buses 206, 207. **Open** 9am-5pm daily.
Admission ¥600. **Map** p81 C3 ❿

When Hideyoshi Toyotomi, the warrior who unified Japan, died in 1598, his grieving widow Nene was granted land in Higashiyama to build a retreat for her final years. Celebrated landscaper Kobori Enshu designed her gardens, tea master Sen-no-Rikyu created her teahouses, and Nene lived out her years as a nun in this Rinzai sect temple. Only the Founder's Hall and Mausoleum survive from Nene's days, but the temple has gained a large *karesansui* garden and is now one of the most popular sights in the area. In early March and December, the temple stays open late and is illuminated to stunning effect.

Ryozen Kannon

Kyoto Museum of Contemporary Art

271 Gionmachi Kitagawa, Shijo Dori, Higashiyama-ku (075 525 1311/ www.kahitsukan.or.jp). Gion Shijo station (Keihan line). **Open** 10am-5.30pm daily. **Admission** ¥1,000. Map p81 A2 ⑪

Check the artwork in the entrance to see whether the current exhibition at this five-floor solo-show specialist piques your interest.

Maruyama Park

Higashiyama-ku. Bus 206. **Open** 24 hrs daily. **Admission** free. Map p81 B2/B3 ⑫

Though best known for a *shidarezakura* (weeping cherry tree) that lures visitors galore in cherry blossom season, this park also boasts some great places to eat at (see Imobo Hiranoya, p88) and an open-air concert space.

Namikawa Cloisonné Museum of Kyoto

338 Horiike-cho, Sanjo Dori Kita-ura, Shirakawasuji Higashi-iru, Higashiyama-ku (075 752 3277/www. kyoto-namikawa.jp). Higashiyama station (Tozai line). **Open** 10am-4pm Tue, Wed, Fri-Sun. **Admission** ¥600. Map p81 B1 ⑬

The main reason to visit the old home of Yasuyuki Namikawa (1845-1927) is

to see examples of his cloisonné work. The leading enamel artist of his era, Namikawa was known for his intricate 'shippo' cloisonné work of bold colours framed with gold or silver lines. The museum stands in the artist's finely preserved 1894 house and garden.

Ryozen Kannon

Kodai-ji Shimokawara-cho, Higashiyama-ku (075 561 2205). Buses 100, 206, 207. **Open** 8.40am-4pm daily **Admission** ¥200. Map p81 C3 ⑭

Kodai-ji's next-door neighbour is a 24m-high concrete bodhisattva that towers over a small complex commemorating the soldiers, foreign and Japanese, who died in World War II. It's most impressive from afar, but you can climb inside the Kannon to see Zodiac-themed Buddhist statues.

Ryozen Museum of History

1 Ryozen-cho, Seikan-ji, Higashiyama-ku. (075 531 3773/www.ryozen-museum. or.jp). Buses 100, 206, 207.

KYOTO BY AREA

Open 10am-4pm Tue-Sun.
Admission ¥500. **Map** p81 C3 🅖
This museum covers the characters and details of the Meiji Restoration, when the Shogunate was overthrown and imperial rule restored. It has some interesting exhibits, including the sword used to kill Ryoma Sakamoto, one of the key figures of the Restoration, but it's a text-heavy museum that will frustrate anyone who doesn't read Japanese.

Shoren-in

69-1 Sanjobo-cho, Awataguchi, Higashiyama-ku (075 561 2345/www. shorenin.com/english). Buses 5, 100; or Higashiyama station (Tozai line).
Open 9am-4.30pm daily. **Admission** ¥500. **Map** p81 C2 🅖
A *monzeki* temple, meaning the head priest has to be of imperial blood, Shoren-in has been home to some auspicious guests. It was here that Shinran, founder of the Jodo Shinshu sect, began his religious life in 1181, and in 1788 it became a temporary Imperial Palace after fire ravaged the Emperor's main digs. For all this history and a wonderful stroll garden with carp ponds, this temple draws surprisingly few visitors. All the more reason to go.

Yasaka Jinja

625 Gionmachi-kitagawa, Higashiyama-ku (075 561 6155). Bus 206; or Gion Shijo station (Keihan line). **Open** 24 hours daily.
Admission free. **Map** p81 B2 🅖
Before there was Kyoto, there was Gion Temple, established in 656. By the mid tenth century, Gion Temple had gained a Tenjin-do – a Shinto hall for rituals to placate *goryo*, the ghosts of exiled or shamed leaders. A few centuries later, the Tenjin-do was the focal point of the institution, so when the 19th-century Meiji government ordered a separation of Shinto and Buddhist worship, Gion Temple disappeared, and the Tenjn-do was renamed Yasaka Jinja. These days the shrine is best known for New Year celebrations and the Gion Festival (p31).

Eating & drinking

Bunnosuke-jaya

373 Yasaka Kamimachi, Shimogawa Higashi-iru, Higashiyama-ku (075 561 1972/www.bunnosuke.jp). Bus 206.
Open 10am-5.30pm Mon, Tue, Thur-Sun. **¥**. **Café**. **Map** p81 B4 🅖
On your pilgrimage to the nearby mega-temples, stop here for some uniquely Japanese desserts. *Warabi mochi* is a sweet, glutinous confection made from bracken starch and coated in toasted soybean flour. Think jelly, but gummier. You can pair it with green tea or *amazake*, a sweet non-alcoholic drink made from fermented rice.

Chourakukan

604 Maruyama-cho, Yasaka Torii-mae Higashi-iru, Higashiyama-ku (075 5610 001/www.chourakukan.co.jp). Buses 100, 206. **Open** *Café* 10am-10pm, *Afternoon tea* 1-5pm daily. **¥¥**. **Café**. **Map** p81 B3 🅖
You probably didn't come to Kyoto for rococo European architecture, but the style of this former home of a tobacco baron is a hit with locals, and has been designated a historical landmark. Today it houses a pair of restaurants (Italian and French) and a café, but the most fun is taking afternoon tea in the salon (¥3,000, minimum of two people).

Il Ghiottone

388-1 Yasaka Kamimachi, Shimokawara Dori, Tounomae-sagaru, Higashiyama-ku (075 532 2550/www. ilghiottone.com). Bus 206. **Open** noon-2.30pm, 6-9.30pm daily. **¥¥¥**.
Italian. **Map** p81 A2 🅖
One of Japan's few celebrity chefs, and the only one known for Italian fare, Yasuhiro Sasajima uses Kyoto ingredients and techniques twist classic Italian recipes. He boils pasta in kelp for an *umami* boost, and uses veg more common to *kaiseki* than a *ristorante*. This flagship restaurant, near Kodai-ji (p84), takes bookings from the first of the preceding month, and fills up fast. A more

casual *cucineria* opened in 2008 a few blocks away (p123), and is often where you'll find the Capo these days.

Gion Hamadaya

Nawate Dori, Shijo-agaru Hitosujime Higashi-iru, Higashiyama-ku (075 561 6841/www.kyo-hamamatsuya.com). Gion Shijo station (Keihan line). **Open** 6pm-midnight Mon-Sat. ¥¥. **Eel**. Map p81 B3 ㉑

When the summer humidity kicks in, the Japanese scoff eels for a stamina boost. Most places baste their eels, but this Gion restaurant uses skewers to drain more of the oil and leave a soft, light fish, served with salt or *ponzu* sauce. The chef's rolled omelette is a highlight, creamier than elsewhere.

Gion Hatanaka

Yasaka-jinja Minamimon-mae, Gion machi Minamigawa, Higashiyama-ku (075 541 5315/ www.kyoto-maiko.jp). Gion Shijo station (Keihan line). **Open** 6pm onwards, days vary. ¥¥¥. **Traditional Japanese**. Map p81 A3 ㉒

Dining with *maiko* is a typical Kyoto experience that few visitors get to try.

Securing their services usually requires more money and better connections than a tourist enjoys. But in 2009, Gion's Hatanaka ryokan began hosting *maiko* dinner parties, which are open to anyone with ¥18,000 to spare. A pair of *maiko* perform a traditional dance, lead you in some drinking games, and make nervous conversation as you tuck into top quality Kyoto cuisine. Foreigners are welcome, but don't expect to have a fluent chat. You can book online in English.

Gion Matsudaya

507-123 Gionmachi Minamigawa, Higashiyama-ku (075 561 3338). Gion Shijo station (Keihan line). **Open** 6-9.30pm Tue-Sun. ¥¥¥. **Sushi**. Map p81 B4 ㉓

A top sushi restaurant in a traditional Gion *machiya* is never going to be cheap, but at least this place is welcoming and worth the outlay. You won't get bowls of soy sauce here – the chef serves his delicacies just as they are intended to taste. An ¥8,000 *makase* course comprises 14 pieces of the chef's choice, including some unique creations.

Yasaka Jinja

Ikkyu-an

Kodai-ji Minamimonzen, Higashiyama-ku (075 561 1901). Buses 206, 207.
Open noon-6.30pm Mon, Wed-Sun.
¥¥¥. Vegetarian. Map p81 B3 ㉔
Japan's most Zen city still has several restaurants that serve the monks' traditional meatless meals. This one, in a beautiful building that once belonged to Kodai-ji (p84), offers *fucha ryori*, a rich, multi-course cuisine with hints of Chinese influence. The menu varies by the season, but always includes their specialities: miso-covered aubergine and *gomadofu*, a tofu-esque creation made from ground sesame. Reservations essential.

Imobo Hiranoya

Chion-in Minami-monzen, Maruyama Koen-nai, Higashiyama-ku (075 561 1603/www.imobou.net/english.html). Bus 206. **Open** 10.30am-8pm daily. **¥¥.**
Traditional Japanese. Map p81 B2 ㉕
For 300 years, this restaurant in Maruyama Park has survived on one simple recipe – cod and potato. The dish was devised by a gardener from Shoren-in (p86) long before inland Kyoto had access to fresh fish, so he used dried cod from the north of Japan – as does the restaurant. The fish is reconstituted for ten days, then boiled with the spuds for a further day. Luckily, it tastes far better than it sounds. There are six set menus here, all of which include the signature dish.

Issen Yoshoku

Shijo Dori, Nawate-agaru, Higashiyama-ku (075 533 0001/www.issen-yosyoku.co.jp). Gion Shijo station (Keihan line). **Open** 11.30am-3am Mon-Fri; 10.30am-9.30pm Sat, Sun. **¥.**
Okonomiyaki. Map p81 A2 ㉖
Issen Yoshoku is a local legend. An oversized menu unfolds to offer just a single dish: a kind of *okonomiyaki* topped with beef, scallion, shrimp and a sweet or spicy sauce. At ¥630, it's a bargain. The store is just as renowned for its logo – a dog pulling at the underwear

of a young boy – and a unique interior that has kimono-clad mannequins sitting at each table like stunned hostesses.

Junidanya Honten

570-128 Gionmachi Minamigawa, Higashiyama-ku (075 561 0213/www.junidanya.com). Gion Shijo station (Keihan line). **Open** 11.30am-1.30pm, 5-8.30pm daily. **¥¥¥. Shabu shabu.** Map p81 A3 ㉗
Prince Charles once dined at this historic *shabu shabu* restaurant. It's one of several establishments claiming to have invented the dish (credit usually goes to Osaka's Suehiro restaurant), but first or not, Junidanya certainly helped popularise the swishing of beef strips in boiling water. A *shabu shabu* dinner here will set you back ¥10,500-¥16,800, but you can pick up a bento lunch for far less.

Kikunoi

459 Shimokawara-cho, Yasaka Torii-mae, Shimokawara Dori, Higashiyama-ku (075 561 0015/www.kikunoi. jp/english). Buses 100, 206. **Open** noon-2pm, 5-8pm daily.
¥¥¥¥. Kaiseki. Map p81 C3 ㉘
Yoshihiro Murata is the Gordon Ramsay of Japanese cuisine. From TV shows to newspaper columns to coffee table books, he's everywhere. This makes him a controversial figure in a city that considers self-promotion vulgar, but if you book a meal at Kikunoi, you'll understand what the fuss is about. One of Murata's signature dishes arrives garnished with burning pine needles, another is cooked in a vacuum pack. Not all the food will be familiar, even to fans of Japanese cuisine, but adventurous palates will be well rewarded.

Kyouen

137 Daikoku-cho Higashigawa, Yamatooji Dori, Sanjo-sagaru, Higashiyama-ku (www.kyouen.jp/english/index.html). Sanjo station (Keihan line). **Open** varies. Map p81 A1 ㉙

Issen Yoshoku

An American landscape designer used glistening pools, raked gravel, bamboo plants and other Japanese garden staples to create a low-rise dining and shopping complex with a Zen theme. The restaurants, most of which try to match the spectacular setting, include a designer dessert café, a branch of a Hokkaido ramen chain, a cheap and cheerful potato-obsessed restaurant and a Japanese health-food restaurant.

Loop Salon

71-9 Motoyoshi-cho, Shinbashi Dori, Yamatoo-ji Higashi-iru, Higashiyama-ku (075 533 6009/www.kidoinc.com). Gion Shijo station (Keihan line). **Open** 6pm-3am daily. **Bar**. **Map** p81 A2 ③⓪

Shinbashi Dori is one of Kyoto's most romantic streets, lined with quaint wooden buildings, some built with windows revealing the geishas entertaining inside. The area is also an inscrutable place, with few establishments announcing their business on signs, which means that most visitors just stroll through. One place at which you will get a warm welcome is this cute bar, which opened in 2008, with English-speaking bartenders, decent cocktails and a second-floor lounge.

Oku

570-119 Gionmachi Minamigawa, Higashiyama-ku (075 531 4776/ www.oku-style.com). Gion Shijo station (Keihan line). **Open** 11am-7pm Mon, Wed-Sun. **¥**. **Café**. **Map** p81 A3 ③①

Lacquerware brand Oku launched in 2006 with a range of voluptuous designs that fuse traditional artistry with modern tastes and techniques. The brand was the brainchild of Hisato Nakahigashi, who is proprietor of Miyamasou, a celebrated ryokan that lies just north of Kyoto. His bulbous dishes were designed to emphasise the sensuality of dining, and you can judge the success for yourself in this townhouse-turned-elegant café. Opened in 2008, it loads Nakahigashi's lacquerware with his trademark mountain herb cuisine and some of the best desserts that you'll find anywhere in Kyoto. If you like the designs, you can buy them on your way out, so that you can take a taste of Oku home.

KYOTO BY AREA

Sfera Bar Satonaka

Scorpione

381 Kiyomoto-cho, Hanamikoji Dori,
Shibashi-sagaru, Higashiyama-ku
(075 525 5054/www.kiwa-group.co.jp).
Gion Shijo station (Keihan line).
Open *11.30am-2pm, 6-10pm daily.*
¥¥¥. Italian. Map p81 A2 ㉜
Everything about this beautiful restaurant is utterly Japanese, from the cushion seats to the lacquerware to the chopsticks – except for the menu, which is Kyoto-influenced Italian. Scorpione offers three set menus (¥5,800-¥11,800) of extravagant, inventive and seasonal dishes, such as tagliatelle in stewed wild boar sauce and chrysanthemum risotto with fried oysters.

Sfera Bar Satonaka

3F Sfera Building, 17 Benzaiten-cho,
Higashiyama-ku (075 541 1197/www.
ricordi-sfera.com). Gion Shijo station
(Keihan line). **Open** *7pm-3am; Mon,*
Tue, Thur-Sun. **Bar.** Map p81 A2 �33
Gion's best cocktail bars often serve up frosty receptions to foreign faces. Satonaka doesn't. In a subtly lit interior with walls that evoke black lacquer, bartender Michito Satonaka offers friendly service and great drinks, including an impressive range of Japanese whiskies and 15 kinds of champagne cocktail. Bring a date.

Tsujiri Honten

Gionmachi Kitagawa 275, Higashiyama-
ku (075 561 2257). Gion Shijo station
(Keihan line). **Open** *10am-8pm daily.*
¥. Café. Map p81 B2 �34
Tsujiri Honten used to be as famous for its queue as for its green tea and desserts. At peak times, it could take around an hour to get a seat. Things have improved since March 2009, when the café moved temporarily into larger premises across the road, so that the original could have a facelift. From mid 2010, the café will return to its former address – as no doubt, will the long queues.

Yorozuya

555-1 Komatsu-cho, Futasujime
Nishi-iru, Hanamikoji, Shijo-sagaru,
Higashiyama-ku (075 551 3409).
Gion Shijo station (Keihan line).
Open *noon-10pm daily. No credit*
cards. **¥. Udon.** Map p81 A3 �35
Like so many Kyoto restaurants, Yorozuya has built its business on the reputation of one special dish. *Negi udon* is a bowl of noodles served in a rich bonito broth, topped with chopped spring onions – but this joint smothers its noodles in a mountain of them. Luckily, they blanch them first to temper the flavour.

Shopping

Aero Concept

223-1 Nishino-cho, Shinmonzenmae Dori, Yamatoo-ji Higashi-iru, Higashiyama-ku (075 533 7161/www.aeroconcept.co.jp). Gion Shijo station (Keihan line). **Open** noon-7pm Wed-Sat. **Map** p81 A2 ㊱
A manufacturer of parts for aircraft and bullet trains uses its metalwork expertise to produce a range of ultra-durable aluminium-alloy suitcases, card holders, keyrings and diary cases. They also make custom cases to fit whatever you need to protect.

Art Yoshikiri

246 Nakanocho, Shinmonzen Dori, Higashiyama-ku (075 541 2989/ www.artyoshikiri.jp). Gion Shijo station (Keihan line). **Open** 10am-6pm daily. **Map** p81 A2 ㊲
The store looks brand new, but it has been in business for two decades, selling antique woodblock prints. The English-speaking owner is passionate about his prints, which range in price from ¥2,000 to well over ¥10 million.

Disney+WA-Qu

463-29 Shimokawara-cho, Shimokawara Dori, Yasaka Torii-mae-sagaru, Higashiyama-ku (075 531 3111/www.ten-qoo-ann.jp). Buses 100, 206, 207. **Open** 11am-6pm; Mon, Wed-Sun. **Map** p81 B3 ㉝
Top local designers and architects turn their hands to Disney merchandise. (See box p93).

Ihee

577-1 Gionmachi Minamigawa, Higashiyama-ku (075 551 3500/ www. ihee.jp). Gion Shijo station (Keihan line). **Open** 11am-8pm daily. **Map** p81 A3 ㊴
Cotton wholesaler Eirakuya was established in 1615, and almost four centuries later, the company is flourishing. In 2007 it launched a sub-brand, Ihee, selling cotton tote bags with modern Japanese motifs such as cherries, bamboo or the *torii* gates of a shrine. Upstairs, another Eirakuya brand sells all kinds of headwear, from flat caps to trilbies, emblazoned with the signature prints.

Japanese Arts Watanabe

236-7 Nakano-cho, Shinmonzen Dori, Hanamikoji Nanseikado, Higashiyama-ku (075 532 1238). Gion Shijo station (Keihan line). **Open** 10am-6pm daily. **Map** p81 A2 ㊵
This antique scroll specialist gives you a shopping experience akin to buying a kitchen, car or cosmetic surgery. Most of the Japanese Arts Watanabe store is devoted to consultation areas, with just a handful of 16th- to 19th-century scrolls on display. Once the English-speaking staff understand your taste, they will bring a selection from the stockroom. The names and dates of the artists are noted for each scroll. Expect to pay ¥80-130,000.

Tsujiri Honten

Kagoshin

Shichiken-cho, 4 Ohashi, Sanjo Dori, Higashiyama-ku (075 771 0209). Sanjo station (Keihan line). **Open** 9am-6pm daily. **Map** p81 B1 ④

Back when Kyoto was divided into blocks of merchants, this area specialised in crafting bamboo. These days just a couple of shops remain, including this 19th-century establishment, which offers bamboo baskets made to order, as well as bamboo beer mugs, toys, ear cleaners, chopsticks, coasters and cutlery.

Mamekichi Honpo

21 Tsukimi-cho, Shimokawara Yasui, Higashiyama-ku (075 533 6064/ www.mame-kichi.jp). Bus 206. **Open** 10am-7pm daily. **Map** p81 B3 ④

Matcha-coated coffee beans and pickled plum-flavoured peanuts are among the treats at this delightful bean-and-nut obsessed store. The shop stocks more than 70 flavours, all of which are beautifully packaged, and lets you sample half of them. Good for snacking, great for souvenirs.

Sfera Archive/Sfera Shop

1F, 2F Sfera Building, 17 Benzaiten-cho, Higashiyama-ku (Archive 075 532 1106, Shop 075 532 1105/www.ricordi-sfera. com). Gion Shijo station (Keihan line). **Open** *Archive* 11am-8pm; *Shop* noon-8pm; Mon, Tue, Thur-Sun **Map** p81 A2 ④

The Sfera Building, designed by Swedish group Claesson Koivisto Rune in 2003, is an oasis of good taste on a street which is loaded with hostess clubs and borderline brothels. It's cloaked in titanium, with holes punched out to depict cherry tree leaves. Inside, there's a five-storey 'culture centre', incorporating a gallery, Japanese and Italian restaurants, and Sfera Bar Satonaka (p80). Shoppers will find plenty to keep themselves amused, including the Archive, selling CDs and design books in English and Japanese, and the Shop, stocked with modern Japanese interior goods.

Shichimiya

2-221 Kiyomizu, Higashiyama-ku (075 551 0738/www.shichimiya.co.jp). Bus 206. **Open** 9am-6pm daily. **Map** p81 B4 ④

The granddaddy of *shichimi* (Japanese 'seven spice') shops has been trading here since the mid 17th century. Today you can buy their blend of peppers, sesame seeds and spices in supermarkets nationwide, but since you're here, do like all the other tourists and pick up a packet from the flagship store.

Shinzaburo Hanpu

Higashioji Dori, Furumonzen-agaru, Higashiyama-ku (075 541 0436/ www.ichizawashinzaburohanpu.co.jp). Bus 206; or Higashiyama station (Tozai line). **Open** 9am-6pm Mon-Sat. **Map** p81 B2 ④

A family squabble turned Kyoto's most famous bag store into two bag stores. Ichizawa Hanpu had been in business since 1905, producing durable and colourful canvas tote bags. In 2006, one of the founder's great-grandsons left with most of the craftspeople to establish a new brand and set up a store virtually on the doorstep of the original. Ichizawa Hanpu stands just a few doors away, along the same street, but Shinzaburo has the best designs. You can see the bags being produced in the workshop a block to the north of the store.

Yachibe

560-25 Komatsu-cho, Yamatoo-ji Dori, Shijo-sagaru 4-chome, Higashiyama-ku (075 561 1055/www.yuruli.com). Bus 207. **Open** noon-8pm Mon, Tue, Thur-Sun.Wed. **Map** p81 A4 ④

Bucking the trend of *machiyas* getting slick makeovers, the owners of this clothing store have made their time-worn townhouse even more rustic by caking the walls in rough clay. The interior of Yachibe suits the merchandise, however, which is mainly gentlemen's clothing made from hemp and organic cotton.

Mouse in the house

Kyoto designers play with Disney's famous creation.

Can you see anything familiar in the lamps pictured? What if we told you they were tessellations of the world's most famous mouse? Believe it or not, the Kirie lamps (above) are Disney merchandise.

They come from a product range that was created for the entertainment behemoth by the **Kyoto design collective WA-Qu** (see p91). The nine-member group was founded in 2002, when furniture company director Shigeki Nakatsuka invited his favourite local creators to join forces. If you spend any time at all in Kyoto, you're likely to see their solo handiwork: Genzo Sugiki produced the interiors of Marukyu Koyamaen and Ogawa Coffee's Sanjo branch (p57). Kazuya Taniguchi gave Il Ghiottone (p86) its look and Hisanobu Tsujimura designed Loop Salon (p89) and Sfera Bar Satonaka (p90).

The collective exhibited their early designs at Milan's Salone in 2004. When they repeated the show at Tokyo's Big Sight the following year, the Disney people took notice.

'They asked us to develop a range of premium products, which sounded like fun,' says WA-Qu's Seiichi Nakamura.

The results went on sale in Kyoto's Ten Qoo An gallery in 2008. Though planned as a year-long showcase, the designs proved so popular that the run was extended for at least another year.

Ten Qoo An is tucked away at the end of a stone path near Kodai-ji (p84). The entrance is graced by a bamboo curtain with cutaways of a bulbous mouse ear.

Inside, there are lamps, incense holders and paper umbrellas, all of which have apparently traditional Kyoto designs, yet, on closer inspection, turn out to be modelled on Walt's most famous creation.

Many of the items cost a little more than your average Disney souvenir. A Mickey-shaped *washi* paper lamp from Eriko Horiki, whose *washi* work adorns Narita Airport, Tokyo's Midtown complex and Setsugekka, goes for ¥1.8 million, whereas the Kirie lamps (pictured) will each set you back ¥69,000. Less flush fans can pick up a coaster (¥600) or wooden confectionery picks (¥2,100).

So was it difficult to work with the mouse? 'To blend American pop culture with classic Kyoto style? Extremely difficult,' says Nakamura.

You wouldn't know it from the designs, which make the mouse look as though he was born to be a Kyoto motif. And yes, it's OK to want them.

Yume Koubou

*Shinmonzen Dori, Hanamikoji
Nishi-iru, Higashiyama-ku. (075 541
7025). Gion Shijo station (Keihan line).*
Open varies (typically noon-5pm
daily). **Map** p81 A2 ㊼

The highlight of Kyoto's street of
antique stores is this enormous six-
room townhouse, crammed with every
conceivable kind of antique, from soy
sauce dispensers to full samurai
regalia. Everything you see is for sale,
though price tags are scarce.
Even if you don't have the budget to
splurge on historic artefacts, this is a
wonderful store to wander around.

Nightlife

Dalia

*5F Louis 1 Building, 5 Benzaiten-cho,
Yamatoo-ji, Sanjo-sagaru, Higashiyama-
ku (075 551 8355/www1.odn.ne.jp/dalia).
Gion Shijo station (Keihan line).* **Open**
8pm-3am Mon-Thur; 8pm-4am Fri, Sat.
Map p81 A2 ㊽

The most welcoming gay bar in Kyoto
is a Barbarella-meets-Fisher Price
lounge that thrives on the banter of
bartender 'Match'. Dalia is a great

place for an introduction to the scene,
and one of the few gay bars in Kyoto
to let in straight or female visitors.

Laugh

*B1 Garnet Building, Gionmachi
Kitagawa, Higashiyama-ku (075 551
1628/www.laughkyoto.com). Gion Shijo
station (Keihan line).* **Open** 8pm-3am
daily. **Map** p81 A2 ㊾

Although the sign suggests that it's a
members-only bar, that's just to prevent any straight boys from wander-
ing in. Bartender Genki occasionally
takes to the turntables with a techno
set that fits this industrial-looking
blue-lit basement bar. Semi-monthly
party 'Rookie' is designed for newbies
and people curious about the scene.

Whoopee's

*493-1 Kiyoi-cho, Yasaka Torii-mae-
sagaru, Higashiyama-ku (075 551 2331/
www.whoopees.net). Bus 206.* **Open**
varies. **Map** p81 B3 ㊿

The name might suggest a corny
revue, but Whoopee's is actually a
bunker for bands and DJs playing hip-
hop, electronica or rock. It's rougher
and more underground than the other

Minamiza

nightspots in this guide. You'll find it beneath Hotel U's, an old love hotel.

Arts & leisure

Gion Corner

Yasaka Kaikan, 570-2 Gionmachi Minamigawa, Higashiyama-ku (075 561 1119/www.kyoto-gion-corner. info/gion_corner/top/index.html). Gion Shijo station (Keihan line) **Open** *1 Mar-10 Nov* 7pm, 8pm daily. *1 Dec-28 Feb* 7pm Sat, Sun, hols. **Map** p81 A3 ⑤

This crash course in Japanese culture squeezes seven traditional art performances into less than an hour. An English brochure and voiceover provides some context, but as the show hurtles through each art form, it does little to demystify them. Still, it's the cheapest place in which to see a *maiko* dance, and the only place to watch *gagaku*, a performance art featuring a flamboyantly attired fantasy creature dancing to what sounds like the death throes of a bagpipe.

Gion Kaikan

323 Gionmachi Kitagawa, Higashiyama-ku (075 561 0160/ www.gionkaikan.jp). Gion Shijo station (Keihan line). **Open** varies. **Map** p81 B2 ⑤

Double bills of second-run movies are the speciality of this half-century-old cinema, but in early November (usually 1st until 10th November), it stages Gion Odori geisha dance shows.

Gion Kobu Kaburenjo

570-2 Gionmachi Minamigawa, Higashiyama-ku (075 561 1115). Gion Shijo station (Keihan line). **Open** varies. **Map** p81 A3 ⑤

Most of the year, this is where geishas and *maikos* practice their routines; occasionally it hosts concerts and other shows. But each April, this *kaburenjo* (arts theatre) puts on the geisha dance spectacular Miyako Odori (Dance of the Capital). First performed in 1872 as

a measure to stave off Kyoto's decline after the city relinquished her title as Japan's capital, it is still one of the highlights of the Kyoto's calendar.

Kashogama Pottery School

3-343 Kiyomizu, Higashiyama-ku (075 531 0056/www.kashogama.com). Bus 206. **Open** 9am-5pm daily. **Map** p81 B4 ⑤

Kiyomizu-yaki is a celebrated local style of ceramics that developed when Kyoto was flourishing as a cultural capital. This store, run by third- and fourth-generation potters, sells top-quality examples of the genre, but it also lets visitors take to the in-store potter's wheel to create some less exemplary items. A class costs ¥1,500-¥3,000, depending on what you wish to produce. For an extra ¥1,000, they'll glaze your creation and mail it to you.

Minamiza

Shijo Ohashi Higashigawa, Higashiyama-ku (075 561 1155/ www.shochiku.co.jp/play/minamiza). Gion Shijo station (Keihan line). **Open** varies. **Map** p81 A3 ⑤

When Tokyo's Kabukiza theatre is demolished in 2010, the Minamiza will be unrivalled as the home of kabuki in Japan. The building dates from 1929, although there's been a Minamiza in some form since the early 17th century. These days, the theatre plays host to various kinds of classical theatre arts, but the highlight of the year is still the Kaomise season, a kind of kabuki all-star show that runs each December to mark the start of the theatrical season.

Miyagawa-cho Kaburenjo

Kawabata Dori, Shijo-sagaru, Higashiyama-ku (075 561 1151). Gion Shijo station (Keihan line). **Open** varies. **Map** p81 A3 ⑤

For two weeks every April, the Miyagawa-cho geisha troupe stages its annual Kyo Odori show here, dancing to the sound of *shamisen*.

Heian Jingu

Northern Higashiyama

It's scenic, romantic and boasts two of the city's best temples (Ginkaku-ji and Nanzen-ji), as well as the legendary path that links them. The verdant Higashiyama mountain range provides a backdrop that many of the area's gardens incorporate. In a picture-postcard city, this is a district that lures even locals with its looks.

Northern Higashiyama is also a major art hub. Two heavyweight museums face each other in Okazaki Park, one exhibiting contemporary art, the other showing classic works. Many of the city's best independent galleries lie between the park and Sanjo Dori, and fans of traditional art have the Nomura and Hosomi collections, as well as museums dedicated to painter Kansetsu Hashimoto and calligrapher Kampo Harada.

For gastronomes, there are two celebrated restaurants, Hyotei and Nakahigashi, plus many of the best noodle restaurants, although it's not an area that presents a huge choice of dining options. Unlike its southern neighbour, Northern Higashiyama is a place where you come for peace and quiet, not city life. A day will do.

Sights & museums

Eikan-do

48 Eikando-cho, Sakyo-ku (075 761 0007/www.eikando.or.jp/English). Buses 5, 100; or Keage station (Tozai line). **Open** 9am-4pm daily. **Admission** ¥600. **Map** p99 F4 ❶ Eikan-do calls itself 'the Temple of Maple Leaves', but that's a little modest for a complex that looks great all year round. Perhaps because it lies in

the shadow of the mighty Nanzen-ji, this place of worship is a relatively calm and unfrequented attraction, except when the autumn leaves turn crimson and the crowds arrive. The temple dates from 853 and belongs to the Jodo-shu sect.

Ginkaku-ji

2 Ginkaku-cho, Sakyo-ku (075 771 5725/ www.shokoku-ji.or.jp). Buses 5, 32, 100, 203, 204. **Open** *Mar-Nov 8.30am-4.30pm daily. Dec-Feb 9am-4pm daily.* **Admission** ¥500. **Map** p99 F1 ❷

While Kinkaku-ji, the Golden Pavilion (p107) lives up to its dazzling name, Ginkaku-ji (the Silver Pavilion) is a simple wooden building. That sounds disappointing, but it's not. The two-storey structure impresses with its modesty in an exceptional garden of gravel, moss, pine trees and ponds. It may not have been the intention: the pavilion was built by the same Ashikaga shogun family that created Kinkaku-ji, but whether penury, time or modesty intervened, no silver leaf was ever applied to the structure. The complex was built in 1482 as a retreat for shogun Yoshimasa Ashikaga, and became a Zen temple eight years later on his demise. At press time, the famous pavilion is concealed as it undergoes renovations, scheduled for completion in March 2010 – but the grounds alone are worth the trip.

Heian Jingu

97 Nishitenno-cho, Okazaki, Sakyo-ku (075 761 0221/www.heianjingu.or.jp). Higashiyama station (Tozai line). **Open** *15 Mar-31Aug 6am-6pm daily. 11 Sept-28 Feb 6am-5pm daily. 1-14 Mar, 1-10 Sept 6am-5.30pm daily.* **Admission** *Courtyard* free. *Garden* ¥600. **Map** p99 C4 ❸

To mark its 1,100th birthday, Kyoto built itself an enormous shrine, complete with a 24m-high vermillion gate and 33,000sq m of garden. The buildings and gardens were designed to evoke the Heian period (794-1185),

when Kyoto's aesthetic began to flourish. The main building is a scaled-down replica of the first Imperial Palace, and the gardens employ the lake-island-bridge style imported from China by Heian landscape designers. The stone pillars of the central garden once supported the original Sanjo and Gojo bridges. The shrine looks best during the New Year celebrations, when the grounds are full of kimono-clad ladies; in April when the cherry blossom works its magic; and on the 1st and 2nd June, when it hosts an outdoor Noh performance.

Hosomi Museum

6-3 Saishoji-cho, Okazaki, Sakyo-ku (075 752 5555/www.emuseum.or.jp). Buses 5, 32, 46, 206; or Higashiyama station (Tozai line). **Open** 10am-6pm Tue-Sun. **Admission** ¥1,000. **Map** p98 C4 ❹

Three generations of the Hosomi family built an extraordinary private collection of Japanese art, now on display in an award-winning piece of modern architecture designed by Tadasu Oe. The gift shop stocks modern Japanese design goods, including Lisn (p61) and Iremonya Design Labo (p78) products.

Kampo Museum

35 Minami Gosho-cho, Okazaki, Sakyo-ku (www.kampo-museum.co.jp). Buses 5, 100; or Higashiyama station (Tozai line). **Open** 10am-4pm daily. **Admission** ¥600. **Map** p99 D4 ❺

The 'Kampo' Museum is named after Kampo Harada, the most eminent calligrapher of the 20th century. Harada saw calligraphy as a way to advance peace and self-fulfilment, and he passed on his wisdom to several million students via his Japan Calligraphy Education Federation. Some of his masterpieces are on display at this quaint museum, along with examples of calligraphy and writing tools from around the world. The museum will also stage a calligraphy workshop if you call in advance.

KYOTO BY AREA

Northern Higashiyama

A   **B**   **C**

Kyoto University
Campus

1

- **1** Sights & museums
- **1** Eating & drinking
- **1** Shopping
- **1** Nightlife
- **1** Arts & leisure

HIGASH-ICHIJO DORI

KAWABATA DORI

2

Kamgawa

KAWARAMACHI DORI

HIGASHIOJI DORI

YOSHIDA

Kyoto
University

3

Hospital   SHOGOIN

Marutamachi

22

15
26

MARUTAMACHI DORI

27   **25**

Heian Ji

3

4

Kamgawa

Okazaki

4

HIGASHIOJI DORI

NIJO DORI

8

NIJO DORI

11

KAWABATA DORI

14
19

5

28

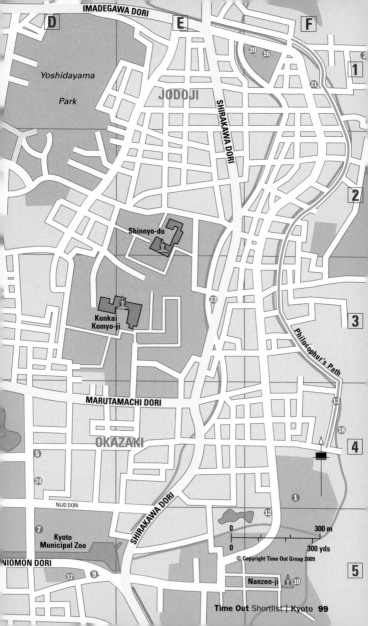

D

E

F

1

Yoshidayama

Park

JODOJI

SHIRAKAWA DORI

20 16

21

2

Shinnyo-do

Konkai
Komyo-ji

23

Philosopher's Path

3

MARUTAMACHI DORI

13

OKAZAKI

18

4

5

24

1

NIJO DORI

12

0   300 m

7   Kyoto
Municipal Zoo

0   300 yds

SHIRAKAWA DORI

© Copyright Time Out Group 2009

NIOMON DORI

5

17   9

Nanzen-ji   10

Kyoto Municipal Museum of Art

Enshoji-cho, Okazaki, Sakyo-ku (075 771 4107/www.city.kyoto.jp/bunshi/kmma/en/index.html). Buses 5, 100; or Higashiyama station (Tozai line). **Open** 9am-4.30pm Tue-Sun. **Admission** varies. **Map** p98 C5 **6**

The 'City of Kyoto' is listed as the official architect of this monumental building. If so, the bureaucrats have unusual design skills: the bronze-roofed modern creation attracts the eye, even in the shadow of the Heian Jingu (p97). Although not quite as impressive inside, Japan's second oldest municipal art museum holds major shows of Japanese and international art. It also loans space to independent art groups for staging exhibitions.

Kyoto Municipal Zoo

Hoshoji-cho, Okazaki, Sakyo-ku (075 771 0210). Buses 5, 100; or Higashiyama station (Tozai line). **Open** *Mar-Nov* 9am-4.30pm Tue-Sun. *Dec-Feb* 9am-4pm Tue-Sun. **Admission** ¥500. **Map** p99 D5 **7**

It may be Japan's second largest zoo, but it's rather a sorry home for around 700 beasts. The lions and gorillas should keep the kids amused, but grown-ups will be itching to explore the area's more impressive sights.

Kyoto Museum of Traditional Crafts

9-1 Seishoji-cho, Okazaki, Sakyo-ku (075 762 2670/www.miyakomesse.jp/fureaika). Buses 5, 32, 46, 206; or Higashiyama station (Tozai line). **Open** 9am-5.30pm daily. **Admission** free. **Map** p98 C5 **8**

What this museum lacks in depth, it makes up for in breadth, with introductions to every conceivable form of traditional craft. There are brief English-language summaries and samples of many artistic pursuits, ranging from dyed kimonos to Noh masks to bamboo fishing rods to roof tiles. It's a useful crash course in local culture.

Kyoto Municipal Museum of Art

Murin-an

31 Kusakawa-cho, Nansen-ji, Sakyo-ku (075 771 3909). Keage station (Tozai line). **Open** 9am-4.30pm daily. **Admission** ¥350. **Map** p99 D5 **9**

In 1903, the year before the Russo-Japanese War, four leaders gathered to plan foreign policy here. The meeting room has been preserved, complete with gold leaf walls. This villa is known for its garden, produced by Jihei Ogawa, the creator of Heian Jingu's grounds. Finished in 1896, the design reflects the era's openness to western influences, juxtaposing lawns with Japanese elements, such as a pond and the scenery of the Higashiyama mountains.

Nanzen-ji

Fukuchi-cho, Nanzen-ji, Sakyo-ku (075 771 0365/http://nanzenji.com). Buses 5, 100; or Keage station (Tozai line). **Open** *Mar-Nov* 9am-5pm daily. *Dec-Feb* 9am-4.30pm daily. **Admission** *Grounds* free. *Abbot's quarters* ¥500. *Sanmon* ¥500. *Sub-temples* ¥300-¥400. **Map** p99 F5 **10**

Japan loves to rank its attractions, and since the 14th century Nanzen-ji has been rated the country's top Rinzai sect Zen temple. Its exalted position is partly a political gesture: the Muromachi government was fearful of fellow Rinzai temples Myoshin-ji and Daitoku-ji, so it announced a Big Five list that failed to mention them. Still, there is no disputing the fact that Nanzen-ji is an awesome sight, and has played a significant part in popularising Zen Buddhism in Kyoto.

It was built by Emperor Kameyama during the 13th century, and a towering *sanmon* (main gate) was added to the structure in 1628. The gate offers impressive views across the city, but is most famous as the hiding place of Japan's version of Guy Fawkes. After a failed attempt to assassinate ruler Hideyoshi Toyotomi in 1594, robber Goemon Ishikawa hid away inside the gate until he was discovered and boiled alive in oil. More peaceful, Zen-like reasons to visit Nanzen-ji include the 'Leaping Tiger' dry Zen garden of the Abbot's quarters and a trio of tranquil sub-temples, all of which feature impressive gardens.

National Museum of Modern Art, Kyoto

Enshoji-cho, Okazaki, Sakyo-ku. (075 761 4111/www.momak.go.jp). Buses 5, 46, 100, 206; or Higashiyama station (Tozai line). **Open** 9.30am-4.30pm Tue-Sun. **Admission** ¥850. **Map** p98 C5 ⑪

A big, grey box designed by Pritzker Prize-winner Fumihiko Maki is the unbecoming home of Kyoto's top contemporary art venue. The 2,600sq m of floor space hosts an impressive permanent collection of around 10,000 pieces, including works by Piet Mondrian and Marcel Duchamp, as well as Japanese paintings, textiles and ceramics. There are strong temporary exhibitions, occasional performances and cinema screenings. The National Museum is always worth a visit.

Green machines

Not everyone took the Kyoto Protocol to the UN Framework Convention on Climate Change seriously, but the host city certainly did. Shortly after the treaty was signed, Kyoto launched a biodiesel project, collecting used cooking oil from households and restaurants, and refining it into fuel for the city's buses and rubbish trucks.

Kyoto now collects 1.5 million litres of used oil per year to power 106 low-emission buses. If you see a cartoon character with twisting arrows for their hair and three bubbles floating from their hand, it means that your bus is eco-friendly.

When hailing a taxi, look for one with a fan on the roof. The wind turbines on these Ecolo Taxis power the car's lights and a charger for passengers' mobile phones. The taxis claim to generate 20% less CO_2 than a regular vehicle, largely thanks to Toyota technology. The Ecolo Taxi company purchases 'Green Power' vouchers to offset the remaining CO_2. With bicycle racks on the rear, you can cycle to the bar and catch a cab home.

Green transport is just one policy in a drive to keep Kyoto at the forefront of the eco movement. Schools grow gourds on their rooftops to reduce their energy costs and produce cheap food for pupils and teachers; the semi-annual *hanatouro* nocturnal illuminations are hydro-powered; and private households collect used oil from some restaurants to refine their own biofuel.

Nomura Art Museum

61 Shimokawaracho, Nanzen-ji, Sakyo-ku (075 751 0374/www.nomura-museum.or.jp). Bus 5 or Keage station (Tozai line). **Open** 10am-4.30pm Tue-Sun. **Map** p99 ⑫

Like all good magnates, the founder of the Nomura financial conglomerate had a passion for art. His collection suggests that he had a particular enthusiasm for Noh and tea ceremony. With plenty of local treasures on display, it's worth a nose around before (or after) you stroll along the Philosopher's Path.

Philosopher's Path

Sakyo-ku. Buses 32, 100. **Map** p99 F4 ⑬

It's easy to see why philosopher Kitaro Nishida chose this route for his meditative strolls. The canalside path connects the area's two greatest temples, Ginkaku-ji and Nanzen-ji, and is lined with cherry trees, 450 of which were donated by the great artist Kansetsu Hashimoto (p103). Of course, Nishida never had to deal with the hordes of tourists who swarm along the route during peak season. Nor was his path lined with souvenir shops. Still, amble along the route on an off-peak weekday and you'll be able to recapture the old thinker's enthusiasm. The walk takes 30 minutes, but you'll want to stop at teashops and smaller temples en route, so allow a couple of hours.

Weissraum Gallery

12 Magohashi-cho, Kawabata Dori, Nijo-sagaru, Sakyo-ku (075 761 8565/www.geocities.jp/weissraum). Sanjo station (Keihan line). **Open** 5pm-5am Mon-Sat; 5-11pm Sun. **Map** p98 A5 ⑭

The name 'white room' suggests an archetypical modern art gallery: an open, symmetrical cube. In fact, the Weissraum is anything but. One of the two rooms is only viewable from the street, and the other is accessed via a bar that consumes most of the floorplan. The exhibitions are often graphic, fun installations by European artists.

Eating & drinking

Etw

2F Ebisu Building, 82 Shimotsustsumi-cho, Kawabata Dori, Marutamachi-agaru, Sakkyo-ku (075 771 3979/www.etw.jp). Marutamachi station (Keihan line). **Open** 3pm-3am Mon, Wed-Sun. **¥**. **Café**. **Map** p98 A4 ⑮

The unusual café hours reflect this spot's role as an unofficial chill-out space for nightclub Metro. It sits two floors above the club, and serves coffees and basic café fare in a cosy setting furnished with local artwork.

Hakusason-so

37 Ishibashi-cho, Jodoji, Sakyo-ku (075 751 0446/www.kansetsu.or.jp). Buses 5, 32, 100. **Open** Zuibensan 4.30-8.30pm daily. *Oshokujidokoro Hashimoto* 11am-5.30pm daily. **¥/¥¥¥**. **Japanese/Kaiseki**. **Map** p99 F1 ⑯

If you've visited Kyoto's major temples and palaces, you'll have seen the art of

Philosopher's Path

Weissraum Gallery

Kansetsu Hashimoto (1883-1945), whose paintings adorn the sliding doors of some of the city's biggest attractions. His vast home and studio now hosts a pair of restaurants and a museum dedicated to his work. Zuibensan is the fancier destination, with *kaiseki* meals at western-style tables and a view of the painter's garden with pond. A more affordable option is the outer restaurant, Oshokujidokoro Hashimoto, with tempura rice bowls, hot tofu dishes and a street view. Admission to the garden, designed by the master painter, is included with your meal at either venue.

Hyotei

35 Kusakawa-cho, Nanzen-ji, Sakyo-ku (075 771 4116/hyotei.co.jp). Buses 5, 100; or Keage station (Tozai line). **Open** 11am-7.30pm daily; closed 2nd, 4th Tue of month. **¥¥¥¥**. **Kaiseki**. **Map** p99 D5 ⑰

For some, Hyotei is the best restaurant in Kyoto. For others, it's overhyped, overpriced and overly simple. Which side of the fence you stand on depends on how you feel about a plain soft-boiled egg being the highlight of a ¥27,000 meal. Hyotei is all about simplicity. Diners are guided to a sparsely decorated, private tearoom and served a parade of straight-up dishes that might

include a tender snapper sashimi, fresh bamboo simmered in bonito or a white miso soup. And a tasty soft-boiled egg.

Kano Shojuan

2-1 Nyakuoji, Sakyo-ku (075 751 1077/ www.kanou.com/teahouse.php). Buses 32, 100. **Open** 10am-4.30pm Mon, Tue, Thur-Sun. **¥**. **Tea**. **Map** p99 F4 ⑱

The Philosopher's Path (p112) is lined with countless cafés, but this is the pick of the bunch. A waiter whisks a bowl of *matcha* at your table and pairs it with a *namagashi* bean-paste sweet, sculpted into a seasonal motif.

Kansou

12 Magohashi-cho, Kawabata Dori, Nijo-sagaru, Sakyo-ku (075 771 7969/ www.cleanbrothers.net/kanso/kanso_kyo to.html). Sanjo station (Keihan line). **Open** 5pm-5am Mon-Sat; 5-11pm Sun. **Bar**. **Map** p98 A5 ⑲

Fancy some tinned bear? Take a look at the snack menu, made of a collection of cans on Kansou's wall. Chick peas and olives are among the tamer options, whereas boiled bear, curried whale and silkworm chrysalids will satisfy fearless appetites. The bar, inside the Weissraum Gallery (p112), is a fun, no-frills spot with friendly staff and rock-bottom prices.

Nakahigashi

*32-3 Ishibashi-cho, Jodo-ji, Sakyo-ku
(075 752 3500). Bus 5.* **Open** noon-
1pm, 6-9pm Tue-Sun. **¥¥¥¥**. **Kaiseki**.
Map p99 F1 ⑳

The most sought-after seats in Kyoto
are found at the eponymous *kaiseki*
restaurant of Hisao Nakahigashi,
brother of the brains behind Oku (p89).
Diners from across Japan compete for
reservations and then plan their trips
around the meal, and it's worth joining
the scramble. Each morning, the chef
heads to the bucolic Ohara countryside
to forage for wild herbs, shoots and
greens. His menu depends upon what
he finds outside, but the dishes are
always restrained and unpretentious.
The best seats are at the counter, where
Nakahigashi explains the background
of each course to his attentive fans. To
bag a seat at this popular restaurant,
try calling at 8am on the first day of the
month before your visit.

Omen

*74 Ishibashi-cho, Jodoji, Sakyo-ku
(075 771 8994/www.omen.co.jp).
Buses 5, 32, 100.* **Open** 11am-8.30pm
Mon-Wed, Fri-Sun. No credit cards. **¥**.
Udon. **Map** p99 F1 ㉑

With great udon, low prices, a cheerful
atmosphere and one of the city's
biggest attractions, Ginkakuji, as a
neighbour, it's no surprise that this
udon restaurant is always bustling.
The signature dish is a bowl of vegetables topped with roasted sesame seeds,
served alongside udon and sauce.
There are three spin-off branches of
Omen: two in downtown Kyoto and
one in New York.

Sumibi Torito

*Marutamachi Dori, Kawabata Higashi-
iru, Sakyo-ku (075 752 4144/www.
sumibi-torito.jp). Marutamachi station
(Karasuma line).* **Open** 5.30-11pm
daily. **¥¥**. **Yakitori**. **Map** p98 A3 ㉒

It's yakitori, but not as you know it.
Forget about eating smoky shops with
grizzled men gnawing cheap grills –

this is top-end chicken in a designer
setting for young urbanites. Almost
every part of the bird is featured on the
menu: bite-sized slices of skin, tail,
wings, neck or heart, all of which are
grilled over charcoal. The highlight is
the *tsukune* – minced chicken cooked
on a skewer and served with a fresh
egg yolk. Adventurous diners can sample the raw chicken liver, dipped in
salted sesame oil.

Tranq Room

*162-2 Shinnyo-cho, Jodoji, Sakyo-ku
(075 762 4888/http://home.att.ne.jp/
sun/tranqroom). Buses 5, 93, 203, 204.*
Open noon-midnight Mon, Wed-Sun.
¥. **Café**. **Map** p99 E3 ㉓

Sleepy Northern Higashiyama is the
last place you'd expect to find a trendy
café hosting avant-garde art shows, DJ
sets and live music. Even odder is the
fact it was founded by a local Indian
restaurant (hence the curries and lassis
on the menu). Nevertheless, this is one
of the hipper hangouts in Kyoto, and
has been for a decade.

Yamamoto Menzo

*34 Minami Gosho-cho, Okazaki,
Sakyo-ku (075 751 0677). Bus 5; or
Higashiyama station (Tozai line).* **Open**
11am-7.45pm Mon, Tue, Fri-Sun; 11am-
2.30pm Wed. **¥**. **Udon**. **Map** p99 D4 ㉔

Menzo is famous for three things: enormous lunchtime queues, divine noodles
and a handsome chef. Don't be daunt-
ed by the queue – service is fast, and
the extra-thick udon is well worth the
wait. The extensive menu is only available in Japanese, but the pick of the list
is udon topped with delicate, crispy
veggie tempura.

Shopping

Kyoto Handicraft Center

*21 Shougoin Entomi-cho, Sakyo-ku
(075 761 8001/ www.kyotohandicraft
center.com). Bus 206; or Higashiyama
station (Tozai line).* **Open** 10am-7pm
daily. **Map** p98 C3 ㉕

You will find better, more authentic handicrafts elsewhere, but nothing like the variety. This seven-storey emporium stocks everything from lucky charms to kimonos to samurai swords. It also has a decent English-language book section with Kyoto- and Japan-related publications. Buy all your gifts in one swoop, then head elsewhere to pick up the good stuff for yourself.

Nightlife

Metro

B1 Ebisu Building, 82 Shimotsutsumi-cho, Kawabata Dori, Marutamachi-agaru, Sakyo-ku (075 752 4765/www.metro.ne.jp). Marutamachi station (Keihan line). **Open** varies. **Map** p98 A4

When it opened in 1990, Metro was the only choice for serious clubbers in Kyoto or Osaka. These days, it has bigger and more central rivals, but it's still the best. Musically, anything goes, but current favourites are drag queen disco Diamonds are Forever and club jazz night Cool to Kool, which has been running since the venue opened. Friendly staff and a just-industrial-enough interior makes this the highlight of the city's nightlife.

Zac Baran

18 Sanno-cho, Marutamachi Dori, Higashioji Higashi-iru, Sakyo-ku (075 751 9748). Bus 206. **Open** 6pm-4am daily. **Map** p98 C3

One night it's a rock bar, the next it's a jazz club, or perhaps a house of blues. Zac Baran has had 30 years in which to figure out its identity, but it still feels like a different place each time you visit. It's most fun as a live venue that hosts a wide spectrum of events, ranging from bamboo flute recitals to raucous student rock bands. Its proximity to Kyoto University keeps the crowd young and hip, while the food and drink is cheap and cheerful.

Arts & leisure

Kanze Nohgakudo

44 Enshoji-cho, Okazaki, Sakyo-ku (075 771 6114/www.kyoto-kanze.jp). Higashiyama station (Tozai line). **Open** varies. **Map** p98 C5

Kanze is Japan's largest and Kyoto's most prolific Noh school, and claims a direct line back to Noh founder Zeami. The theatre stages around three shows of the traditional Japanese masked drama per week, though none with English explanations.

Hakusason-so p102

Kinkaku-ji

North-west

Change comes slowly to north-western Kyoto. This is a district of ancient Zen temples and businesses that measure their history in centuries. Most visitors make directly for the world-famous attractions (Myoshin-ji, Kinkaku-ji and Ryoan-ji), then head straight back out again. For time-pressed visitors it's a good strategy, but for those with a little more time, there are a number of endearing attractions that deserve attention. First and foremost, two sub-temples in the Myoshin-ji complex (Taizo-in and Shunko-in) allow you to talk Zen with eloquent, English-speaking priests. If you start your trip with a visit to one of these two, the rest of the city will make more sense.

On Kuramaguchi Dori, there is a pair of historic bathhouses; Funaoka Onsen looks just as it did almost a century ago, and Sarasa Nishijin is now a café with pan-Asian food and live music. Walk south to reach the weaving district of Nishijin. Though shifting fashions and the relocation of power to Tokyo ought to have killed off the traditional weaving industry, looms are still clacking away. Your souvenir kimono probably began life here, as did more contemporary clothes.

Tokiwazushi and Toyoukejaya are eateries known across the city, as is Daiichi, although the latter serves boiled turtle at gastronomic prices, and even many local lips curl at the thought.

The public train system barely grazes this area, so bring a bus pass, a bicycle or plenty of stamina.

Sights & museums

Insho Domoto Museum of Fine Arts

26-3 Kamiyanagi-cho, Hirano, Kita-ku (075 463 0007/www2.ocn.ne.jp. Buses 12, 50, 59. **Open** *9.30am-4.30pm Tue-Sun.* **Admission** *¥500.* **Map** *p108 B2* ❶

Painter and sculptor Insho Domoto (1891-1975) built his own museum in 1966, and he clearly wasn't in the mood for subtle architecture. Reportedly an abstract rendering of a ship, the building is splattered with graffiti-like relief work. Insho began his career as a textile designer in the Nishijin district, but became one of Japan's great modern artists, producing an unusually diverse canon of work. This museum traces his career, ranging from traditional Japanese themes to his involvement with abstract expressionism.

Kinkaku-ji

1 Kinkakuji-cho, Kita-ku (075 461 0013/www.shokoku-ji.or.jp). Bus 205. **Open** 9am-5pm daily. **Admission** ¥400. **Map** p108 C1 ❷
Kyoto's most iconic structure is a three-storey pavilion that literally dazzles visitors when the afternoon sun hits the gold leaf. It's the centrepiece of the temple grounds of the Rokuon-ji, which was an aristocrat's villa and then shogun's retreat before becoming a Zen temple in 1422. The pavilion, its upper two floors are coated in gold leaf, appears to float upon the aptly named 'Mirror Pond', against a backdrop of verdant mountains. It's the most modern of Kyoto's star attractions, dating back only as far as 1955, after a monk set fire to the original structure.

Kitano Tenmangu

Bakuro-cho, Kamigyo-ku (075 461 0005/www.kitanotenmangu.or.jp). Buses 50, 101; or Kitanohakubai-cho Station (Keifuku line). **Open** *Mar-Nov* 9am-6pm daily. *Dec-Feb* 9am-5.30pm daily. **Admission** free. **Map** p109 D3 ❸
A political conflict saw Heian period statesman Sugawara no Michizane demoted to a menial position on the island of Kyushu, where he died in 903. When earthquakes and storms ravaged Kyoto shortly after his passing, locals feared that Sugawara was exacting revenge on the city. Their solution was to build Shinto shrine Kitano

Tenmangu and deify the vengeful spirit. The grounds were decorated with Sugawara's favourite plum trees, about 2,000 of which blossom each February. To celebrate the occasion, a festival with local *maiko* and *geiko* has been held here on 25 February since 1109 (the temple now opens 7am-9pm on the 25th of each month). Kitano Tenmangu is also known for its Tenjin-san flea market (see p28). The rest of the year it's a peaceful and photogenic shrine, with a more restrained colour scheme than most of its Shinto brethren.

Myoshin-ji

Myoshinji-cho, Hanazono, Ukyo-ku (075 463 3121/www.myoshinji.or.jp/ english/index.html). Myoshinji station (Keifuku line). **Open** 24 hours daily. **Tours** 9.10am-3.40pm. **Admission** free. *Tours* ¥500. **Map** p108 A4 ❹
When Emperor Hanazono officially achieved enlightenment, his villa was converted into a Zen temple. Over the following six centuries, Myoshin-ji grew into the most influential Rinzai-sect temple in Japan, with around 3,500 affiliated temples nationwide. You wouldn't know it to walk the hushed streets of this enclave. Even though its scale is awe-inspiring, with 46 sub-temples covering a vast area, it's a dreamy, tranquil place. The treasures include the oldest bell in Japan (dated 698) and several works by Tanyu Kano, such as a dragon on the roof of the Lecture Hall. Depending on the angle from which you view the beast, he appears to be either ascending or descending, but his eyes glare at you wherever you stand.

Nishijin Textile Centre

Horikawa Dori, Imadegawa-sagaru, Kamigyo-ku (075 451 9231/www. nishijin.or.jp). Buses 9, 12, 51, 59; or Imadegawa Station (Karasuma line). **Open** 9am-5pm daily. **Admission** free. **Map** p109 F3 ❺
In the Nishijin weaving district, where a fabric auction house once stood, this multi-storey celebration of local textiles

North-west

gives visitors the chance to watch a kimono fashion show, try their hand at weaving, view historic garments, and spend their yen in the sizeable souvenir section. English-speaking staff make it a great place for tourists. Entrance and the kimono show are free; the weaving workshop costs ¥1,800 and should be booked at least a day ahead.

Ryoan-ji

13 Goryonoshita-machi, Ryoan-ji, Ukyo-ku (www.ryoanji.jp). Buses 50, 55, 59. **Open** *Mar-Nov* 8am-5pm daily. *Dec-Feb* 8.30am-4.30pm daily. **Admission** ¥500. **Map** p108 A2 ❻
The Ryoan-ji complex occupies 50 ha at the foot of the Kitayama mountains, but it's famous for just 248sq m: the *karensansui* (dry mountain water). Often described as the world's finest Zen garden, it is said to contain 'infinite teachings', although you may have to settle for just admiring its simplicity. Neither the garden's designer nor his or her intentions are known, but leading theories about the layout suggest that it represents either the branches of a tree or a tigress leading her cubs across a river. The rest of the grounds receive less attention but are no less beautiful, and the Seigen-in tofu restaurant (p112) offers one of the best views of any eaterie in the city.

Shunko-in

42 Myoshinji-cho, Hanazono, Ukyo-ku (075 462 5488/www.shunkoin.com). Hanazono station (Sagano line); or Myoshinji station (Keifuku line). **Classes** 9am, 10.40am, 1.30pm. **Tickets** ¥2,000 **Map** p108 A4 ❼
Crypto-Christian artworks and the Jesuit bell of Kyoto's first church are the unlikely treasures you'll discover in this Myoshin-ji sub-temple. Shunko-in even received visitors from the Vatican in recognition of its support for Christians while their religion was officially banned, and for burying the historic Bell of Nanban-ji to save it from being turned into World War II munitions.

The temple offers thrice-daily tours and seated meditation lessons from the English-speaking vice-abbot.

Taizo-in

35 Myoshinji-cho, Hanazono, Ukyo-ku (075 463 2855/www.taizoi.com). Hanazono station (Sagano line) or Myoshinji station (Keifuku line). **Open** 9am-5pm daily. **Admission** ¥500. **Map** p108 A4 ❽
The oldest and most famous of Myoshin-ji's sub-temples is renowned for its tranquil gardens. A rock creation by master painter and former resident Motonobu Kano (1476-1559) resembles a cascade of water, while a mid 20th century stroll garden with pond features a verdant landscape of azaleas. Several times a month, the temple offers English speakers a chance to experience Zen practice. The half-day events take in calligraphy, meditation, a tea ceremony and a *shojin ryori* lunch. It's an invaluable introduction to the ideas behind some of Kyoto's star attractions.

Urasenke Research Centre

Horikawa Dori, Teranouchi-agaru, Kamigyo-ku (075 431 6474/www.urasenke.or.jp/texte/index.html). Buses 9,12; or Kuramaguchi station (Karasuma line). **Open** 9.30am-4.30pm daily. **Admission** ¥500. **Map** p109 F2 ❾
At least you can be sure that you'll get a good bowl of *matcha* at Urasenke, Japan's leading school of tea. Though teaching the art of tea is the centre's raison d'être, it also allows visitors in for a cuppa and a snoop at some of its most treasured tea tools. For the very keen, there's access to the library.

Eating & drinking

Daiichi

6-371 Shimochojamachi, Senbon Nishi-iru, Kamigyo-ku (075 461 1775). Bus 206. **Open** 12.30-1.30pm, 5-7.30pm Mon, Wed-Sun. **¥¥¥¥**. **Turtle**. **Map** p109 E4 ❿

Shunko-in

Turtle hotpot isn't everyone's idea of a dream dinner, especially at these prices, but this 12th generation restaurant claims to have served every prime minister of Japan, as well as the cream of feudal-era Japanese society. Slashes on the entrance beams are said to have been made by frustrated samurai, who arrived after closing time. Everyone has the same set meal here: an appetiser of stewed turtle followed by a steaming turtle hotpot and then a bubbling turtle broth with eggs and rice. In case you're wondering, it tastes a little like chicken. If you're here for thrills, try the sake with turtle blood.

Jumbo

35-16 Minami-machi, Toji-in, Kita-ku (075 462 2934). Bus 26; or Toji station (Keifuku line). **Open** 11am-2pm, 4.30-11pm Wed-Sun. Closed 4th Sunday of month. **¥**. No credit cards. **Okonomiyaki & yakisoba**. Map p109 B4 ⑪

The name refers to the super-sized portions of okonomiyaki (around 30cm in diameter) and yakisoba (the cabbage almost falls off the hotplate). The functional interior is a throwback to the late 1970s, enlivened only slightly by the autographs of celebrities who have eaten here. If you would like to dine where the locals eat, this is the place.

Happily, while the servings are hefty, the prices are reasonable.

Kintame

576 Botanboko-cho, Senbon Dori, Itsutsuji-agaru, Kamigyo-ku (075 461 4072/www.kintame.co.jp). Buses 50, 206; or Imadegawa station (Karasuma line). **Open** 11am-2pm Mon, Tue, Thur-Sun. Shop 9am-5pm daily. **¥**. **Pickles**. Map p109 E3 ⑫

Pickles play a supporting role in most Japanese meals, but at Kintame they are the headline act. The staff cut the local veggies by hand and press them by stone, just as their predecessors have done since 1879. At the front of house, you can buy packs of pickles, whereas out the back, in the garden-view tatami room, the pickles star in a multi-course lunch – which includes top-quality pickle 'sushi', white miso soup, sun-dried radish and grilled fish.

Oimatsu

Kitano, Kamishichiken, Kamigyo-ku (075 463 3050). Bus 50. **Open** 8.30am-6pm daily. **¥**. No credit cards. **Confectionery**. Map p109 D3 ⑬

In Kamishichiken, a maiko district that flies below most radars, you'll find this former purveyor of confectionery to the imperial family (the Emperor no longer has official suppliers). The goodies are,

Ryoan-ji p110

of course, seasonal: in summertime, look for the bitter oranges filled with bitter-sweet jelly, and in winter try the *kokamochi* (a complex sweet with orange peel, pine nuts, raisins and almonds). Oimatsu offers a 75min confectionery-making class each morning (reservations essential).

Raku Raku

2-3 Inoke-cho, Hanazono, Ukyo-ku (075 462 9156/http://sites.google.com/ site/ kitchenrakuraku). Bus 26; or Toji station (Keifuku line). Open 11.30am-2pm, 5.30-10pm Tue-Sat; 5.30-10pm Sun. Closed 3rd Tuesday of month. ¥. **Modern Japanese**. Map p108 B4 🔞

As Japan's most traditional city, Kyoto suffers a reputation for being haughty and aloof. Here's the counterpoint: a bar-restaurant where staff might break into an impromptu musical jam and customers are likely to strike up a conversation with any fresh face. Indeed, the place's name means 'easygoing' in Japanese. Even though the menu won't excite you ('spaghetti' and 'mixed fry' are two of the options), the dishes are down-to-earth, and taste better than

they sound. The friendly atmosphere makes a great contrast to the Zen hush of neighbouring Myoshin-ji (p107).

Sarasa Nishijin

11-1 Higashi Fujinomori-cho, Murasakino, Kuramaguchi Dori, Kita-ku (075 432 5075/http://sarasa n2.exblog.jp). Bus 206. Open noon-9.30pm Mon, Wed-Sun. ¥. **Café**. Map p109 F1 🔞

Due to fire safety and size restrictions, baths were never a part of traditional *machiya* (townhouse) design. Instead, people bathed communally in *sento* (public bathhouses). Thus, as machiya life disappeared, so did the sento. This 1920s bathhouse closed at the end of the last century, but re-opened in 2000 as a 50-seat café serving coffees, cakes and bowls of rice. The renovation was gentle, preserving the wooden beams, ceramic tiles and an ivy-covered façade, but adding sofas and a kitchen. This is a highlight among the cafés in Kyoto.

Seigen-in

13 Goryonoshita-machi, Ryoan-ji, Ukyo-ku (075 462 4742). Buses 50, 55, 59. Open 10am-5pm daily. ¥¥. No credit cards. **Tofu**. Map p108 A2 🔞

The scenic garden of a World Heritage site is a wonderful backdrop to this eaterie. Guests sit around stone hearths, tucking into tofu, while a stream trickles between moss-covered rocks and miniature pine trees in the grounds of the famous Zen temple Ryoan-ji. The vegetarian set meal is good value, with a pot of tofu and local veggies paired with a tray of appetisers. No reservations necessary; minimum of two guests.

Tawaraya

918 Bakuro-cho, Onmae Dori, Imakoji-sagaru, Kamigyo-ku (075 463 4974). Bus 50. Open 11am-3.30pm daily. ¥. No credit cards. **Udon**. Map p109 D3/D4 🔞

You only get two noodles in a bowl of Tawaraya udon. Luckily, they're probably the world's thickest noodles, with

the texture of pounded rice. The dish couldn't be simpler: two noodles in a rich, smoky broth, with just a dab of wasabi on the side. If you're hungry, you might want to order one of the heartier bowls of udon standards.

Tokiwazushi

Senbon Dori, Motoseiganji-sagaru, Kamigyo-ku (075 441 7162). **Open** 11am-9.30pm daily. **¥¥¥**. **Sushi**. **Map** p109 E3 ⓲

This family-run establishment usually features on the best sushi lists, but it offers great value. You can eat well here for about ¥6,000. The third-generation chef serves sublime *tessa* (paper-thin sashimi) and *teppi* (skin) during winter's blowfish season, and a seared *toro* roll that regulars rave about.

Toriiwaro

75 Itsutsuji-cho, Itsutsuji Dori, Chiekoin Nishi-iru, Kamigyo-ku (075 441 4004). **Open** noon-9pm Mon-Wed, Fri-Sun. **¥¥¥**. **Chicken hotpot**. **Map** p109 F3 ⓳

Every day, 30 chicken carcasses are simmered for eight hours to make the broth for the next day's meals here. For lunch, there is just one option: a ¥800 chicken soup and *oyako-don*, a rice bowl topped with chicken and egg. It's unlikely that you'll find somewhere that does this better in Kyoto. For dinner, the price rockets to ¥6,000 for a choice of set meals, all with chicken hotpot. The restaurant started in Gion in the early 20th century, but relocated to a Nishijin townhouse after World War II, preceding the current *machiya* restaurant boom by half a century.

Toyoukejaya

822 Kamiyagawa-cho, Imadegawa Dori, Onmae Nishi-iru, Kamigyo-ku (075 462 3662/www.toyoukeya.co.jp/shiten.htm). Buses 50, 101; or Kitanohakubai-cho station (Keifuku line). **Open** *Restaurant* 11am-3pm Mon-Wed, Fri-Sun. *Shop* 10am-6.30pm Mon-Wed, Fri-Sun. **¥**. **Tofu**. **Map** p109 D3 ⓴

The Toyouke tofu store opened in 1897, but it took 95 years for them to add a kitchen and start cooking their widely praised curd. With just 12 tables, the restaurant is as famous for its queue as its filling *kyo yasai* to *nama yuba* lunch set. A similar story prevails across the street, where Tofu Café Fujino draws a lively crowd with its menu of tofu burgers and soy desserts. Locals argue about which is best. We're backing Toyouke.

Shopping

Kato Shoten

Ichijo Nakadachiuri, Kamigyo-ku (090 5131 7688). Buses 50, 101; or Kitanohakubai-cho station (Keifuku line). **Open** 9.30am-4.30pm daily. **Map** p109 D4 ㉑

Gion's Shichimiya (p92) may be the most famous place to buy the Japanese spice mix *shichimi*, but Kano Shoten is the best. A block south of Kitano Tenmangu (p107), septagenarian Masao Kato blends the seven ingredients to suit your taste and grinds them in his mortar. He sells devilishly hot chilli powder.

Funaoka Onsen p114

KYOTO BY AREA

Ohashi Kobo

16-5 Tenjugaoka-cho, Hanazono,
Ukyo-ku (075 464 3303). Bus 26.
Open 10am-6pm Mon-Fri. **Map**
p108 A3/A4 **㉒**

Nowhere takes chopsticks more seriously than this tiny establishment. Ohashi Kobo creates bespoke sticks that carefully pay attention to your height, gender and hand-size. You'll need to be patient, though – it takes around a year from order to delivery. There is a small ready-made selection for impatient shoppers.

Tozando

451-1 Shinhakusuimaru, Kamigyo-ku
(075 432 1600/www.tozandoshop.com).
Bus 50. **Open** 10am-6pm Mon-Sat.
Map p109 F4 **㉓**

For martial art fans or wannabe warriors, this is where you'll find all the swords, knives, *gi*, *hakama* and full samurai suits of armour you could possibly want. The store has English-speaking staff, and will ship your purchases worldwide.

Ukai Shoten

Omiya Dori, Teranouchi-agaru,
Kamigyo-ku (075 441 3885). Buses
9, 12. **Open** 9am-8pm Mon-Sat.
Map p109 F2 **㉔**

It's quite a trek from anywhere, but this sake store is by far the best in the city. Owner Hiroaki Ukai visits breweries throughout Japan and selects the top products, including aged and deep-sea water sakes. If you can speak Japanese, Ukai will discuss the drinks' characteristics at length; if you can't, pick the bottle with the prettiest label – there are no fillers on these shelves.

Nightlife

Jittoku

815 Hishiya-cho, Omiya Dori,
Shimodachiuri-sagaru, Kamigyo-ku
(075 841 1691/www2.odn.ne.jp/
jittoku). *Bus 9.* **Open** varies. **Admission**
free-¥3,000. **Map** p109 F5 **㉕**

Kyoto's most attractive live venue opened back in 1973, in what was once a sake brewery. And it still feels like a brewery, with stone floors, sake barrel seats and flowing alcohol. This live venue encourages you to sit, eat and drink, although the beverages are far better than the food. The venue books anybody who wants to play, but expect to hear blues, rock, jazz or folk.

Arts & leisure

Funaoka Onsen

82-1 Minami Funaoka-cho,
Murasakino, Kita-ku (075 441 3735).
Bus 206. **Open** 3pm-1am Mon-Sat;
8am-1am Sun. **Admission** ¥410.
Map p109 E1 **㉖**

Technically it's a *sento* (Japanese bathhouse) rather than an *onsen* (hot spring) since the heat is artificial, but why quibble over details when the place is as atmospheric and historic as this. The interior has barely changed since this bathhouse opened more than eight decades ago, so you can still admire the elm carvings depicting Japanese troops invading Manchuria. The nostalgic decor draws Kyoto's traditional types, which means that ladies might find themselves bathing with geisha, and gents often have the dubious privilege of sharing their tub with tattooed yakuza. The wide range of baths include steaming hot and freezing cold water, a bath with Chinese medicines, and a tub that zaps bathers with a mild current.

Kamishichiken Kaburen-jo

742 Shinsei-cho, Onmae Dori,
Kamishichiken, Kamigyo-ku
(075 461 0148). Bus 50, 101;
or Kitanohakubai-cho station (Keifuku
line). **Open** varies. **Map** p109 D3 **㉗**

This is the most remote of the city's five traditional arts theatres, and thus is often the easiest place to score tickets to see *maiko* perform their spring dances (shows 1pm and 3pm during 15-25 April, ¥3,800).

Arashiyama

Even the relentless swirl of tourists can't spoil the beautiful sights of Arashiyama. Set against a verdant mountain range, this idyllic retreat is famous for its picturesque scenery and tranquil pace of life. It takes just 20 minutes to reach the area from Kyoto Station, and it makes the city centre look like Manhattan. The scenery is attractive all year round, and looks particularly magnificent during cherry blossom or maple leaf season.

The landscape has been depicted on everything from sliding doors to alcohol adverts, described in poetry and sung about by emperors, so don't expect to have the place to yourself. The great thing is that Arashiyama is a compact area, so if you make an early start, you can whizz through the best parts in a day.

Sights & museums

Bamboo Forest

Ukyo-ku. Arashiyama station (Keifuku line) or Saga Arashiyama station (JR Sagano line). **Map** p117 A2 ❶
A five-minute stroll that you'll never forget, this route from the northern gate of Tenryu-ji past Okochi Sanso and on to Nonomiya-jinja is a winding path of towering bamboo. Light and wind stream through the canes to create an eerie but romantic scene. For two weeks each December, the path is lit with lanterns for evening strolls.

Jojakuko-ji

Ogura-cho, Ogurayama, Saga, Ukyo-ku (075 861 0435). Arashiyama station (Keifuku line), Saga Arashiyama station (JR Sagano line). **Open** 9am-4.30pm daily. **Admission** ¥400. **Map** p117 A1 ❷
On autumn evenings, when the long ascent to this temple is framed by maple

leaves and lit by lanterns, this is an essential stop on the tourist route. For the rest of the year, give it a miss.

Monkey Park Iwatayama

8 Genrokuyama-cho, Arashiyama Nishikyo-ku (075 872 0950). Arashiyama station (Keifuku line), Saga Arashiyama station (JR Sagano line). **Open** *mid-Mar-31 Oct* 9am-5pm daily. *1 Nov-mid March* 9am-4pm daily. **Admission** ¥520. **Map** p117 B3 ❸
Free of fences or cages, this animal-friendly park has almost 200 wild *macaques* (snow monkeys) roaming around the mountaintop. Visitors can feed the monkeys from an enclosure, and although it's a trek, they will be rewarded with a great view.

Nonomiya-jinja

Saga Nonomiya-cho, Ukyo-ku (075 871 1972/www.nonomiya.com). Arashiyama station (Keifuku line), Saga Arashiyama station (JR Sagano line). **Open** 24 hours daily. **Admission** free. **Map** p117 B1 ❹
Kyoto's most propitious shrine for lovers is packed with ways in which to boost your romantic fortunes or cement your relationship. Although modest in scale, it has been mentioned in countless poems and novels, including the millennium-old Japanese text *The Tale of Genji*, and its reputation lures crowds of love-seeking girls. Supplicants can scrawl their wishes on wooden *ema* (votive boards), and visitors wishing to rid themselves of a certain misfortune can pay ¥300 to dunk a description of their woe into a barrel of water; as the ink washes away, so too, they say, will your problem.

Okochi Sanso

8 Tabuchiyama-cho, Ogurayama, Saga, Ukyo-ku (075 872 2233). Arashiyama station (Keifuku line); or Saga Arashiyama station (JR Sagano line). **Open** 9am-5pm daily. **Admission** ¥1,000. **Map** p117 A2 ❺
Denjiro Okochi was one of Japan's earliest silent movie superstars, and although he died in 1962, his mountainside villa has been meticulously maintained and is now open to the public. Unlike his Hollywood counterparts, Okochi displayed good taste in building an elegant house and stroll garden with the best view in Arashiyama. From the highest point in the garden, you can scan the city to the east, or look west towards the tiny, rickety temple Daihi-ji, nestled alone in the Arashi mountains. The ¥1,000 entrance fee may seem steep, but it includes a bowl of green tea, a Japanese sweet and a postcard.

Tenryu-ji

68 Susukinobaba-cho, Tenryu-ji, Saga, Ukyo-ku (075 881 1235). Arashiyama Station (Keifuku line), Saga Arashiyama station (JR Sagano line). **Open** 8.30am-5.30pm daily. **Admission** *Garden and Main Hall* ¥600, *Garden* ¥500 *Lecture Hall* ¥500. **Map** p117 B2 ❻
Arashiyama's World Heritage site is a Rinzai Zen temple that dates from 1259. It was built to soothe the spirit of the late emperor Go-Daigo, and now achieves much the same thing for tourists with its superb landscaped stroll garden. The scenery changes dramatically with the seasons, thanks to its cherry, peach and maple trees. Tenryu-ji, whose name means Temple of the Heavenly Dragon, also has a dragon painted onto the ceiling of the Lecture Hall, with eyes that appear to follow you around the room. The image dates from 1997, when a local artist was commissioned to replace an original work that was beyond restoration. If you have seen the dragon in other Zen temples (especially Myoshin-ji, p107), you're likely to find this version less impressive, so you can save yourself the extra ¥500 for a viewing.

Togetsu-kyo

Nakanoshima-kanyuchi, Saga, Ukyo-ku. Arashiyama station (Keifuku line), Saga Arashiyama station (JR Sagano line). **Map** p117 B2 ❼

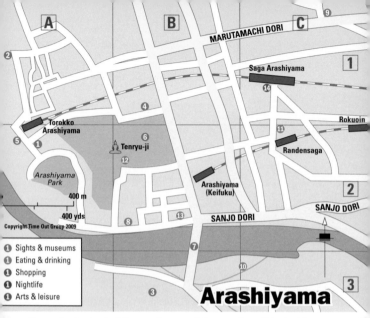

MARUTAMACHI DORI

Saga Arashiyama

Torokko
Arashiyama

Rokuoin

🛕 Tenryu-ji

Randensaga

Arashiyama
Park

Arashiyama
(Keifuku)

400 m

SANJO DORI

400 yds

SANJO DORI

Copyright Time Out Group 2009

❶ Sights & museums
❶ Eating & drinking
❶ Shopping
❶ Nightlife
❶ Arts & leisure

Arashiyama

Togetsu-kyo has inspired photographers and poets for centuries. Its name, which literally means 'Moon Crossing Bridge', derives from an emperor's poetic notion that the arc of the bridge over the river resembles the path of the moon as it crosses the sky. The current version, mainly built of concrete, dates from 1934.

Eating & drinking

Kitcho

55 Susukinobaba-cho, Tenryu-ji, Saga, Ukyo-ku (075 881 1101/www.kitcho.com/kyoto). Arashiyama station (Keifuku line), Saga Arashiyama station (JR Sagano line). **Open** 11.30am-3pm (last seating 1pm), 4.30-9pm daily (last seating 7pm). **¥¥¥¥. Kaiseki**. Map p117 B2 ❽
This is often described as Kyoto's most exclusive restaurant, but it's only the cost that keeps the hoipolloi away (lunch starts at ¥36,750, dinner at ¥42,000). Chef Kunio Tokuoka produces food that's seasonal, colourful

and almost too beautiful to eat. Elegant service, antique ceramic dishes and impeccable rooms with garden views still don't quite account for the immoderate price tag, but for gastronomes looking to tick boxes, this is one of the city's big-name restaurants.

Nishiki

Nakanoshima Koen-nai, Saga, Arashimaya, Ukyo-ku (075 881 8888/ www.kyoto-nishiki.com). Arashiyama station (Keifuku line), Saga Arashiyama station (JR Sagano line). **Open** 11am-9pm Mon, Wed-Sun. **¥¥¥**.
Kaiseki. Map p117 C1 ❾
As you arrive at this riverside restaurant, you'll notice that the stone entrance is wet, regardless of the weather. It's a subtle way of saying that the place is spotless and ready to welcome guests. The maids will usher you to a private room with cherry branches brushing the window, then deliver a miniature lacquer chest of drawers containing traditional Kyoto cuisine. For service,

food and a great view, it's astonishingly good value, and even cheaper if you don't mind dining in a shared, no-frills dining room. Book a day or two ahead off-peak, or several months ahead for peak season private rooms.

Le Plat Plus

72-1 Shingu-cho, Saga, Ukyo-ku (075 881 9329). Saga Arashiyama station. **Open** 11.30am-2pm, 5.30-8.30pm Mon, Wed-Sun. No credit cards. **¥¥**. **French**. Map p117 C3 ⑩
Just far enough from the tourist trail to keep the hordes away, but always packed with locals, this cute French bistro is your best bet for Western grub in Arashiyama. It's not food to write home about, but you'll recognise it, understand it and enjoy it.

Sagano-yu

4-3 Imahori-cho, Tenryu-ji, Saga, Ukyo-ku (075 882 8985/www. sagano-yu.com). Arashiyama station (Keifuku line), Saga Arashiyama station (JR Sagano line). **Open** 11am-8pm daily. **Café**. Map p117 C2 ⑪
Showerheads line the ceramic walls of this bathhouse-turned-café that teams non-slip mats, lockers and washbasins from its former life with wooden floorboards, desks and tables for a feminine, European interior. It's glistening, spotless and not nearly as cosy as Kyoto's other bathhouse café (Sarasa Nishijin, p112), but it's a fun place to pop into for a sandwich and a cup of tea.

Shigetsu

Tenryu-ji, Saga, Ukyo-ku (075 882 9725). Arashiyama station (Keifuku line), Saga Arashiyama station (JR Sagano line). **Open** 11am-2pm daily. **¥¥**. **Shojin ryori**. Map p117 B2 ⑫
'Eat to live, don't live to eat,' says the pamphlet in the garden of Tenryu-ji (p116), so you would be forgiven for expecting gruel. Luckily, only monks-in-training eat so ascetically. Here, you'll be seated on the floor of a long tatami room; off-season

you might have the room to yourself, whereas in peak season you'll have dozens of fellow diners. Waitresses flutter about with lacquer trays bearing colourful vegetarian dishes. Meat and fish are proscribed, of course, but so are overpowering ingredients, such as onions, garlic and spices. There are three sets (¥3,000, ¥5,000 or ¥7,000), but even the cheapest will fill you up. It's a good idea to book ahead.

Yoshimura

2 Togetsukyo Kitazumenishi, Arashiyama, Ukyo-ku (075 863 5700/ www.arashiyama-yoshimura.com). Arashiyama station (Keifuku line), Saga Arashiyama station (JR Sagano line). **Open** 11am-5pm (10.30am-6pm in cherry blossom or maple season) daily. **¥**. **Soba**. Map p117 B2 ⑬
You'll want a window seat here. With Mount Arashi in the background and the Togetsu Bridge stretching across the Oi in the foreground, the view is wonderful. The food's not bad either: home-made buckwheat noodles, served hot or cold, followed by buckwheat-flavoured desserts. Try the *Nishin soba*, a Kyoto speciality of noodles in a hot broth, topped with smoked herring. There's also an English menu.

Arts & leisure

Hozu River Boats

Hozu-cho, Kameoka (077 122 5846). Kameoka Torokko station (Sagano line). **Open** *1 Dec-9 Mar* 10am-2.30pm. *10 Mar-30 Nov* 9am-3.30pm. Map p117 C1 ⑭
Take the aptly named Sagano Scenic Railway from Saga Torokko Station (adjacent to JR Saga Arashiyama Station) to Kameoka Torokko Station (the journey costs ¥600, but doesn't run on Wednesdays), then ride the Hozu river back to Arashiyama. A trio of oarsmen propels each boat, carrying up to 20 passengers on a two-hour ride through the picturesque canyon, over rapids and past some of the most idyllic scenes in the area. Boats depart hourly.

Byodo-in p128

Further Afield

Some of the biggest attractions can be found on the outskirts of town. Luckily, Kyoto is such a compact city that even the outskirts are just a quick bus or train ride away. Listed below are the best of the attractions that didn't fit on the maps, including restaurants, cafés and a live venue that are no more than a stroll from the city centre.

Kyoto is also a stepping stone to several other great towns and cities, and the efficient rail network means that getting away for a day is a breeze. Looming largest on the radar is Osaka, Japan's second largest city and a great contrast to the sophistication of Kyoto with its earthy ambience. There's also Nara, the country's capital prior to Kyoto, and several other restful escapes. All these destinations make easy day trips.

Greater Kyoto

Sights & museums

Daitoku-ji

53 Daitokuji-cho, Murasakino, Kita-ku (075 491 0019). Kitaoji station (Karasuma line). **Open** *varies by season.* **Admission** *Main temple free. Koto-in* ¥400. *Daisen-in* ¥400. *Ryogen-in* ¥400. Like so much of Kyoto, Zen temple Daitoku-ji was destroyed in the Onin War (1467-77). The monk who rebuilt it was Ikkyu Sojun, a keen practitioner of tea and calligraphy. Under his guidance, the reborn temple became a centre of the arts. The temple gave great tea master Sen no Rikyu his Zen education, but also lead to his death. The ruling Hideyoshi Toyotomi was incensed to discover that Rikyu had placed a statue of himself in the grand Sanmon gate. Since Toyotomi regularly walked

through the gate, he considered the statue to be an insult to his authority and ordered Rikyu to commit ritual suicide. The temple is still renowned for its artworks, gardens and connections to tea culture. Of the 24 sub-temples in this vast complex, four are open to the public. Koto-in, Ryogen-in and Daisen-in are the ones not to miss. There is also a *shojin ryori* restaurant, Izusen (075 491 6665; open 11am-4pm Mon-Wed, Fri-Sun) near the Zuihoin sub-temple.

Fushimi Inari Taisha

68 Fukakusa Yabunouchi-cho, Fushimi-ku (075 641 7331/www.inari.jp). Inari station (JR Nara line); or Fushimi-Inari station (Keihan line). **Open** dawn until dusk daily. **Admission** free.

You may have seen the photographs of Fushimi Inari, but you won't be prepared for the scale of this place. A line of more than 5,000 vermillion shrine gateposts snakes around four kilometres of mountainside just south of the city. The shrine is dedicated to the gods of rice, sake and business. As a result, businesses and sake brewers nationwide pay to erect gateposts. If you're feeling flush, you can too: prices range from ¥200,000 to tens of millions of yen, depending on size and location.

Kamigamo Jinja

339 Motoyama, Kamigamo, Kita-ku (075 781 0011/www.kamigamojinja.jp/ english/index-e.html). Bus 9. **Open** Apr-Oct 9am-5pm daily. Nov-Mar 9.30am-5pm daily. Tours 9.30am. **Admission** free. *Tours* ¥500 tours.

Even though it's a trek to reach from the city centre, this World Heritage site is worth the effort for its English-language tours each morning. These offer an insight into the Shinto religion and its oldest Kyoto shrine. Kamigamo was constructed by Emperor Tenmu to the north of the city in an attempt to ward off evil. The brilliant red that dominates the buildings was thought to repel malicious spirits, which were believed to always attack from the north.

Katsura Rikyu

Misono-cho, Katsura, Nishikyo-ku (075 211 1215/http://sankan. kunaicho.go.jp/guide/katsura.html). **Admission** free (by appointment only).

Perhaps the greatest garden in Kyoto. As you stroll through the 7ha site, an enchanting transformation takes place, with ponds, islets, teahouses and miniature landscapes moving in and out of the frame. The buildings, notably the Sho-in, are considered exemplars of the *sukiya* style – the restrained, teahouse-inspired wooden architecture that influenced so many of Kyoto's constructions. Visitors need to apply in advance to the Imperial Household Agency (p12).

Koke-dera (Saiho-ji)

56 Jingatani-cho, Matsuo, Nishikyo-ku (075 391 3631). Bus 29. **Admission** ¥3,000 (by appointment only).

This major league attraction doesn't make things easy for visitors. You'll need to apply in advance p12), pay ¥3,000 and then spend an hour copying sutras by hand before being allowed to view the famous moss gardens of this Zen temple. It's worth it. There are two gardens: one is the oldest dry garden in Japan and the template for the dry gardens at Kinkaku-ji and Tenryu-ji; the other is a stroll garden with a pond in the shape of the Chinese character for 'heart'. Both are blanketed with more than a hundred varieties of moss. Zen monk and legendary landscape architect Muso Soseki designed the gardens, although he never planned for them to be green. It was only in the mid 19th-century that temple funds were too low to maintain the garden and the moss swept the grounds. The fairytale landscape looks its best in June during the rainy season.

Kyoto Botanical Garden

Shimogamo Hangi-cho, Sakyo-ku (075 701 0141/www.pref.kyoto.jp/plant). Kitayama station (Karasuma line). **Open** 9am-4pm daily. *Greenhouse* 10am-3.30pm daily. **Admission** ¥200.

In any other city this would be a major attraction: 12,000 plants occupying 24ha, with colourful scenes throughout the year. There are zones for cherry blossom and autumn leaves, Western-style lawns and a bamboo grove. There is a greenhouse with tropical and sub-tropical plants, including the popular carnivores. It's a great place to while away an afternoon, but who needs to while away time in a city like this?

Miho Museum

300 Momodani, Shigaraki, Shiga (074 882 3411/www.miho.or.jp). Ishiyama station (Tokaido line) then bus. **Open** *Mar-May, July-mid Dec* 10am-4pm Tue-Sun. **Admission** ¥1,000.
One of the tenets of the 'new religion' Church of World Messianity is that art and beauty can elevate humanity. Consequently, the church and its offshoots have amassed treasuries of art, including the Shumei collection. The collection's home is a 1997 geometric creation by Pritzker Prize-winner IM Pei. The museum occupies a 100ha area of mountainside an hour south of Kyoto. Its works come from all areas and eras, with the emphasis on beauty rather than curatorial coherence.

Shugaku-in Rikyu

Shugaku-in yabu-cho, Sakyo-ku (075 211 1215/http://sankan.kunaicho.go.jp/guide/shugakuin.html). Shugaku-in station (Eizan line). **Admission** free (by appointment only).
Emperor Go-mizuno abdicated his throne at the tender age of 34 to focus on aesthetic pursuits, including the creation of this 28ha villa. During his reign (1611-29), he was in regular conflict with the shogun (the true holder of power at the time), but on his abdication he received funding from the Tokugawas to create this exquisite landscape. One of Kyoto's best examples of 'borrowed scenery', it incorporates a mountainous panorama into the view from the garden's upper level. Visits are by appointment only.

Suntory Yamazaki Whisky Distillery

5-2-1 Yamazaki, Shimamoto-cho, Mishima (075 962 1423/www.suntory. co.jp/factory/yamazaki/index.html. Yamazaki station (JR Kyoto line). **Tours** 10am-3pm daily (groups of two or more). **Admission** free (by appointment only)
Japanese whisky has been booming in the last decade, winning medals and market share worldwide. Suntory's Yamazaki brand is one of the biggest names, and the company offers hour-long tours of the distillery. Reservations are required at least one day in advance. Free English audio guides.

Tofuku-ji

15-chome Honmachi, Higashiyama-ku (075 561 0087/www.tofukuji.jp). Tofuku-ji station (Keihan or Nara lines). **Open** 9am-4pm daily. **Admission** ¥400.
This temple, south-west of Kyoto Station, boasts one of Japan's top-rated Zen gardens, as well as spectacular scenes of autumn foliage. A pair of wooden bridges face each other, with a ravine of maple trees in between. The scene is a photo-opportunity any time of year, but it's breathtaking in November. Don't miss the *tousu*; nicknamed the '100-man loo', this Important Cultural Property is the largest and oldest communal commode in Japan. Although it is no longer in use, it was once a major source of income for Tofuku-ji, which sold the excrement for compost.

Toji

Kujo-cho, Minami-ku (075 691 3325). Toji station (Kintetsu line). **Open** *20 Mar-19 Sept* 8.30am-5.30pm daily. *20 Sept-19 Mar* 8.30am-4.30pm daily. **Admission** ¥500.
World Heritage site Toji is best known for its landmark pagoda, Japan's tallest, but is also home to a host of National Treasures. Kobo Daishi, the founder of Shingon Buddhism and the monk credited with creating Japan's syllabary, took charge of the temple in the eighth century and set about creating a 3-D

Kyoto Botanical Garden p121

mandala to help people visualise his ideas. Even though much of Toji has been repeatedly destroyed and rebuilt, the 21 statues of the mandala have survived and are on display in the Kodo building. On the 21st of each month the temple hosts a flea market, nicknamed Kobo-san after the visionary monk.

Eating & drinking

A Womb

35-2 Hinokuchi-cho, Ichijoji, Sakyo-ku (075 721 1357/www.awomb.com). Bus 5. **Open** noon-2pm, 6-9pm Mon, Tue, Thur-Sun **¥¥**. **Modern Japanese**.
A restaurant this far from the action needs to be special to survive. A Womb's formula is top-class modern Japanese cuisine in an airy, minimalist interior with custom-made furniture from Iremonya Design Labo (p78). The menu is unusually broad, veering from sushi to curry to rice bowls to *obanzai* (daily dishes). If you've made it this far, you may as well indulge in the Hisago sushi *kaiseki* set (¥7,000).

Il Ghiottone Cucineria

160-2 Izumiya-cho, Kiyamachi Dori, Mastubara-agaru, Shimogyo-ku (075 353 8866/www.cucineria.jp). **Open** noon- 2pm; 6-11pm Mon, Tue, Thur-Sun. **¥¥**. **Italian**.

The main branch of Il Ghiottone is famously booked up weeks in advance. In 2008, chef Sasajima opened this casual, riverside cucineria and keeps several tables for walk-ins. Like the main branch, the cucineria serves top-grade Italian dishes with a Kyoto twist, and these days you're more likely to find the celebrated chef here than at the ever-popular original branch.

Ranhotei

64 Kamikawara-cho, Sanjo Dori, Omiya Nishi-iru, Nakagyo-ku (075 801 0790/ www.ranhotei.com). Nijojo-mae station (Tozai line). **Open** 10am-8pm daily. **¥**.
Tea salon.
The burly Canadian owner of Ranhotei looks more like a Bond villain than a tea master, but appearances can be deceptive. Randy Channell has been practising tea ceremony for more than two decades, teaching it since 1996, and in 2008 opened this beautiful tea salon, in which you can enjoy traditional tea-and-sweet sets or more modern twists on desserts such as green tea affogato or cheesecake. Channell's hour-long tea primers are a great way to learn about the history and significance of tea in Japan, as well as enjoy a brew by the master (¥2,500, reservations are required).

Nightlife

Taku Taku

Tominokoji Dori, Bukkoji-sagaru,
Shimogyo-ku (075 351 1321).
Kawaramachi station (Hankyu line).
Open varies. **Admission**
¥1,000-¥4,000.

Once a sake brewhouse, now one of the
city's most popular live venues, Taku
Taku has hosted several legends of
blues and rock since opening in 1974.
It still draws some recognisable names
(Roy Ayers was a recent visitor), but
most days you'll find hot Japanese acts
on stage. It is located two blocks south
of the Downtown map.

Arts & leisure

Nishi-Kyogoku Stadium

32 Shinmeicho, Nishi Kyogoku, Ukyo-ku.
(075 313 9131/www.sanga-fc.jp). Nishi-
Kyogoku station (Hankyu line).

The home ground of Kyoto Sanga FC,
the city's perennially under-performing
J-League football team, is a 20,000-
capacity piece of drab concrete. All but
a few premium seats are exposed to the
vagaries of the elements. Even though
local support is usually thin, the stadium can light up when more popular
teams, such as the Urawa Reds, come
to play in town.

Toei Uzumasa Eigamura

10 Higashi Haschigaoka-cho,
Uzumasa, Ukyo-ku (075 864 7716/
www.eigamura30.com). Open Mar-Nov
9am-5pm daily. *Dec-Feb* 9.30am-4pm
daily. **Admission** ¥2,200.

It's Universal Studios with samurai
but without the rides in this movie-set
theme park from Toei, producer of
Japanese period dramas and superhero
shows. It even has a mechanical sea
monster where the shark should be. The
full-scale street sets depict a Japan
of yore, but so does most of Kyoto
itself. Nostalgia seekers will find more
value elsewhere; children may see
things differently.

Nara

Looking at Nara today, it's hard to
imagine this was once the capital
of Japan. It feels more like a village
than a city, albeit one furnished
with breathtaking architecture. In
the 69 years during which Nara was
the seat of power (710-740, 745-784),
the emperors bestowed on it temples,
shrines and a palace, which are now
collectively known as the Historic
Monuments of Ancient Nara.

The aim was to establish Nara as
the permanent, peaceful capital of a
united country. Instead, the temples
were a little too successful and the
emperor soon moved his palace
away from the meddling clergy.
Since then, Nara has never had a
chance to blossom as a capital, so
those great monuments dominate
a quaint, unspoiled destination.
Almost as soon as you step out of
Nara station you will discover a
500-hectare park containing the
city's two greatest temples and its
deer. The animals have been seen

Ranhotei p123

as messengers of god ever since a Shinto deity reportedly came riding into Nara on the back of a white deer. They enjoyed official divine status until the mid 20th century, and it was once a capital offence to harm a Nara deer. The estimated 1,200 deer have since been downgraded to the status of Natural Monuments. They roam Nara Park and its nearby streets, surviving on crackers offered by visitors.

Kasuga Taisha

160 Kasugano-cho (074 222 7788/ www.kasugataisha.or.jp). **Open** *Apr-Oct* 6.30am-5.30pm daily. *Nov-Mar* 7am-4.30pm daily. **Admission** *Main hall* ¥500. *Treasure house* ¥400. *Botanical garden* ¥500.

To appreciate just how powerful the Fujiwara family was during the eighth century, head first to Kofuku-ji, the family temple, then here to the family shrine. Officially established in 768, though likely to be older, this shrine does for lanterns what Fushimi Inari Taisha does for shrine gateposts. There are about 2,000 stone lanterns and a further 1,000 hanging bronze lanterns decorating the shrine and its grounds. Between 2nd and 4th February and 15th and 16th August, crowds flock to see them illuminated. Other good times to visit are 13th March for a performance of *gagaku* (the music and dance of the imperial court) and late April to early May, when the wisteria are in bloom.

Kofuku-ji

48 Noborioji-cho (074 222 4096/www. kohfukuji.com). **Open** 9am-5pm daily. **Admission** *Grounds* free. *Eastern Golden Hall* ¥300. *Treasure Museum* ¥500.

This temple was perhaps partly to blame for Nara losing its role as capital city. The emperor wanted to distance the court from the powerful temples, and Kofuku-ji was the epitome. Founded by the mighty Fujiwara clan in south-eastern Kyoto in 669, it was moved twice to stay close to the seat of power. At its peak, Kofuku-ji

was a military and political force, but when the Fujiwara clan's influence waned, so did interest in their temple. Just a handful of buildings remain, although one is Japan's second-largest pagoda and another contains the remnants of the Fujiwara's treasure.

Okumura Commemorative Museum

4 Kasugano-cho (074 226 5112/ www.okumuragumi.co.jp). **Open** 10am-5pm daily. **Admission** free.

Museum is too grand a name for a building that touts a 'rest area' as one of its main attractions, but this construction company's corporate folly also hosts an earthquake simulator that recreates two of Japan's most destructive temblors. A fun diversion on the way to visit the temples.

Todai-ji

406-1 Zoshi-cho (074 222 5511/ www.todaiji.or.jp). **Open** *Nov-Feb* 8am-4.30pm daily. *Mar* 8am-5pm daily. *Apr-Sept* 7.30am-5.30pm daily. *Oct* 7.30am-5pm daily. **Admission** ¥500.

In 752, when Emperor Shomu still had grand plans for Nara, he built a temple of such a staggering scale that it would bring together all Japan's Buddhists. The unification never happened, but the temple still stands on the edge of Nara Park and has become the city's greatest attraction. From the towering wooden gate to the 47m-high Daibutsu Hall with its 250-ton bronze Buddha, everything here is scaled to impress visitors. The strange wooden character in a red cape just outside the Daibutsu Hall is Binzuru, a master of occult powers. Rub Binzuru, then the corresponding part of your body, and any ailments there, so they say, will disappear.

Getting there

Take the Kintetsu line from Kyoto station to Nara station (¥610, 46 minutes). All the attractions listed here are within walking distance of the station.

Ohara

An hour from Kyoto, Ohara offers quintessentially Japanese scenery and architecture. Wooden farmhouses and temples are nestled together at the foot of forested hills that rise abruptly from lush paddy fields. Monkeys amble across the fields, as do *oharame* – female sellers of firewood or flowers who dress in a distinctive local costume and carry their wares on their heads.

The town is bursting with stalls selling all sorts of curios and goodies, including iced cucumbers pickled in seaweed water to munch as you stroll around. For hikers, Ohara is the start point of several mountain trails.

Sights & museums

Jakko-in

187 Shorinin-cho, Ohara, Sakyo-ku (075 744 2537/www.jakkoin.jp). **Open** 9am-4.30pm daily. **Admission** ¥600.
Jakko-in was founded in the seventh century, but its importance was established, so the story goes, through tragedy. In 1185, when the army loyal to child emperor Antoku was beaten in a sea battle by a rival clan, the boy's grandmother leapt into the ocean with him, drowning both. Antoku's mother retreated to Jakko-in to become a nun. The main hall of Jakko-in was lost to arson in 2000, but has since been restored.

Sanzen-in

540 Raigoin-cho, Ohara, Sakyo-ku (075 744 2531/www.sanzenin.or.jp). **Open** *Mar-Nov* 8.30am-4.30pm daily. *Dec-Feb* 8.30am-4pm daily. **Admission** ¥700.
The origins of this Tendai sect temple date back to 985. The buildings that now comprise this temple are more recent but, together with the moss-carpeted gardens, they still ooze history. The temple's main treasure is a gold-coated statue of Amida Buddha in the photogenic main hall, Ojo Gokuraku-in. The

two pond gardens were built in the 17th century, and although they are more crowded and chaotic than some of Kyoto's most scenic landscapes, they are rich, extensive and full of surprising treasures and tranquil nooks.

Arts & leisure

Ohara Sansou

17 Kusao-cho, Ohara, Sakyo-ku (075 744 2227/www.ohara-sansou.com/english/index.htm).
There's no need to be a guest at this luxurious ryokan to use their indoor and outdoor hot springs. You can simply pop in for a restorative soak, followed by a *sukiyaki* dinner. It's also possible to reserve a small hot spring bath for private use.

Getting there

From Kyoto Station, take the Karasuma subway line to Kokusaikaikan station (¥260, 20 minutes). Then take bus 19 (¥340, 20 minutes, two buses per hour). Alternatively, take bus 17 directly from Kyoto Station to Ohara (¥580, 60 minutes).

Osaka

Kyoto's gregarious big sister is only 29 minutes away by train, but a world away in atmosphere. Where Kyoto is refined, elegant and not a little snooty, Osaka is earthy, intolerant of affectation and knows how to have fun.

The city has a national reputation for its culinary and comedy cultures. Local specialities include the cheap 'n' cheerful *takoyaki* (octopus dumplings) and *okonomiyaki* (savoury pancakes), but there is plenty of fine dining as well, and in recent years the city has witnessed a proliferation of foreign cuisines.

Architecturally, the place is a post-modern wonderland, with a

wealth of cutting-edge constructions. Waterfront developments have lead the city's promoters to brand it the 'Venice of the East', although a swankier Manchester is perhaps closer to the mark.

Umeda is the city centre proper, with high-end shopping and a money-magnet atmosphere. Minami is the collective name for the districts of Namba, Shinsaibashi, Amerika-mura and Dotonbori, and is almost a synonym for eating, drinking and consumer fun. The area's labyrinth of narrow streets is made for strolling and people-watching. Next door are Horie, full of hip eateries and boutiques, and Nipponbashi, Osaka's geek central for electrical shops, manga and cosplay cafés.

Sights & museums

National Museum of Art, Osaka

4-2-55 Nakanoshima, Kita-ku (066 447 4680/www.nmao.go.jp/english/home.html). Watanabebashi station, exit 1 (Keihan Nakanoshima line); or Higobashi station, exit 3 (Yotsubashi line). **Open** 10am-4.30pm Mon-Thur, Sat, Sun; 10am-6.30pm Fri. **Admission** ¥420.

In 2004, Osaka razed its old National Museum of Art and replaced it with an eye-popping piece of architecture by César Pelli. Dubbed 'the submarine' because of its subterranean location, the 13,500sq m museum is entirely concealed, but for an explosion of steel and glass at ground level, representing reeds waving in the wind. The galleries are home to modern art by Japanese and international masters, including Cézanne, Picasso and Ernst.

Osaka Castle

1-1 Osakajo, Chuo-ku (066 941 3044/ www.osakacastle.net/English). Osakajokoen station (JR loop line); or Tanimachi 4-chome station (Chuo line). **Open** 9am-5pm daily. **Admission** ¥600.

One of Japan's best-known castles, Osaka-jo was built to flaunt the power of warlord Hideyoshi Toyotomi. The main tower is a 1931 ferroconcrete reconstruction of the 1598 original, with all but the moat and outer walls having fallen to mishaps, manmade or natural. The main tower is now a museum narrating the history of the castle through art, armour and weaponry. The grounds accommodate an extensive and popular park, which hosts amateur music, sport and picnickers.

Shitenno-ji

1-11-18 Shitennoji, Tennoji-ku (066 771 0066/www.shitennoji.or.jp). Shitennoji-mae Yuhigaoka station (Tanimachi line). **Open** Nov-Feb 8.30am-4.30pm daily; Mar-Oct 8.30am-4pm daily. **Admission** Chushingaran ¥300. Treasure House ¥200. Honbo Garden ¥300. All area pass ¥700.

Kyoto is the city of shrines and temples, but Osaka also has its fair share, and Shitenno-ji is the pick of the lot. It is said to have been the first Buddhist temple in Japan, dating back to 593. When Buddhist-leaning Prince Shotoku defeated the Shinto-favouring Mononobe clan, he built this temple as a monument. Shitenno-ji hosts a lively flea market on the 21st of each month.

Tsutenkaku Tower

1-18-6 Ebisuhigashi, Naniwa-ku (066 641 9555/www.tsutenkaku.co.jp). Shin Imamiya station (JR, Yamatoji and Nankai lines); Ebisucho station (Sakaisuji line); or Dobutsuen-mae station (Midosuji line). **Open** 10am-6.30pm daily. **Admission** ¥600.

Paris has the Eiffel Tower and Tokyo has the Tokyo Tower, so Osaka had to build the 91m-high Tsutenkaku ('Tower Reaching to Heaven'). The tower is the city's best-known landmark after the castle and was once the biggest crowd puller. It stands in an eccentric but flamboyantly imitative area called Shinsekai, a great place for people-watching and a glimpse of Osaka's earthy side.

Nightlife

Onziemme

11F Midosuji Building, 1-4-5 Nishi-shinsaibashi, Chuo-ku (066 243 0089/ www.onzi-eme.com). Shinsaibashi station (Midosuji, Nagahori Tsurumi-ryokuchi lines). **Open** varies. **Admission** ¥3,000-¥3,500.

There was a time when Osakans travelled to Kyoto for clubbing. Now, it's the other way around, and Onziemme is the biggest lure. Since it opened in 2007, this 700-capacity venue has seen Sasha, Digweed, Freeland, Emerson and many other stars fill the dancefloor. Monthly party 06 is the highlight of the schedule.

Triangle

2-18-5 Nishi-shinsaibashi, Chuo-ku (066 212 2264/www.triangle-osaka.jp). Shinsaibashi station (Midosuji and Nagahori Tsurumi-ryokuchi lines). **Open** varies. **Admission** ¥2,000-¥3,000

Run by the same folks as Kyoto's Lab Tribe, Triangle is a cosy three-storey club with a rooftop jacuzzi. Events cover all the usual dancefloor genres, but house and hiphop are the favourites.

Arts & leisure

National Bunraku Theatre

Nipponbashi, Chuo-ku (066 212 2531/ www.ntj.jac.go.jp/english/index.html). Nipponbashi station (Sakaisuji line). **Shows** vary **Admission** ¥2,300-¥5,800.

Osaka is the home of *bunraku* (a traditional Japanese form of theatre, which features large puppets on stage and narrative recited off stage) and in 1984 this 750-seat theatre was opened to keep the art alive. English-language summaries and audio guides assist you in keeping up with the storylines, but it's enough just to watch the action and marvel at the expressions eked out of these puppets made of wood and cloth. There are several bunraku runs a year, with other forms of theatre filling the gaps in the schedule.

Universal Studios Japan

2-1-33 Sakurajima, Konohana-ku (www.usj.co.jp/e). Universal City station (JR Yumesaki line). **Open** varies. **Admission** ¥5,800; ¥3,900 reductions.

Not so different from Universal Studios in the United States, Osaka's top theme park opened in 2001 with paradesand rides based on *Backdraft*, *Back to the Future* and other films that your kids have never heard of.

Getting there

The fastest route is by bullet train from Kyoto station to Shin-Osaka station (¥2,730, 14 minutes). Better value is the rapid train between the two stations (¥540, 29 minutes). You can also take the Keihan line to central Osaka (Sanjo to Yodoyabashi costs ¥400 and takes 51 minutes), or Hankyu line from Kawaramachi to Umeda (¥390, 45 minutes).

Uji

The green tea you've been drinking in Kyoto probably came from Uji, the second largest city in Kyoto Prefecture. The third Ashikaga shogun, the man responsible for Kinkaku-ji, was a tea enthusiast who encouraged the cultivation of plantations in this town, renowned for the purity of its water. Tea giants Ippodo, Marukyu-Koyamaen and Fukujuen all grow their leaves here, and there is no shortage of tea salons. This town of just 200,000 people also boasts a pair of World Heritage sights, one of which is an unforgettable sight.

Sights & museums

Byodo-in

116 Uji Renge (077 421 2861/www. byodoin.or.jp). Uji station (JR Nara line). **Open** *Mar-Nov* 8.30am-5.15pm daily. *Dec-Feb* 9am-4.45pm daily. **Admission** ¥600.

Toei Uzumasa Eigamura p124

The temple etched into the back of every ¥10 coin has more national treasures than any temple in Kyoto. Byodo-in's Phoenix Hall is a piece of ostentation that has survived intact since 1053. It is thought to be an embodiment of paradise, with a lake marking the boundary between Heaven (the temple) and Earth. The resident of the hall, a 3m-high Amida Buddha, was carved by the era's most renowned sculptor, Jocho, who also worked on the 52 floating deities in the museum.

Tale of Genji Museum

45-26 Uji Higashiuchi (077 439 9300/ www.uji-genji.jp). **Open** 9am-5pm Tue-Sun. **Admission** ¥500.
Proud of its prominent role in the world's oldest novel, Uji opened this dedicated museum in 1998. Suprisingly large for a museum based on a single book, the galleries include recreations of aristocratic life in the Heian period and audio-visual renderings of the story. Whether or not you care about the Tale, the museum should whet your appetite to explore its setting.

Ujigami Jinja

59 Uji Yamada (077 421 4634). **Open** 8.30am-4.30pm daily. **Admission** free.
Uji's other World Heritage site plays second fiddle to the more dazzling Byodo-in, but it's worth a look while you're here. The Main Hall is the oldest shrine building in Japan. Even though the precise date of construction is unknown, a team of researchers recently dated the wood back to the mid 11th century, making it contemporaneous with Byodo-in. In the grounds lies *kirihara-mizu*, the only remaining spring of what was once a septet of famously pure water sources in Uji.

Arts & leisure

Cormorant fishing

Ujigawa (077 423 3334). **Open** late June-late Sept. **Tickets** ¥1,800.
In place of nets or rods, Uji's fishermen use cormorants on leashes. The birds dive for the fish, store them in their beaks and are then hauled back to the boat to give up their prey. Snares around the birds' throats prevent them from swallowing the fish, so this is not an attraction that will amuse bird lovers. At night, the fishing takes place by flaming torchlight, and the local tourist bureau organises boat trips for a close-up view.

Getting there

Take the Nara line from Kyoto station to Uji station (¥230, 25 minutes).

KYOTO BY AREA

Make the most of London life

Essentials

Tawaraya p141

Hotels

Where else in the world can you choose between staying in a modern hotel, a classic inn, a converted townhouse, an old storehouse, a Buddhist temple, an imperial villa or a budget hostel? Accommodation in Kyoto can mean sharing a tatami mat floor with half a dozen strangers, or encountering hospitality as an art form.

Your first decision is whether or not to make the accommodation integral to the experience. If you want a concierge, a spa and a bar, stick to the hotels. Kyoto has some impressive options, with the Hyatt Regency, Granvia and Westin Miyako standing out: for service, style and comfort, these three are hard to fault.

There is a quartet of top-class boutique hotels: The Screen (see box p138), which attracted a blaze of attention when it opened in 2008; the Chourakukan Hotel, which

opened later the same year but far more quietly; the Hotel Mume, which arrived in mid 2009; and the Prinz Apartotel, whose two rooms make it a boutique, though perhaps not quite a hotel.

For those that want to live, breathe, eat and sleep Kyoto, a stay at one of the many ryokan is a must. These traditional inns exist throughout Japan, but nowhere else will you find such a high standard of hospitality. At the best establishments there will be a short curtain to welcome you, not a door to block you. The stone entrance will have been freshly sprayed with water, telling guests that everything is in order. When you enter your room, you may find the lingering hint of an incense stick lit hours before your arrival. Such is the precision of ryokan hospitality.

The rooms are sparingly furnished. The decor will usually

be composed of calligraphy and freshly cut flowers. The furniture is just a low table and perhaps a lacquered chest, whereas the bedding, a futon, is rolled out by the maid each night.

These aren't just places to slumber. The high-end ryokan experience involves a *kaiseki* meal delivered to your room, a soak in a wooden bathtub, and lounging in a *yukata* gown, absorbing the garden. Some orthodox ryokan operate just as they did a century or more ago; others are keeping pace with progress, while retaining the essence of Japanese hospitality. Needless to say, the ones with a contemporary outlook are the most comfortable, which is just as well because some of the more conservative places don't welcome foreigners. The ryokan listed here all cater to international visitors.

For the Old Kyoto atmosphere without the fine dining and fastidious service, there are classic townhouses (*machiya*) for private rental. At the very top end are the Iori establishments, decked out in fine arts and luxury furnishings. For those on a tighter budget, there are a number of machiya now operating as hostels. Though atmospheric and great value, they don't always stand up well to the elements. In the humid summer months, you would be wise to avoid the cheapest Japanese-style dorms.

Curfews

Some of the more economical ryokan and guesthouses impose curfews, usually from around 11pm. Others lock the doors but provide guests with access codes or keys. The pricier places rarely have such rules, but in a ryokan, with their wooden floors and thin walls, make sure that to return to your room quietly.

SHORTLIST

Best new
- Chourakukan Hotel (p142)
- Hotel Mume (p135)
- K's Guest House (p137)
- The Screen (p138)

Best budget
- Hannari Guesthouse (p144)
- K's Guest House (p137)
- Utano Youth Hostel (p145)

Superlative service
- Hiiragiya (p137)
- Hyatt Regency Kyoto (p135)
- Tawaraya (p141)
- Yoshikawa (p141)

Affordable ryokan
- Ishihara (p139)
- Nishiyama Ryokan (p142)

Designer digs
- Hotel Mume (p135)
- New wing of Hiiragiya (p137)
- Prinz Apartotel (p145)
- The Screen (p138)

Best city views
- ANA Hotel Kyoto (p141)
- Chourakukan Hotel (p142)
- Granvia (p135)

City on your doorstep
- Ishihara (p139)
- Kanamean Nishitomiya (p139)
- Kyoto Hotel Okura (p142)
- Kyoto Royal Hotel & Spa (p139)

Machiya life
- Iori Sanbo Nishinotoin-cho (p139)
- Suisen-Kyo Shirakawa (p143)

Best spas
- Kotoran at Kyoto Royal Hotel & Spa (p143)
- Riraku at Hyatt Regency Kyoto (p135)

ESSENTIALS

Location

For peace and quiet but easy access to the wonderful sights, anywhere in Higashiyama is a good choice to stay. If you're planning to do plenty of temple-hopping, pick a place near Kyoto station, with easy access to all train and bus routes. Downtown and Gosho district accommodation will suit anyone who likes their cities served straight up. Even though the North-west is a little far from the action, it's worth considering a night or two here as a base for exploring this endearing district and its legendary temples.

Prices

Be careful when comparing room rates. Though prices for deluxe hotels and ryokan are comparable, the hotels are charging per room, while the ryokan rate is usually per person. Some offer reduced rates if you don't wish to have the evening meal. The deluxe price bracket here (¥¥¥¥) assumes a regular night with full dinner. Expect to pay ¥40,000-¥90,000 per person per night. At the other end of the spectrum, a futon in a dormitory can cost as little as ¥2,500.

Booking ahead

If you wish to see the cherry blossom, autumn leaves, Gion Festival or New Year celebrations, book at least three months ahead and expect to pay up to double the off-peak rates. If visiting off-peak (after New Year until the end of February, and in June), you may find a few of the fancier establishments become surprisingly affordable.

Kyoto Station Area

APA Villa Hotel

533 Shiokoji-cho, Shichijo-sagaru, Higashinotoin-dori, Shimogyo-ku (075 341 8111/www.apahotel. com/hotel/kansai/02v_kyoto-ekimae). Kyoto station (JR, Kintetsu and Karasuma lines). ¥¥.

The quirky amenities here include a branch of Seattle's Best Coffee and a microwave in the lobby. Rooms are clean, if cramped, and have free internet access. Members of staff aren't always attentive. The best reason to stay here is the location, just a couple of blocks away from Kyoto station.

Gojo Guest House

3-396-2 Gojobashi-higashi, Higashiyama-ku (075 525 2299/

Granvia

www.gojo-guest-house.com).
Gojo station (Keihan line). ¥.
A light renovation has turned a century-old townhouse into one of the city's most economical hostels. If you choose the cheapest option of a dormitory room, you'll sleep just as the original owners would have – with futons on rush mat floors – although with half a dozen strangers as company. The young, English-speaking owners have created a cosy, friendly place to crash.

Granvia

901 Higashi Shiokoji-cho, Karasuma Dori, Shiokoji Sagaru, Shimogyo-ku (075 344 8888/www.granviakyoto. com). Kyoto station (JR, Kintetsu and Karasuma lines). ¥¥¥.
The Granvia has one great advantage to brag about, over other hotels: most of the city's buses, trains and subways stop only a few metres away from its front door. Located inside Kyoto Station, this 500-room hotel also offers impressive views of the city, a dozen restaurants and, in its premium rooms, a seven-headed massage shower and a startle-free wake-up system that uses sound and light to ease you ever so gently from your slumber over the course of around 30 minutes. Within the Granvia, there are no less than 13 bars and restaurants inside the hotel, including an affordable branch of Arashiyama's Kitcho (p117).

Guest House Tomato

135 Shimizu-cho, Shiokoji Dori, Horikawa Nishi-iru, Shimogyo-ku (075 203 8228/http://pascon.gozaru.jp/ enindex.html). Kyoto station (JR, Kintetsu and Karasuma lines). ¥.
This foreigner-friendly guesthouse is wonderfully intimate, with just two private rooms and a small dormitory. Attractions include a Wi-Fi-equipped living room and a communal kitchen. On the downside, there are only two showers to serve up to 14 people; a nearby public bathhouse makes a pleasant alternative.

Hotel Mume

261 Umemoto-cho, Shinmonzen Dori, Higashioji Nishi-iru, Higashiyama-ku (075 525 8787/http://www.hotelmume. com). Gion Shijo station (Keihan line). ¥¥¥.
The thin tower of ferroconcrete doesn't promise much, but ring the doorbell and the bright red door will open to reveal Kyoto's newest boutique hotel. Mume arrived in May 2009 with seven stunningly appointed rooms that will surely rival The Screen (p138) for the attention of the design crowd. Aptly for a hotel found amid the antique stores of Shinmonzen Dori, Mume is furnished with exquisite collectibles, including works from China, the UK and Vietnam. The suite is positively regal, with guests sleeping on a platform bordered with bamboo screens.

Hotel New Hankyu

Higashi Shiokoji-cho, Shiokoji Dori, Shimogyo-ku (075 343 5300/ www.hankyu-hotel.com). Kyoto station (JR, Kintetsu and Karasuma lines). ¥¥.
The name hasn't been accurate since the early 1980s, but the 320-room New Hankyu began renovating its rooms in 2005 and the newer ones enjoy modern Japanese furnishings in a stylish palette of beige and brown. The older rooms are far less attractive, but all benefit from a location opposite Kyoto Station.

Hyatt Regency Kyoto

644-2 Sanjusangendo-mawari, Higashiyama-ku (075 541 1234/ www.kyoto.regency. hyatt.com). Shichijo station (Keihan line). ¥¥¥.
Readers of *Condé Nast Traveller* voted the Hyatt Regency the best hotel in Kyoto (and Japan's second best), and it's very easy to see why: the gorgeous interior. Designed by Super Potato's Takashi Sugimoto, it includes a knockout lobby surrounded by oversized kimono patterns, clever in-room lighting, and a granite

Hotel Mume p135

bathroom that you could live in. The
service is on a par with the top ryokan,
the hotel bar is the best in the city and
you can enjoy a feast of a breakfast.
There's impeccable concierge service
too. It doesn't hurt to be next door
to one of the city's best temples
(Sanjusangen-do, p50) and opposite
the National Museum (p48).

K's Guest House
*418 Naya-cho, Dotemachi Dori
Shichijo-agaru, Shimogyo-ku
(075 342 2444/www.kshouse.jp).
Shichijo station (Keihan line). ¥.*
From wireless internet to shoe-dryers
to two fully equipped kitchens, this
backpacker hostel has more facilities
than you could ever need. It's also
pristine and spacious, with several
lounges, two terraces and a surprisingly well-appointed bar. The profes-
sional, English-speaking staff help
make K's Guest House the best option
in the cheap-as-chips price bracket.

Downtown

Hiiragiya
*Fuyacho Dori, Anekoji-agaru,
Nakagyo-ku (075 221 1136/
www.hiiragiya.co.jp). Karasuma Oike
station (Karasuma and Tozai lines).
¥¥¥¥.*

Much has been written about Hiiragiya
since it opened in 1861, usually rich
with superlatives. Along with its cross-
street neighbour Tawaraya (p141), it's
considered the city's greatest ryokan.
The traditional element of the inn is the
most famous – the 21 original rooms
exude historic charm, with furnishings
including a Tokugawa-family dresser
and Karacho screens. Less famous is
the seven-room new wing, completed
in 2006 by Jun Michida, a young architect who also worked on the Miho
Museum (p122). Where Hiiragiya's old
wing displays the aesthetics of Japanese
nobility, the new wing is a model of contemporary Japanese design; where a
scroll would hang in a traditional room,
a window frames a scene from outside.
In the daytime, sunlight draws the
inn's holly leaf logo on the interior
walls, thanks to cut-aways in the concrete – a technique you will also find at
many temples.

Hotel Monterey
*Karasuma Dori, Sajo-sagaru,
Nakagyo-ku (075 251 7111/
www.hotelmonterey.co.jp/ kyoto).
Karasuma Oike station (Karasuma
and Tozai lines). ¥¥.*
You'll either love or hate the design
here. The lobby of black marble and
mirrors, crystal chandelier, and Renoir

ESSENTIALS

Screen show

Kyoto's first bona fide boutique hotel opens.

Kyoto always had plenty of boutique accommodation. The two most famous ryokan, the Tawaraya (p141) and Hiiragiya (p137), have less than 50 rooms between them. Other inns have fewer than ten. So perhaps the city never felt the need to join the boutique hotel boom at the start of the century.

Some had flirted with the idea of a design hotel. The Prinz rental apartments (p145) are the work of a top local creator. When the Hyatt group took over the former Kyoto Park Hotel in 2006, it tapped Japan's top interior designers to give it a dazzling makeover (Hyatt Regency Kyoto, p135). But it wasn't until **The Screen** (p142) arrived in 2008, that the city got its first true boutique hotel.

The format is now a familiar one: each room has a different designer. But unlike Copenhagen's Hotel Fox or Bratislava's 21 Cakov-Makara, The Screen didn't opt for boundary-pushing novelties. The 13 rooms here are all elegantly appointed with modern furnishings.

Boycott creative director Satoru Tanaka and design consultant Akiko Masuda gave their rooms a moody black interior, punctuated by spotlights and white furniture. Other designers opted for white, producing brilliant, bleached rooms crowned with chandeliers. In 403, lighting designer Sam Liu gave his room a misty look with billowing muslin drapes separating the sleeping and living areas. *Nihongaka* (traditional Japanese painter) Tetsuei Nakamura furnished room 101 with bold screen doors, which the hotel spiel suggests is a nod to Nijo Castle's opulent decor.

It was left to Italy's Salvatore Barbiera to produce the most playful room. He used stylised trees and spotlights to suggest that the guest is sitting in a forest clearing. Even here, the concept is executed so delicately that it never feels like a gimmick.

Any self-respecting design hotel needs a name-dropping amenity list, and The Screen's roster of names includes Bose, iPod, Simmons, Nespresso and Ren. Consider also a 13-dish Japanese breakfast, a rooftop lounge and giant jacuzzi baths, and you might start to see why a night at The Screen costs as much as a room at a luxury ryokan or a suite in a top-flight hotel.

and Hendricks originals looks more like the entrance to a Bubble-era nightclub than a hotel. The odd design continues in the guest rooms, with burgundy and cream stripes conveying the look of an upmarket Punch 'n' Judy booth. Beneath the quirky surface is a great hotel, with comfortable rooms, helpful staff and, for girls, a *ganbanyoku* hot stone spa.

Iori Sanbo Nishinotoin-cho

Nishinotoin Dori, Oike-sagaru, Nakagyo-ku (075 352 0211/www. kyoto-machiya.com). Karasuma Oike station (Karasuma and Tozai lines). **¥¥¥¥**.

For the last five years, the Iori company has been turning classic townhouses into luxury rental apartments. One of their latest is the former home of a local painter, tucked behind green-tea salon Marukyu Koyamaen (p57) on the edge of the Downtown district. The renovations include nods to classic Kyoto with a gold kimono sash across the futons, an old storehouse door now employed as a table, and some oversized calligraphy from author Alex Kerr, one of the founders of Iori. The modern amenities include underfloor heating, wireless internet and a sci-fi toilet, though curiously no toothbrush. Other Iori branches are located in Karasuma Oike and Gion, and there are several properties just south of Shijo Dori. Visit their website for details.

Ishihara

Yanaginobanba Dori, Aneyakoji-agaru, Nakagyo-ku (075 221 5612/www. yado-web.com). Karasuma Oike station (Karasuma and Tozai lines). **¥¥**.

Even though Ishihara was famously the favourite inn of cinema legend Akira Kurosawa, there are much better reasons to stay here. First and foremost, the welcome and service from the *okami* (proprietress) equals that of a top-end ryokan. With just six rooms to attend to, your host provides attentive,

amiable hospitality. There's also the prime location in the Downtown district. Best of all, it's superb value for money – the traditional ryokan experience without the bruising price tag.

Kanamean Nishitomiya

Tominokoji Dori, Rokkaku-sagaru, Nakagyo-ku (075 211 2411/ www.kanamean.co.jp). Karasuma station (Hankyu line); Shijo station (Karasuma line); or Sanjo station (Keihan line). **¥¥¥¥**.

This beautiful two-storey house has been welcoming guests since 1873. The hospitality is classic Kyoto, as is the dinner. The inn stands a block and a half away from the gourmet wonderland of Nishiki-koji market, from where most of the ingredients for the evening's *kaiseki* are sourced.

Kyoto Royal Hotel & Spa

Kawaramachi, Sanjo-agaru, Nakagyo-ku (075 223 1234/www. ishinhotels.com/kyoto-royal/en). Kyoto Shiyakusho-mae station (Tozai line); or Sanjo station (Keihan line). **¥¥**.

The Kyoto Royal may have opened in 1972, but it still looks brand new, courtesy of a makeover in 2005. The singles are named 'Superior Singles' and it's not such an outlandish conceit – they're spacious and well-appointed, so long as you aren't fussy about having a big bathroom. In the suites, however, the bathrooms are a highlight, furnished with multi-headed massage showers. The titular spa is the kind you find in the world's best hotels, with over-the-top treatments including green tea body wraps and caviar facials.

Super Hotel Kyoto

538-1 Nakano-cho, Shinkyogoku Dori, Shijo-agaru, Nakagyo-ku (075 255 9000/www.superhotel.co.jp). Kawaramachi station (Hankyu line). **¥**.

This is a super hotel in the same way that Tesco's is a super market: it's convenient and cheap. And for such reasonable prices, what can you expect?

Airline flights are one of the biggest producers of the global warming gas CO_2. But with **The CarbonNeutral Company** you can make your travel a little greener.

Go to **www.carbonneutral.com** to calculate your flight emissions then 'neutralise' them through international projects which save exactly the same amount of carbon dioxide.

Contact us at **shop@carbonneutral.com** or call into the office on **0870 199 99 88** for more details.

Everything is automated, from the check-in (via something resembling an ATM) to the bar (a vending machine). The hotel opened in late 2008, so the spartan rooms are still shiny and new.

Tawaraya

Fuyacho Dori, Anekoji-agaru, Nakagyo-ku (075 211 5566). Karasuma Oike station (Karasuma and Tozai lines). ¥¥¥¥.

Tawaraya is rightly hailed as one of Japan's finest ryokan. Some have even gone so far as to call it the 'world's best hotel'. Established in the early 18th century, the inn is an exemplar of classic Japanese hospitality, even though it never feels anything less than contemporary. There is every modern convenience that you could hope for, but almost all are artfully concealed. Dinner is a lavish *kaiseki* meal served in your room, or tempura at Tenyu (p58). In the morning, when you awake and slide the screen door to reveal the Japanese garden, it's difficult to believe that this idyllic place lies in the heart of the bustling city centre. On Fridays and Saturdays guests can take part in a tea ceremony with the owner's daughter-in-law.

Yoshikawa

Tominokoji Dori, Oike-sagaru, Nakagyo-ku (075 221 5544/ www.kyoto-yoshikawa.co.jp). Kyoto Shiyakusho-mae station (Tozai line). ¥¥¥¥.

Ryokan owners like to talk of their inns as family homes, and Yoshikawa may be the most convincing example. With just eight rooms, the inn provides attentive and friendly service, and the lobby's dramatic hearth is a great place to sip tea and chat to staff or fellow guests. The building has changed little since it was built over a century ago, but rooms now boast modern luxuries such as internet access and underfloor heating. The best rooms have views of the fabulous garden and carp pond.

Gosho

ANA Hotel Kyoto

Nijojo-mae, Horikawa Dori, Nakagyo-ku (012 067 7651/www.ana-hkyoto.com). Nijojo-mae station (Tozai line). ¥¥.

Perhaps the city's most attractive mid-range hotel, the ANA occupies a plum spot opposite Nijo Castle (p70). You will, of course, have to cough up more for a castle view, but it's worth it. Ceiling-height screens slide open to reveal the old shogun's stronghold, with a backdrop of mountains. Staff, dressed in elegant pink and white kimonos, speak English and attend to guests' every need. The hotel dates back to the 1980s, but it still looks good for its age.

Hearton Hotel

Higashinotoin Dori, Oike-agaru, Nakagyo-ku (075 222 1300/ www.heartonhotel.com/hearton_ hotel_kyoto.htm). Karasuma Oike station (Karasuma and Tozai lines). ¥¥.

The granite façade promises grand things, but the Hearton is a strange place. The lobby is a sterile café; there's a barely perceptible difference between single and double rooms; and if you want a newspaper you have to buy it from the front desk. The service is efficient but, like the heavily annotated, hand-drawn area map that you'll find on your dresser, the Hearton is a little unconventional.

Hirota Guest House

665 Seimei-cho, Nijo Dori, Tominokoji Nishi-iru, Nakagyo-ku (075 221 2474). ¥¥.

Among historic lodgings, few offer as authentic an experience of traditional city life as the Hirota Guest House. Run by the spry Hiromi Hirota, the *machiya* has been in the family for five generations and was once a sake factory. Visitors sleep upstairs in the main building or slip through the back garden to the *kura* storehouse, which is now an atmospheric private cottage.

ESSENTIALS

Make sure that you get some travel tips from Ms. Hirota, a former interpreter who will point you to some of Kyoto's most intriguing sites.

Kyoto Brighton Hotel

Shinmachi Nakadachiuri, Kamigyo-ku (075 441 4411/www.kyotobrighton. com). Imadegawa station (Karasuma line). ¥¥¥.

Of all the top-end hotels in Kyoto, this is the one that most desperately needs a makeover. The cavernous atrium lobby and much of the in-room furnishings are throwbacks to a design sense that won't be resurfacing anytime soon. On the plus side, the staff is five-star, the rooms are spacious and there's a swimming pool on the roof.

Kyoto Hotel Okura

Kawaramachi Oike, Nakagyo-ku (075 211 5111/www.kyotohotel.co.jp). Kyoto Shiyakusho-mae station (Tonzai line); or Sanjo Station (Keihan line). ¥¥¥.

The Okura claims to be the oldest hotel in Kyoto, but since it was razed and rebuilt in the early 1990s, that doesn't really count. It can boast of being the tallest in the area, with 17 floors, but the best reason to stay is the location, above a subway station in the Downtown district. In terms of style and service, it meets rather than exceeds expectations for a high-end hotel.

Nishiyama Ryokan

Gokomachi Dori, Nijo-sagaru, Nakagyo-ku (075 222 1166/ www.ryokan-kyoto.com). Kyoto Shiyakusho-mae station (Tozai line). ¥¥.

Kyoto's most foreigner-friendly ryokan has English-speaking staff who can point guests in the direction of English-language activities around the city. It even has an English-language cartoon guide to ryokan life, covering basics such as protocol for the communal bath and how to don the yukata. Rooms are spacious, spotless and good value.

The Screen

640-1 Shimogoryomae-cho, Nakagyo-ku (075 252 1113/www.the-screen.jp). ¥¥¥¥.

Kyoto's first boutique hotel is a playground of modern design with 13 unique rooms from 13 different creators. See box p138.

Southern Higashiyama

Ayado

3F Sakura Building, Shinmonzen Dori, Yamatooji Higashi-iru, Higashiyama-ku (075 531 5849/www.ayado.net). Gion Shijo station (Keihan line). ¥.

In a city packed with picturesque places to stay, Ayado is an odd proposition: two rooms in a concrete office block. But what it lacks in physical charm, it makes up for with genial staff and, for the price, great amenities. There's free internet access, free tea and coffee, a spacious lounge and a manga library. Bedding is dormitory style, with two rooms of five comfy bunk beds. One gripe: the en suite showers mean that early risers usually wake the rest of the dorm.

Chourakukan Hotel

604 Maruyama-cho, Yasaka Torii-mae Higashi-iru, Higashiyama-ku (075 561 0001/www.chourakukan.co.jp). Bus 206. ¥¥¥.

Chourakukan is best known as a historic dining complex that serves European fare in Rococo and neo-classical settings (p86). Since 2008, there has also been a hotel tucked inconspicuously into the rear of the building. If you can reserve one of the six rooms, you're in for a treat. The sumptuous furnishings include a real log fire, a wood and brick interior, and jacuzzi baths with views of Maruyama Park. The Chourakukan lies somewhere between a boutique hotel and a rental apartment, with a club lounge that offers food and drink, but otherwise few of the services that you might be used to in a hotel.

Hyatt Regency Kyoto p135

Gion Hatanaka

*Yasaka Jinja Minamimon-mae, Gion,
Higashiyama-ku (075 551 0553/
www.thehatanaka.co.jp). Gion Shijo
station (Keihan line).* **¥¥¥¥**.
Though fast approaching its cente-
nary, this gleaming ryokan isn't
showing its age at all. In a superb location for shopping or temple-hopping,
the Hatanaka has the look of an old
ryokan but the feel of a modern hotel.
Located within sight of Yasaka Jinja
and walking distance of many spectacular landmarks, and with several
English-speaking staff, Hatanaka is a
great choice for sightseers. The main
building has some enormous rooms,
but the annexe is more atmospheric.

Motonago

*511 Washio-cho, Kodaiji-michi,
Higashiyama-ku (075 561 2087/
www.motonago.com). Bus 206.* **¥¥¥**.
The Motonago has got everything that
a great ryokan should have: pristine
rooms epitomising the *wabi-sabi* aesthetic, a *kaiseki* dinner of local delicacies, a tailored garden and world-class
hospitality. It also has an incredible

location on a picturesque street in front
of Kodai-ji (p84). Great value.

Suisen-Kyo Shirakawa

*473-15 Umemiya-cho, Higashiyama-ku
(075 712 7023/www.suisenkyo.com).
Higashiyama station (Tozai line).* **¥¥**.
'Home away from home' is a hoary old
cliché, but it suits this hotel perfectly.
Although your usual abode probably
isn't a century-old *machiya*, you'll discover this two-bedroom townhouse,
renovated in 2008, is cosy and relax-
ing. The friendly owner will pop in
to say hello, but otherwise you'll
have the house all to yourself. The
building lies in a quiet, residential
area, but only a few blocks from the
Downtown district.

Northern Higashiyama

Rakuyoso

*77 Hosshoji-cho, Okazaki, Sakyo-ku
(075 762 0788/www.eisu.co.jp/eisu
club-rakuyoso/ top.html). Jingu
Marutamachi station (Keihan line).*
¥¥¥.
The building's history stretches back
to the early 20th century, when it
served as a viscount's villa, but it only
became a luxury lodging in 2003. Of
the seven rooms, 'Mangetsuan' and
'Sanjo' are the highlights, and the only
two with private baths. The former is
a detached teahouse with kitchen and
veranda, and the latter has a wonderful view of the garden. The other
rooms share facilities, although the
windowside cypress tubs are no hard-
ship. Rooms 'Wakasa' and 'Tanba' are
the cheapest options, at less than
¥30,000 for two people. Rakuyoso is
not actually a ryokan, so you lose the
meals but gain a bar.

Three Sisters Inn

*18 Higashi Fukunokawa-cho, Okazaki,
Sakyo-ku (075 761 6336). Bus 206.*
¥¥.
Some ryokan refuse foreign guests,
others welcome them. This one insists

on them: since the 1950s, only non-Japanese guests have been able to book a room at this popular inn. The location, which lies a block north of Heian Jingu (p97), is great for those who like their Kyoto surroundings to be tranquil and picturesque, less so for anyone who wants to feel the pulse of the city. Rooms are designed in a Japanese style and are great value (the inn keeps prices low by not offering dinner). There is also a nearby annexe, in which en suite bathrooms are a feature of all the rooms.

Westin Miyako Hotel

1 Awadaguchi Kacho-cho, Sanjo Keage, Higashiyama-ku (075 771 7111/075 751 2490/www.westinmiyako-kyoto. com). Keage station (Tozai line). **¥¥¥**.
The setting can't be faulted: the 501-room Westin sits against a verdant mountain and boasts gardens by master Jihei Ogawa and his son. Inside, there are artworks galore, including door panels by Domoto Insho (p106). The rooms are well appointed, if not particularly inspired, and they feature the chain's trademark 'Heavenly beds'. The lobby is dominated by what appears to be a towering steel-and-glass do-not-disturb sign.

Yoshida Sanso

59-1 Shimo Oji-cho, Yoshida, Sakyo-ku (075 771 6125/www.yoshidasanso. com). Demachiyanagi station (Keihan line). **¥¥¥¥**.
The 16-petal chrysanthemum motifs on the doors and eaves give a clue to this ryokan's former role as the villa of Count Higashi-Fushimi (uncle of the current emperor). The structure was built in 1932, but following World War II, was converted into a ryokan with a reputation for fine cuisine. The ten rooms of the main house each boast a garden view, but the treat here is the *hanare*, a detached cottage made entirely of cypress. The location is great for Ginkaku-ji (pXX) and the student area just north of Higashiyama.

Gekkousou (Moonlight Guest House)

73-18 Minami Funaoka-cho, Murasakino, Kita-ku (075 200 8583/ www.gekkousou.com/2007/kyoto). Buses 6, 46, 206. **¥**.
There are no frills here: there's even a ¥100 surcharge for hot water. But with Funaoka Onsen (p114) as your neighbour, you might never need to pay it. Kinkaku-ji (p107) is only a stroll away, although there's little else in the area. The Japanese-style dorm is probably the cheapest lodging in town, but the private room is much better value.

Hannari Guesthouse

693 Kushige-cho, Higurashi Dori, Shimodachiuri-kudaru, Kamigyo-ku (075 803 1300/www.hannari-guesthouse. com). Buses 10, 93, 202, 204. **¥**.
In 2008, a group of young locals converted this merchant's *machiya* into one of the city's best guesthouses. The bedding is basic (a 'double' here means a room with a bunk bed), but the house is immaculate inside and out, the staff are friendly and fun, and there's a special service: guests can help themselves to free sake.

Shunko-in

42 Myoshinji-cho, Hanazono, Ukyo-ku (075 462 5488/www.shunkoin.com). Hanazono station (Sagano line) or Myoshinji station (Keifuku line). **¥**.
Not many temple lodgings come furnished with wireless internet, air-conditioning and a kitchen, but these rooms within the grounds of the Myoshin-ji complex are surprisingly comfy. Constructed in 2007, five private rooms are available, two of which have en suite showers. Even though its location is far from central, Shunko-in stands close to several major sights and allows guests to borrow its bicycles for the day. The journey back at night through the Myoshin-ji complex is a magical experience.

Hiiragiya p137

Utano Youth Hostel

9 Nakayama-cho, Uzumasa, Ukyo-ku (075 462 2288/www.yh-kyoto.or.jp/ utano). Buses 10, 26, 59. ¥.

One look at the map ought to dissuade you from staying here. The Utano is tucked away in the far north-west of the city – which makes it ideal for visiting Arashiyama and a couple of temples, but not so good for anything else. Yet this is the newest (revamped in 2008), largest and most attractive youth hostel in town. And its location allows for plenty of space, lots of nature and fantastic facilities, including a barbecue pit, a tennis court and a Japanese bath of which any inn would be proud.

Arashiyama

Hoshinoya Kyoto

11-2 Genrokuzan-cho, Arashiyama, Nishikyo-ku (075 871 0001/ www.hoshinoya.com/en). ¥¥¥¥.

While most hotels tout their proximity to the sights, Hoshinoya does the opposite. The latest creation from Japanese luxury resort-maker Hoshinoya is nestled in the Arashiyama mountains. To reach it, you can drive the 20-minute route from Kyoto Station, or head to Arashiyama and take the shuttle – a wooden punt that steers you past spectacular scenery. When you arrive, you'll find 25 rooms of up to 100sq m in area, baths with a river view and fine dining. At press time, the hotel was yet to open (scheduled for winter 2009), but if the other Hoshinoya resorts are any measure, expect luxurious escapism.

Further Afield

Prinz Apartotel

5 Tanakatakahara-cho, Sakyo-ku (075 712 3900/www.prinz.jp/apartotel). Chayama station (Eizan line). ¥¥¥.

Forgive this hotel its name: the 'Apartotel' is one of the most stylish rental abodes in the city. There are just two rooms, furnished in an elegant, minimalist style by local design star Shin Nishibori (Efish, p50). Pick the larger room: for a small price hike, you get a bath and an enormous bed. The Apartotel sits atop the Prinz gallery-café-bar complex, which makes a great place for a nightcap. The downside: it's a long trek from most of the sights.

ESSENTIALS

Getting Around

Arriving & leaving
By air

Three airports serve Kyoto. The largest is Kansai International Airport, 75 minutes away by train, or about an hour and a half by car. Osaka International Airport is a domestic hub, and is a 55-minute bus ride from Kyoto. From Centrair Airport, it is a 28-minute local train ride to Nagoya, then 35 minutes by shinkansen (bullet train) to Kyoto. Centrair connects mainly to airports in East Asia. If you are flying via Tokyo, a connection to Osaka Airport will be most convenient.

Kansai International Airport (KIX)

Flight information 072 455 2500/ www.kansai-airport.or.jp/en.
The Biwako line connects KIX with Kyoto station. The fastest train is an Airport Express Haruka (which usually runs twice an hour between 6.29am and 10.18pm). It takes 75 minutes and costs ¥2,980. There is also a limousine bus service that takes 95 minutes (072 461 1374, www.kate.co.jp). The buses leave once or twice an hour from bus stop 8 and call at Sanjo Keihan station (for Downtown destinations) and Kyoto Station. Tickets, available via vending machines, cost ¥2,500.

Centrair Airport (NGO)

Flight information 056 938 1195/ www.centrair.jp.
The Meitetsu Railroad connects the airport to Nagoya station (¥850, 28 minutes). Trains depart every five to ten minutes between 5.23am and 11.15pm. From Nagoya station,

a *shinkansen* to Kyoto takes 35 minutes and costs ¥5,640.

Osaka International Airport (ITM)

Flight information www.osaka-airport.co.jp.
Better known as Itami Airport, this two-terminal airport serves most domestic destinations, including Okinawa. It's possible, but time consuming, to reach Kyoto from here by monorail and then train. The quickest way to travel into the city is to take the limousine bus (074 222 5110, www.okkbus.co.jp/eng), which runs every 20 minutes between 8am and 9.10pm. The 55-minute journey costs ¥1,280.

By rail

Japan Railways' *shinkansen* offer fast, reliable and expensive access to the rest of the country. It is cheaper to buy *jiyuu seki* tickets (non-reserved seats). If travelling off-peak, this is usually a safe bet. For peak hours, reservations are essential. Not all *shinkansen* are equal: Nozomi trains are fastest.
   The trip takes 2 hours 23 minutes from Tokyo by Nozomi (¥13,220 reserved seat, ¥12,710 unreserved), 36 minutes from Nagoya (¥5,640/ ¥4,930), and 1 hour 47 minutes from Hiroshima (¥10,890/¥10,280). There are also green-sha (first-class seats), but the basic seats are comfortable enough.

By bus

Japan Railways also operates an array of bus routes, which are all significantly cheaper than the train. The journey takes eight hours from

Tokyo and costs ¥4,500-¥8,180. The cheapest option is a *seishun* bus. These no-frills coaches leave from Tokyo's Shinjuku station (New South exit) or Tokyo station (Yaesu exit) and arrive at Kyoto station's Hachijo exit. If reserved at least five days in advance, tickets cost ¥4,500; otherwise they cost ¥5,000. Standard buses offer more leg room for ¥8,180. Night buses, both standard and *seishun*, are called 'Dream Kyoto' and depart from Tokyo station's Yaesu exit (10pm and 11.10pm) or Shinjuku station's New South exit (11.50pm daily, also 10.30pm Fri-Sun). There are 'Ladies Dream' routes for women only, which leave Tokyo station at 10.30pm daily. Tickets for all routes are available at the green *midori no madoguchi* ticket windows inside major train stations.

JR Kousoku bus company

033 844 1950/www.kakuyasubus.jp.

International ferries

Two companies operate ferry routes between Osaka and Shanghai. The trip takes 46-48 hours. Both charge ¥21,500-¥101,500, depending on the room's quality, with the cheapest option being a floor in a shared room with only a blanket and pillow for comfort. At the top end, rooms resemble those of a mid-range hotel.

Shanghai Ferry Company

066 243 6345/www.shanghai-ferry.co.jp.
Private rooms start at ¥39,500. Tickets are available online or via JTB travel agents (www.jtb.co.jp).

Shanghai Ferry Boat Xin Jian Zhen

06 6536 6541/www.shinganjin.com/ index_e.php.
Private rooms start at ¥41,500. Tickets are available online or via JTB travel agents (www.jtb.co.jp).

Public transport

Japan's rail efficiency extends to Kyoto's overground and subway network, with regular trains arriving exactly when they say they will. The stations all have English signage telling you which exit you need. Now the bad news: the rails are run by several different companies, and the lines rarely intersect. They also neglect areas with major sights. The solution: bite the bullet and learn to use the buses.

Buses

Kyoto's bus system serves every part of the city, filling in the gaps in the rail network. In many cases, this is the most efficient way to cross the city. Unfortunately, most information at stops and on buses is only in Japanese. English maps are available from the information bureaus in front of Kyoto station, in Karasuma Oike subway station and at Kitaoji bus terminal. You can download one at www.city.kyoto.jp.

You board most buses via the back door and exit via the front. There is a flat fare of ¥220, payable upon exiting the bus (drop the exact fare in the slot next to the driver). Some buses on further afield routes have staggered fares. If you see a ticket machine by the entrance, take a ticket and check the number. A signboard at the front shows your fare underneath the number.

The main bus terminals are located at Kyoto station, Sanjo station and Kitaoji station.

Trains

There are eleven train lines in Kyoto, including two subways and one line that heads underground when it enters the city. The official Kyoto Municipal Subway network consists of the Tozai line, which

bisects the city from east to west, and the Karasuma line, which runs north to south. Single fares cost from ¥210 to ¥340. The Keihan line links Kyoto with Osaka, and travels underground when it reaches Kyoto. It runs north to south, following the Kamogawa river. Another useful route for visitors is the JR Sagano line, which runs from Kyoto station to Hanazono station (for Myoshin-ji, p107) and Arashiyama.

To purchase tickets for any of the train lines, insert your money into the ticket machine and press the button showing the fare to your destination. If you aren't sure of the fare, you can buy the cheapest ticket and pay the difference at a 'fare adjustment' machine at your destination. These are usually bright yellow and can be found near the exit barriers of all stations.

Travel passes

JR Passes

The Japan Rail Pass (www.japanrailpass.net) allows virtually unlimited travel on the entire national JR network, including *shinkansen*. It cannot, however, be used for the Nozomi super-express *shinkansen*. It costs ¥28,300 for a standard seven-day pass, ¥45,100 for 14 days and ¥57,700 for 21 days. If you plan to make more than two trips per week, the tickets are excellent value.

The pass is available only to visitors from abroad travelling under the entry status of 'temporary visitor', and must be bought before coming to Japan. Buy an Exchange Order abroad, which can then be traded in for a pass at an exchange office in Japan. Orders can be purchased at overseas offices of the Japan Travel Bureau International, Nippon Travel Agency, Kinki Nippon Tourist, Tokyu Tourist Corporation and other associated local travel agents, or at an overseas Japan Airlines or All Nippon Airways office if you are booked on to one of their flights. Check the Japan Rail Pass website for overseas locations.

JR West Kansai Pass

www.westjr.co.jp/english/travel/ jrp/index.html.
Similar to the Japan Rail Pass, but limited to the Kansai area, this pass is good value for foreign visitors wishing to explore Osaka, Nara, Kobe and Kyoto. The passes cost ¥2,000, ¥4,000, ¥5,000 or ¥6,000 for 1, 2, 3 or 4 days respectively, and can be purchased at the same locations as the Japan Rail Pass. As with the Japan Rail Pass, the JR West Kansai Pass must be purchased before arriving in Japan.

ICOCA cards

The ICOCA cards are Western Japan's IC smart cards. Swipe them over the panels at the ticket barriers of JR stations and the minimum fare will be automatically deducted. The remainder is deducted when you swipe again at the exit station. The cards cost ¥2,000, of which ¥500 is a deposit (refundable if you hand the card in to a JR ticket office). The ICOCA cards are good for any JR rail travel. They work on Tokyo's JR network, just as Tokyo's Pasmo and Suica IC cards will work on JR lines in Kyoto.

Bus passes

All-day bus passes entitle you to unlimited travel around most of Kyoto (Arashiyama and Shugaku-in are both outside the pass zone). They cost ¥500 and are sold at bus information bureaus as well as at many hotels. A pass that also allows transport on the city's train lines costs ¥1,200 for one day, or ¥2,000 for two days.

Kansai Thru Pass

www.surutto.com/conts/ticket/3dayeng/index.html.

A ¥3,800 two-day pass or a ¥5,000 three-day pass gives you unlimited travel on all subways, private railways and buses in the Kansai area, covering Kyoto, Osaka, Kobe and Wakayama. The pass entitles bearers to discount entry to various attractions, such as the Kyoto Tower (p48), Toei Uzumasa Eigamura (p124), the National Museum (p101), Kodai-ji and Kennin-ji (p84). Passes are sold at the Kyoto station bus information centre (open 7.30am-8pm) or the KAA travel desk on the first floor of Kansai International Airport (open 7am-10pm).

Cycling

Kyoto is compact, flat and a great city for cycling. Many hotels and hostels have bicycles to lend guests, usually free of charge. The Kyoto Cycling Tour Project (www.kctp.net) rents a variety of bikes, including mountain bikes, and has four locations across the city for pick-up or drop-off, with English-speaking staff. Fees vary by type of bicycle, from ¥1,000-¥2,000 per day. For an extra ¥500, they will deliver the bike to your hotel, hostel or ryokan.

The law states that cyclists must stick to the street (though this law is routinely ignored) and that it's the car driver's responsibility to ensure the cyclist's safety, so you're unlikely to encounter aggressive vehicles.

The only problem with cycling is finding a place to park. Though it's common to see bicycles chained up, regulations demand that cyclists use bicycle parks, of which there are few. The locals park bikes wherever convenient, and periodically the council impounds the bikes, leaving a notice with directions to the place where people can pay ¥2,300 to reclaim their wheels.

Driving

Unless you enjoy crawling along for short distances in heavy traffic, driving a car is the worst way in which to travel around Kyoto. But if you do decide to hire a car, you'll need to have an international driving licence and at least six months' driving experience. A better idea is to rent a scooter, so that you can zip around the sights. For vehicle rental, visit the following:

Japan Automobile Federation
418 Horimatsu-cho, Karasuma Dori, Marutamachi-agaru, Kamigyo-ku (075 212 1100/www.jaf.or.jp).
This local branch publishes a Rules of the Road guide in English (¥1,000).

Kyoto Rental Scooters
3-4 Miyanomoto-cho, Sagano, Ukyo-ku (075 864 1635/www.kyotorentalscooter.com/english.html).
English-speaking staff rent out Honda scooters, starting at ¥4,000 for the first day and ¥2,000 per day onwards. Reserve a scooter online in English, then take your passport and international driving licence to their office near Arashiyama.

Nippon Rent-a-Car Company
64 Higashi-kujo Muromachi, Minami-ku (075 681 0311/www.nipponrentacar.co.jp).
This rental car company has a branch close to the Hachijo Dori exit of Kyoto station and is open 24 hours a day. Rates start at ¥6,500 per day for a small car.

Taxis

Kyoto is so small that travelling by taxi isn't as budget-busting as in many cities. There are far more cabs than the city could possibly need, so it's always easy to hail one regardless of the time of day. The cabs are operated by more than a dozen different private companies and the competition has driven prices down. The cheapest options have either a heart or a price on their roofs. It is not necessary to tip taxi drivers in the city.

ESSENTIALS

Resources A-Z

Accident & emergency

In Japan, the number to call for an ambulance is 119. These hospitals and medical centres offer regular appointments and deal with 24-hour emergencies. The Japan Baptist Hospital has English-speaking staff.

Japan Baptist Hospital
47 Yamanomoto-machi, Kita-Shirakawa, Sakyo-ku (075 781 5191/ www.jbh.or.jp). Buses 3, 5.

Japanese Red Cross Kyoto Daiichi Hospital
749-15 Honmachi, Higashiyama-ku (075 561 1121/www.kyoto1-jrc.org). Tofukuji station (Keihan line).

Kyoto City Hospital
(Kyoto Shiritsu Byouin) 1-2 Higashi Takada-cho, Mibu, Nakagyo-ku (075 311 5311/www.city.kyoto.jp/ hokenfukushi/siritubyoin/index.html). Buses 73, 75, 205.

Customs

The duty-free allowances for non-residents entering Japan are: 400 cigarettes or 100 cigars or 250g of tobacco; three 750ml bottles of spirits; 57g (20oz) of perfume; gifts or souvenirs up to a value of ¥200,000. There is no limit on the amount of foreign currency you can import. Visit www.customs.go.jp.

Dental

For English-speaking staff, visit:

Niimi Dental Clinic
538 Gion-machi Minamigawa, Higashiyama-ku (075 532 0200/ www.niimi-dental.com). Gion-Shijo station (Keihan line). **Open** 9.30am-1pm, 2.30pm-7pm Mon, Tue, Thur, Fri; 9.30am-2pm Wed; 9.30am-1pm Sat.

Disabled

Travelling around Kyoto for wheelchair-bound visitors is easy. Subway and train stations have elevators, and most trains have space for wheelchairs. Ask the staff at each station for assistance. Many of the sights and restaurants are less accommodating. Basic, if dated, information for disabled visitors is available at the following website: http://accessible.jp.org/ kyoto/en/index-e.html.

Electricity

Electric current in Japan runs at 100V AC. Plugs have two flat-sided prongs. If bringing electrical appliances from Europe, you need to purchase an adaptor.

Embassies & consulates

For most nationalities, your nearest consulate is located in Osaka. Canadians have to go to Nagoya.

British Consulate
19th Floor, Epson Osaka Building, 3-5-1 Bakuro-machi, Chuo-ku, Osaka (06 6120 5600/http://ukinjapan. fco.gov.uk). Honmachi station (Chuo, Midosuji, Yotsubashi lines).

Canadian Consulate
Nakato Marunouchi Building, 3-17-6 Marunouchi, Naka-ku, Nagoya (052 972 0450/ www.canadanet.or.jp). Hisaya-odori station (Meijo, Sakura Dori lines).

Irish Consulate
4-1-1 Dosho-machi, Chuo-ku, Osaka (06 6204 2024). Yodoyabashi station (Midosuji lines).

New Zealand Consulate

c/o Daikin Industries, Umeda Center Building, 2-4-12 Nakazaki-nishi, Kita-ku, Osaka (06 6373 4583). Umeda station (Hanshin, Hanyu, Midosuji lines).

US Consulate

2-11-5, Nishitenma, Kita-ku, Osaka (06 6315 5900/http:// osaka.usconsulate.gov). Yodoyabashi station (Midosuji line).

Etiquette

Etiquette is an art form in Japan, and Kyoto-ites are the masters. There are right and wrong ways in which to open a sliding door, pour a drink, sit, walk, eat and bathe. Some locals, such as *geisha* and *ryokan* staff, make it their business to perfect the etiquette maze. Fortunately, the rest of us aren't expected to. Learn some protocol basics and you can survive without offending anyone (too much).

● First and foremost, remove your shoes when entering Japanese-style interiors. If you see a step, or slippers, that's a good indication that you should remove your footwear.

● Do the same again when using the toilet. There will be plastic slippers to wear in the loo.

● If you're on business, load up on cards. Always proffer your card two-handed, and read and comment on the one you receive. Never write on another person's business card.

● When you leave a restaurant, bar or café, say '*gochiso sama deshita*' (thank you for treating me), rather than '*arigato*'.

● At a public bath, wash thoroughly and remove all trace of soap before entering the tub. Enter it naked.

● In bars and restaurants, keep an eye on your companions' drinks and top them up regularly. Never pour your own drinks.

● Never pass food to someone using chopsticks, and never stick your chopsticks upright in a bowl of rice – both actions signify death.

● If you receive a bowl of green tea, rotate the bowl so that the main motif faces away from you.

Internet

Wi-Fi hotspots are sporadic, even in cafés. Café Bibliotic Hello! (p72) and Iyemon Salon (p57) both have Wi-Fi; otherwise, hotel lobbies are the best bet. Most 24-hour manga coffee shops (*manga kissa*) offer cheap internet services.

Money

ATMs

Cash is still the main method of payment in Kyoto, and restaurants, bars and stores may refuse credit cards. ATMs located inside banks are closed overnight (times vary) and all day Sundays.

Citibank and Shinsei Bank, both on Shijo Dori, have 24-hour ATMs with English instructions. Many convenience stores have ATM machines that operate around the clock, although usually they will only accept Japanese bank cards.

Post offices are also convenient for cash: their ATMs allow you to withdraw money using most foreign credit cards and have instructions in English. Some of their ATMs open 24 hours a day.

Credit cards

To report lost or stolen credit cards, dial one of the following 24-hour freephone numbers:

American Express *0120 020 120. English message follows Japanese.*
Diners Club *0120 074 024.*
MasterCard *00531 113 886.*
Visa *00531 78 0112.*

Opening hours

Department stores and larger shops in Kyoto are open daily from 10am or 11am to around 8pm or 9pm. Smaller shops keep shorter hours, with older ones closing as early as 5pm or 6pm, and open six days a week. Sunday is a normal shopping day for most stores in the city.

Most restaurants open at around 11am. Last orders can be as early as 7pm or as late as 4am. Bars and *izakaya* are usually open until at 2am, or 5am on weekends.

Banks are open from 9am to 3pm, Monday to Friday.

Police

For emergencies, call 110. If you are using a green public phone, press the red button.

Post offices

Post offices (*yubin kyoku*) – indicated by a red-and-white sign like a letter 'T' with a line over it – are plentiful. Local post offices open from 9am to 5pm Monday to Friday, and close at weekends and on public holidays.

The Kyoto Central Post Office, close to the station's central exit, is open 9am-7pm Mon-Fri, 9am-5pm Sat, 9am-12.30pm Sun. Post office ATMs accept foreign bank and credit cards.

Smoking & drinking

The legal age for smoking and drinking is 20 years old. Public smoking is prohibited on several streets in the Downtown area (Karasuma, Nishiki-koji, Shijo, Sanjo, Shinkyogku and Teramachi), punishable by disapproving stares and on-the-spot fines of ¥1,000.

Public intoxication is a common sight, so the resulting antisocial behaviours usually go unheard.

Telephones
Dialling & codes

The country code for Japan is 81. The area code for Kyoto is 075, which you don't need to dial when calling from within the city.

If you are phoning from outside Japan, dial the international access code plus 81 plus 75, followed by the main seven-digit number.

Numbers starting with 0120 are **freephone** (receiver-paid or toll-free). For the operator, dial 100; for directory enquiries, dial 104. Both services are Japanese-language only.

International calls

When calling abroad, dial 001 (KDDI), 0041 (Japan Telecom), 0061 (Cable & Wireless IDC) or 0033 (NTT Communications), followed by your country's international code, area code (minus any initial zero) and the telephone number.

The cheapest time to call is between 11pm and 8am, when an off-peak discount of 40 per cent applies. Only public phone booths with 'ISDN' or 'International' marked on the side allow international calls, and you'll need to buy a prepaid card or have a lot of change to spare.

Public phones

Green phones take flexible phone cards and ¥10 and ¥100 coins, but don't allow international calls; grey phones are the same, but allow you to make international calls.

Prepaid phone cards

The KDDI 'Super World' prepaid card for international phone calls is sold at most major convenience stores in denominations of ¥1,000, ¥3,000 or ¥5,000 and can be used with any push-button phone.

Tickets

The largest ticket agency is Ticket Pia (0570 029 111, http://t.pia.co.jp), which has outlets throughout the city, including one in the lobby of the Kyoto Gekijo (p48) inside Kyoto Station. Convenience store chain Lawson (www2.lawsonticket.com) has ticket vending machines in most stores, but navigation is in Japanese.

Tipping

Tipping is not expected in Japan, even in taxis or hotels, and people will often be embarrassed if you try. Some establishments add a service charge to bills.

Tourist information

There are two tourist information centres inside Kyoto Station. The biggest and the best, with internet access, multilingual staff and a library of Kyoto-related magazines and books, is located on the ninth floor of the Isetan department store (p52) inside Kyoto Station (075 344 3300; open 10am-6pm, closed 2nd and 4th Tuesday). A smaller centre is on the second floor, opposite Isetan's entrance (075 343 6655; open 8.30am-7pm daily).

The Japan National Tourist Organisation (JNTO) is the national English-language tourist service for visitors coming to Japan. Its website, www.jnto.go.jp, is packed with useful information.

Visas

It's not necessary to obtain a visa in advance unless you plan to work in Japan or stay longer than 90 days. To change your visa status, visit the immigration bureau at the following address:

Osaka Regional Immigration Bureau, Kyoto Branch
4th floor, Kyoto Chiho Dai-ni, Godo Chosha Building, 34-12 Higashi-Marutamachi Dori, Kawabata Higashi-iru, Sakyo-ku (075 752 5997). Marutamachi station (Keihan line). Open 9am-11am, 1pm-4.30pm.

What's on in Kyoto

Blogs

Deep Kyoto
www.deepkyoto.com.
An expat blog spotlighting some lesser-known destinations

Kyoto Foodie
www.kyotofoodie.com.
Explores local cuisine and restaurants.

Kyoto Kyoto
http://nncj-kyoto.seesaa.net.
The latest cultural topics from Kyoto.

Books & magazines

Kyoto is such a major destination for domestic tourism that bookshops and convenience stores are full of up-to-date guides, although most are Japanese. *Meets* and *Leaf* are two of the best listings magazines, available at kiosks, convenience stores and bookshops across the city. For English listings, see:

Kyoto Visitor's Guide
www.kyotoguide.com.
This monthly, free guide is distributed at bars, hotels, shops and restaurants. It has a comprehensive map.

Kansai Scene
www.kansaiscene.com.
A colourful, pocket-size monthly free magazine published in Osaka, which contains information on Kyoto.

Kansai Time Out
www.kto.co.jp.
No relation to this guidebook, Kansai Time Out is a monthly magazine that has been running since 1977. It's good for current affairs and classified ads.

ESSENTIALS

Vocabulary

Pronunciation

Japanese pronunciation presents few problems for native English speakers, but you must split up the syllables: *made* (until) is pronounced 'ma-de' and *shite* (doing) is 'shi-te' rather than anything else. When a 'u' falls at the end of the word, it is barely spoken: '*desu*' is close to 'dess'.

Consonants are the same as in English, but always hard: ('**g**' as in 'girl', not 'gyrate'), except for the 'l/r' sound, which falls halfway between the English pronunciation of the two letters. As for vowels, say **a** as in car, **e** as in 'bed', **i** as in 'feet', **o** as in 'long' and **u** as in 'flu'. Elongated vowels are pronounced the same way, but longer – an easy distinction to the Japanese, less so for English speakers.

Numbers

1 *ichi*; 2 *ni*; 3 *san*; 4 *yon*; 5 *go*; 6 *roku*; 7 *nana*; 8 *hachi*; 9 *kyuu*; 10 *juu*; 11 *juu-ichi*; 12 *juu-ni*; 100 *hyaku*; 1,000 *sen*; 10,000 *man*; 100,000 *juu-man*. Note that 7 can be read 'shichi,' so 7th Street is 'Shichijo' on maps and street signs, but 'Nanajo' to bus and taxi drivers.

Days, months, times

Monday *getsu-youbi*; Tuesday *ka-youbi*; Wednesday *sui-youbi*; Thursday *moku-youbi*; Friday *kin-youbi*; Saturday *do-youbi*; Sunday *nichi-youbi*; January *ichi-gatsu*; February *ni-gatsu*; March *san-gatsu*; April *shi-gatsu*; May *go-gatsu*; June *roku-gatsu*; July *shichi-gatsu*; August *hachi-gatsu*; September *ku-gatsu*; October *juu-gatsu*; November *juu-ichi-gatsu*; December *juu-ni-gatsu*; excuse me, do you have the time? *sumimasen, ima nan-ji desu ka?*; it's... o'clock... *ji desu*; noon *shougo*; midnight *mayonaka*; this morning *kesa*; this afternoon *kyou no gogo*; this evening *konban*; yesterday *kinou*; tomorrow *ashita*; today *kyou*; last week *sen-shuu*; this week *kon-shuu*; next week *rai-shuu*; the weekend *shuumatsu*

Basic expressions

yes/no *hai/iie*; please (asking favour) *onegai shimasu*; please (offering a favour) *douzo*; thank you (very much); *doumo arigatou*; good morning *ohayou gozaimasu*; good afternoon *kon nichi wa*; good evening *kon ban wa*; goodnight *oyasumi nasai*; how are you? *ogenki desu ka?*; excuse me (getting attention) *sumimasen*; excuse me (may I get past?) *shitsurei shimasu*; sorry *gomen nasai*; it's okay *daijoubu desu*; my name is... ...*desu*; what's your name? *o namae wa?*; pleased to meet you *douzo yoroshiku*; cheers! *kampai!*; do you speak English? *eigo o hanashimasu ka?*; I don't speak (much) Japanese *nihongo o (amari) hanashimasen*; could you repeat that? *mou ichido itte kudasai* do you understand? *wakarimasu ka?*; I understand/don't understand *wakari mashita/masen*; where is it? *doko desu ka?*; when is it? *itsu desu ka?*; what is it? *nan desu ka?*

Hotels

do you have a room? *heya wa arimasu ka?*; I'd like to reserve a single/double *shinguru/daburu no*

heya o onegai shimasu; I've made a reservation *yoyaku shite arimasu*; is there… in the room? *heya ni… wa arimasu ka?*; air-con *eakon*; TV/telephone *terebi/denwa*; we'll be staying… …*tomarimasu*; one night only *ippaku dake*; a week *isshuu-kan*; I don't know yet *mada wakarimasen*; how much is…? …*ikura desu ka?*; does the price include…?; *kono nedan wa…komi desu ka?*; sales tax (VAT) *shouhi zee*; breakfast/ meal *choushoku/ shokuji*; could you wake me up at…? …*ji ni okoshite kudasai*; towel/ blanket/ pillow *basu taoru/moufu/ makura*; what time do we have to check out by? *chekkuauto wa nan-ji made desu ka?*; could I have my bill, please? *kaikei o onegai shimasu*; would you order me a taxi, please? *takushii o yonde kudasai*

Shopping & money

I'd like… …*o kudasai*; do you have…? …*wa arimasu ka?*; how much is that? *ikura desu ka?*; could you help me? *onegai shimasu*; can I try this on? *kite mite mo ii desu ka?*; I'm looking for… …*o sagashite imasu*; I'll take it *sore ni shimasu*; that's all, thank you *sore de zenbu desu*; currency exchange *ryougae-jo*; I'd like to change pounds into yen *pondo o en ni kaetain desu ga*; could I have some small change, please? *kozeni o kudasai*

Health

where can I find a hospital/ dental surgery? *byouin/hai-sha wa doko desu ka?*; I need a doctor *isha ga hitsuyou desu*; is there a doctor/dentist who speaks English? *eigo ga dekiru isha/ha-isha wa imasu ka?*; could the doctor come to see me here? *oushin shite kuremasu ka?*; could I make

an appointment for…? …*yoyaku shitain desu ga*; it's urgent *shikyuu onegai shimasu*; I'm diabetic *watashi wa tounyoubyou desu*; I suffer from asthma *watashi wa zensoku desu*; I'm allergic to… …*arerugii desu*; contraceptive pill *hinin you piru*; I feel faint *memai ga shimasu*; I have a fever *netsu ga arimasu*; I've been vomiting *modoshi mashita*; I have diarrhoea *geri shitemasu*; it hurts here *koko ga itai desu*; I have a headache *zutsuu ga shimasu*; I have a sore throat *nodo ga itai desu*; I have a stomach ache *onaka ga itai desu*; I have toothache *ha ga itai desu*; I have lost a filling/tooth *tsumemono/ ha ga toremashita*

Sights & transport

gallery *bijutsukan*; hot springs *onsen*; mountain *yama*; museum *hakubutsu-kan*; palace *kyuuden*; park *kooen*; shrine *jinja*; temple *tera*; where's the nearest underground station? *chikatetsu no eki wa doko desu ka?*; a map of the underground, please *chikatetsu no rosenzu o kudasai*; to…, please …*made onegai shimasu*; single/return tickets *katamichi/ oufuku kippu*; where can I buy a ticket? *kippu wa doko de kaemasu ka?*; when does the train for… leave? …*iki no densha wa nan-ji ni demasu ka?*; ticket office *kippu-uriba*; vending machines *kenbai-ki*; bus *basu*; train *densha*; bullet train *shinkansen;* subway *chikatetsu*; taxi *takushii*

Local dialect

welcome (shop staff to regulars or customers with reservations) *oideyasu*; welcome (staff to casual visitors) *okoshiyasu*; thank you *okini*

Menu Reader

寿司屋 *sushi-ya* sushi restaurants

イクラ *ikura* salmon roe

タコ *tako* octopus

マグロ *maguro* tuna

こはだ *kohada* punctatus

トロ *toro* fatty tuna

ホタテ *hotate* scallop

ウニ *uni* sea urchin roe

海老 / エビ *ebi* prawn

平目 / ヒラメ *hirame* flounder

アナゴ *anago* conger eel

イカ *ika* squid

玉子 *tamago* yaki rolled omelette

鉄火巻き *tekkamaki* rolled tuna

お新香巻き *oshinkomaki* rolled pickles

蕎麦屋（そば屋）*soba-ya* noodle restaurants

buckwheat noodle restaurants (in udon restaurants, dishes will end in うどん in place of そば)

天ぷらそば *tempura* soba noodles in a hot broth with prawn tempura

にしんそば / ニシンそば *nishin* soba noodles in a hot broth with smoked herring

ざるそば *zaru* soba noodles on a bamboo rack, topped with *nori*

きつねそば *kitsune* soba noodles in broth topped with fried tofu

たぬきそば *tanuki* soba noodles in broth with fried tempura batter

月見そば *tsukimi* soba raw egg broken over noodles in a hot broth

あんかけうどん *ankake* udon noodles served in a thick fish bouillon/soy sauce soup with fishcake slices and vegetables

鍋焼きうどん *nabeyaki* udon noodles boiled in an earthenware pot with stock and other ingredients, mainly eaten in winter

居酒屋 *izaka-ya* Japanese-style bars

literally 'a place where there is sake'; an after-work drinking den that offers extensive and inexpensive food and drink menus

日本酒 *nihon-shu* sake

冷酒 *reishu* cold sake

熱燗 *atsukan* hot sake

焼酎 *shouchuu* distilled barley or potato spirit

酎ハイ *chuuhai* shouchuu with juice, tea or soda

生ビール *nama-biiru* draught beer

黒ビール *kuro-biiru* dark beer

梅酒 *ume-shu* plum wine

焼き魚 *yakizakana* grilled fish

煮魚 *ni zakana* boiled fish in sauce

刺身 *sashimi* thinly sliced raw fish

枝豆 *edamame* boiled soy beans in the pod and sprinkled with salt

揚げ出し豆腐 *agedashi doufu* deep-fried tofu with savoury sauce

おにぎり savoury rice balls

焼きおにぎり grilled rice balls

ふぐ刺し *fugusashi* sashimi of blowfish

唐揚げ *kara-age* deep-fried chicken nuggets

焼き鳥屋 *yakitori-ya*
yakitori restaurants

焼き鳥 *yakitori* chicken skewers

つくね *tsukune* minced chicken balls

タン *tan* tongue

ハツ *hatsu* heart

シロ *shiro* tripe

レバー *rebaa* liver

ガツ *gatsu* pig's stomach

おでん屋 *oden-ya*
oden restaurants

さつま揚げ *satsuma-age* fish cake

昆布 *konbu* kelp

大根 *daikon* radish

こんにゃく *konnyaku* devil's
tongue jelly

Other types of restaurant

懐石 *kaiseki* Japanese haute cuisine

京料理 *kyou ryouri* literally 'Kyoto
cuisine' restaurants; expect local
specialities such as tofu, *yuba* and
vegetables, often served *kaiseki* style

精進料理 *shoujin ryouri*
Zen vegetarian cuisine

おばんざい *obanzai*
rustic, home-style cooking using
local ingredients

湯豆腐 *yudoufu* tofu hotpot

ラーメン屋 *ramen-ya*
ramen restaurants

天ぷらや *tempura-ya*
tempura restaurants

お好み焼き屋 *okonomiyaki-ya*
okonomiyaki restaurants

トンカツ屋 *tonkatsu-ya*
tonkatsu restaurants

すき焼き屋 *sukiyaki-ya*
sukiyaki restaurants

Essential vocabulary

a table for one/two/three/four
hitori/futari/san-nin/yo-nin desu

is this seat free? *kono seki aite
masu ka?*

could we sit…? *…ni suwatte mo
yoroshii desu ka?*

over there *asoko*

outside *soto*

in a non-smoking area *kin-en-seki*

by the window *madogiwa*

excuse me *sumimasen*

may I see the menu, please?
menyuu o onegai shimasu

do you have a set menu? *setto
menyuu/teishoku wa arimasu ka?*

I'd like… *…o kudasai*

a bottle/glass of… *…o ippon/
ippai kudasai*

I can't eat food containing… *…ga
haitteru mono wa taberare masen*

do you have vegetarian meals?
bejitarian no shokuji wa arimasu ka?

have you a children's menu? *kodomo-
you no menyuu wa arimasu ka?*

the bill, please *okanjyou
onegai shimasu*

we'd like to pay separately
betsubetsu ni onegai shimasu

we'd like to pay all together
issho ni onegai shimasu

is service included?
saabisu-ryou komi desu ka?

can I pay with a credit card?
kurejitto kaado o tsukae masu ka?

could I have a receipt, please?
reshiito onegai shimasu

that was delicious, thank you
gochisou sama deshita

Index

ESSENTIALS

Arts & Leisure

ESSENTIALS

1000 ways to spend your weekends

From £12.99/ $19.95

TIME OUT GUIDES
WRITTEN BY
LOCAL EXPERTS
visit timeout.com/shop

Time Out
Guides